Local Societies and Rural Development

Local Societies and Rural Development

Self-organization and Participatory Development in Asia

Edited by

Shinichi Shigetomi

Institute of Developing Economies (IDE), Japan External Trade Organization (JETRO), Japan

Ikuko Okamoto

Toyo University, Japan

INSTITUTE OF DEVELOPING ECONOMIES (IDE), JETRO

Edward Elgar

Cheltenham, UK • Northampton, MA, USA

Published by
Edward Elgar Publishing Limited
The Lypiatts
15 Lansdown Road
Cheltenham
Glos GL50 2JA
UK

Edward Elgar Publishing, Inc.
William Pratt House
9 Dewey Court
Northampton
Massachusetts 01060
USA

A catalogue record for this book
is available from the British Library

Library of Congress Control Number: 2014932630

This book is available electronically in the ElgarOnline.com
Social and Political Science Subject Collection, E-ISBN 978 1 78347 438 7

ISBN 978 1 78347 437 0

Typeset by Servis Filmsetting Ltd, Stockport, Cheshire
Printed and bound in Great Britain by T.J. International Ltd, Padstow

Contents

Contributors

Atsuko Hayama is Associate Professor at the Faculty of Economics, Kurume University in Fukuoka, Japan. Her research interests are in the fields of rural development and forest economics in Asia, with special focus on the Philippines and Japan.

Misaki Iwai is Professor at the Department of Asian Languages, Kanda University of International Studies in Chiba, Japan. Her research interests are in the field of social transformation, migration, and the relationship between the state and society in rural Vietnam.

Ikuko Okamoto is Professor at the Faculty of Regional Development Studies, Toyo University in Tokyo, Japan. Her research interests are in agricultural and rural development, with special focus on Myanmar. She is the author of *Economic Disparity in Rural Myanmar: Transformation under Market Liberalization* (Singapore: National University of Singapore Press, 2008).

Shinichi Shigetomi is Senior Research Fellow at the Institute of Developing Economies (IDE), Japan External Trade Organization (JETRO). His research covers rural development, agricultural economics, and civil society in Asia, with special focus on Thailand. He edited *Protest and Social Movements in the Developing World* (Cheltenham, UK and Northampton, MA, USA: Edward Elgar, 2009).

Motoko Shimagami is Associate Professor, Six-University Initiative Japan Indonesia (SUIJI) Promotion Office, Ehime University in Ehime, Japan. Her research interests are in the fields of village autonomy, community-based resource management, and community organizations in Indonesia and Japan.

Akina Venkateswarlu is Senior Fellow of the Indian Council of Social Science Research (ICSSR), at the Centre for Economic and Social Studies, Hyderabad, India. His research interests are in the fields of agricultural economics, rural development, and political economy of development. He is the author of *The Role of Village Panchayats and Village Development Councils in Rural Development* (Delhi: Abhijeet Publications, 2012).

Nanae Yamada is Research Fellow of the Institute of Developing Economies (IDE), Japan External Trade Organization (JETRO). Her research interests are Chinese agriculture and rural economy issues, with special focus on resource management, institutions and organizations.

Preface

Let us assume that a rural household must host a funeral. Because a funeral requires a considerable amount of resources, people in rural societies commonly organize collective actions to assist the host household. In a Japanese village, a neighborhood group (*kumi*) comprised of approximately 10–20 households assists with all activities related to the funeral. Every household in the *kumi* is required to participate in this collective action, regardless of personal ties with the host family. In the case of a Thai village, the host family's relatives and friends would volunteer to help with the funeral. The personal ties that relatives and friends maintain with the host family serve to connect them with collective actions related to the funeral. In Thailand, no clear-cut criteria for membership or geographical scope appear to exist among those individuals who assist with the funeral. The two contrasting cases clearly demonstrate that, even though the purposes or needs of these collective actions are the same, the forms and the methods employed to organize people differ substantially based on each local society. Thus, local societies have developed their own mechanisms which they can use to create organizations.

Organizing people is an indispensable part of participatory rural development, because local people are expected to tackle their problems collectively. Designers and practitioners of rural development who attempt to apply this approach should become familiar with the mechanisms local people use to organize themselves in their communities. However, the search for these types of mechanisms has rarely been the focus of scholarly studies. Rather, studies have frequently provided discussions of outside agents' roles, and examinations of policy arrangements that might facilitate participatory development.

We do not claim that traditional institutions, such as those involved in funerals, would be applicable to current development needs without the addition of some changes. Nevertheless, rules of conduct should be shared by local people when they attempt to organize themselves. In order to approach local communities, we must know which mechanisms exist in the local community and how they work in the process of creating organizations. If development projects lack adequate knowledge of local mechanisms, those projects may fail to induce participation. Some organizations might not survive once assistance is withdrawn. Even a successful pilot project might not be able to expand to wider areas.

This volume is the product of a joint research project entitled "A Comparative Study on the Organizational Capabilities of Asian Rural Societies." The project was conducted by the Institute of Developing Economies over a two-year period that extended between April 2011 and March 2013. This research project sheds light on local societies. It attempts to identify local mechanisms that might be used to develop organizational activities and to develop methodologies that might be used to locate these local mechanisms. Figuratively speaking, we intend to present maps or a method to draw maps that rural researchers and frontline workers can rely on to uncover self-organizing capabilities of local societies.

The participants in this research project include scholars who possess significant experience in conducting research in rural societies in their personal field countries. In addition to the authors of this volume, when Keiko Sato was a graduate student at Kyoto University she also participated in the project during its first year and contributed to the interim report.

This study project received various types of support and cooperation. In particular, we would like to thank Toshihiro Yogo, a visiting professor from Nihon Fukushi University. He provided a lecture on the importance of local social systems in rural development. He also provided comments related to the scope of our study and case analysis that were remarkably helpful to the development of our ideas. We cordially thank Andrew Walker from the Australian National University, and our colleagues, especially Yutaka Arimoto and two anonymous reviewers, for providing comments on the manuscript.

It would have been impossible to continue this research without the assistance of local leaders, villagers, government officials, and non-governmental organizations during the time we conducted field surveys in each country. Even though we cannot name all of these individuals and institutions here, we are extremely grateful for their valuable assistance.

Shinichi Shigetomi
Ikuko Okamoto

1. Local societies and rural people's self-organizing activities: an analytical framework

Shinichi Shigetomi and Ikuko Okamoto

INTRODUCTION

The importance of community-based and participatory approaches has been emphasized in rural development literature. Rural people, who as individuals are economically and politically weak, can only participate in development projects when they become collectively organized. Therefore, rural people's organizational activities should be considered an indispensable element in participatory rural development.

However, the tasks involved in organizing people are not easy. Frequently, organizations malfunction once development assistance agencies leave project sites. This suggests that the process involved in "making organizations" is not similar to the process involved in "making a system of making organizations" (Shigetomi 2011). The latter process is required to make local organizations spontaneous, sustainable, and transferrable. The main purpose of this volume is to identify the local mechanisms by which rural people organize themselves to meet their development needs.

People create organizations because they expect to derive benefits from those organizations. However, economic opportunities and favorable resource endowments do not always ensure that expectations will be realized. Mechanisms must be instituted to motivate and control members of new organizations as they attempt to achieve organizational goals. This volume assumes that these types of mechanisms exist in local societies in which people relate to one another because they live in close geographic proximity and/or in the same administrative or social units. Based on the purposes of our study, when we refer to "local society," we mean a particular locality, such as an administrative village or a settlement, that is not so large that its residents (hereafter, "local people") are unable to consult one another when they create their organizations.

We focus on local societies for the following reasons. First, some groups of people in local societies may serve as host organizations that incubate new organizations (Chaskin et al. 2001, p. 83). Second, the possibility exists that the behaviors of organization members might be directed towards the achievement of organizational goals by relying on their local society's social norms.

A local society contains groups of people who function as actors, resources used to facilitate people's lives, and institutions that regulate interactions among the people. These actors, resources, and institutions are interrelated in a system we call a "local social system." They function as mechanisms that can be used to make organizations among local people. However, it is not easy for outsiders to single out these systems within complicated societies.

These types of systems become visible only when actual organizing processes occur. Therefore, we must carefully observe how an organization is formed and managed, and how the elements of a local society affect that organization's form and how the organization came about. Then, we must attempt to identify local systems that support organizational activities. We refer to this method as the "organizational process approach."

To gain a better understanding of this approach, case studies can provide indispensable information. In this volume, we will examine a variety of cases that involve organizational activities performed during rural development projects conducted in seven Asian countries. We will identify how these activities were facilitated by the social systems in each locality. Based on a synthesis of the results of each case study, we will propose ways to gain a better understanding of local societies and their functions as social systems.

In the remainder of this chapter, we will explain in more detail the background, research questions, and methodology used to create this volume. Then, we will provide outlines of each chapter's results.

ORGANIZING PEOPLE FOR RURAL DEVELOPMENT

Reasons for Organizing

Rural poverty remains one of the major problems that affect developing countries. The World Bank (2003) reported that 1 billion people live below the poverty line. In fact, 75 percent of these poor people live in rural areas. The persistence of rural poverty suggests that resource distribution through market mechanisms alone cannot fundamentally eradicate the problem. Therefore, some scholars believe deliberate approaches are required to distribute resources to targeted populations. Rural development is one such intervention. However, simultaneously, since the very beginning of rural development practice, scholars have observed that the distribution of resources through hierarchical government channels has not always been successful. Therefore, the concept of achieving development through community efforts has received serious consideration.

Placing emphasis on the community is a method in which local people are considered to be active participants in decision-making processes and the implementation of development projects. According to Oakley et al. (1991), local people's participation can enhance the efficiency, effectiveness, self-reliance, coverage, and sustainability of projects. To realize the advantages offered by popular participation, local people's needs should be collected, discussed, and synthesized into actual proposals. These processes require that local people become organized (Esman and Uphoff 1984; Galjart 1981; Burkey 1993).

Rural organizations function as intermediaries that assist households' abilities to access external resources (Yogo 1996). It can be difficult for individuals to access resources. Hence, people join together to form organizations so that they can more efficiently obtain external resources. People also make organizations to mobilize resources already available in their local societies. These organizations become substitutes for markets and governments to procure resources.

Thus, organizations formed by local people become agents of participatory development, intermediaries which seek and receive external resources, and tools for the creation of resources and services.

Categories of Local Organizations

We define "local organizations" in a broad sense. The term refers to organizations formed by local people, as well as to local people's organizational activities or collective actions that might not necessarily assume the form of a membership organization. They include two different types of organizations, based on their functions. One type consists of an organization formed to achieve specified targets. The other type coordinates and regulates its members' behaviors.[1] In the rural development context, the former type of organizations are exemplified by microfinance organizations that provide low-interest loans, joint marketing groups that attempt to secure better market access, and conservation groups that administer common-pool resources. This type of organization is the direct target of participatory rural development projects. We describe this type of organization as a development organization.[2]

Some organizations that focus on specific targets have also been formed endogenously. These organizations have been in operation for a long time.

Rotating savings and credit associations (ROSCAs) and mutual assistance labor exchanges have operated for long periods in various rural societies. However, the transformation of rural economies has created new reasons for local people to develop new organizations. In these rural development situations, interventions are required. Therefore, the rural development literature usually focuses on organizations that might develop because of some exogenous interventions. This volume shares the same concern.

The second type of local organization also provides examples of both endogenous and exogenous organizations. An endogenous organization is generally described as a social organization (Blau and Scott 1963). Social organizations in rural areas include kinship groups, natural or indigenously formed villages, and caste organizations. These organizations facilitate and/or coordinate members' relationships. Sometimes, these organizations also guide members' behaviors. For example, when two members of the same caste become involved in a conflict, the caste council or elders group from the same caste intervenes and arbitrates the conflict (Zamora 1990, pp. 55–56).

An exogenously formed organization is a unit created to provide local governance and administration (hereafter, "local administrative organization"). For example, an administrative village and its subdivisions fall in this category. Even though an external authority introduces the local administrative organization to a local society, the organization usually has institutions and functions which it can use to coordinate and regulate its residents.

Although the latter types of local organizations are not direct targets of rural development practices, their coordinating and controlling functions are related to the mechanisms used to organize local people. Our primary research goal is to identify local mechanisms that bolster development organizations. Hence, these local organizations that perform coordinating and controlling functions are the prime focus of this study.

Difficulties Involved in Organizing

Although the significance of local organizations has been widely recognized, organizing people is not an easy task. Many community-based development projects have failed to attract villagers' participation. Those projects may have survived solely on assistance provided by outside agencies. Even though many successful cases have been reported, those cases have rarely been reproduced and transferred to wider areas. Chapter 6 of this volume provides a good example of a situation in which a community-based forest management project in the Philippines failed to mobilize local people's collective actions. Ultimately, the "community forest" existed solely in the project's name.

People create organizations because they expect to derive benefits from them. Potential benefits may be affected by economic, political, and natural conditions that exist in local environments. However, favorable environments do not automatically provide benefits during organizing efforts. The benefits of organizations can only be realized when participants begin to act for the benefit of those organizations, rather than for their individual benefits. Therefore, organizations must rely on mechanisms that guide participants' behaviors. Moreover, making organizations is not cost-free. People, especially leaders, must input their private resources. Mechanisms should be developed to save on organizing costs.

Organizational activities will not occur spontaneously unless these mechanisms are used to control members' behaviors and save on organizing costs. Many development organizations fail to become sustainable because they do not develop and rely on these types of mechanisms. Development organizations are not easily transferred to other areas because outside agencies fail to recognize the mechanisms in use at each project site. To make projects sustainable and diffusible, we must identify the types of mechanisms that facilitate local people's self-organizing activities.

FOCUSING ON LOCAL SOCIETIES

To determine these mechanisms, we must focus on local societies for two main reasons. The first reason relates to the cost of making new organizations. In rural societies, people usually rely on existing social institutions to present ideas and generate consensus so they can begin organizing. Therefore, people rarely need to discuss how to proceed with consensus building prior to developing organizations. This reduces organizing costs. On the other hand, if common resources are available in local societies, they are used to reduce the initial costs each participant must pay. This may reduce local people's risks when they participate in those organizations.

The second reason relates to the administration of organizations. Social theory explains that in formal organizations, organization members' behaviors must remain free of the influences of societies that operate outside those organizations (Luhmann 1992).[3] However, in rural local societies, human interactions in both organizations and those societies cannot remain physically separate. Each organization's members are simultaneously members of each local society. Therefore, they cannot behave without considering social relationships that exist in their societies. In other words, the social forces that operate in local societies can easily influence organizations.

Sometimes, these factors can negatively affect the administration of organizations. For example, local leaders may use their power within their local societies to administer organizations for their own benefits. In contrast, some cases have been observed in which the social relationships in a local society worked to support the administration of organizations. For example, social control mechanisms, such as gossiping among neighbors and the provision of warnings by senior relatives, may guide participants to follow the rules of these organizations.

In rural societies, most individuals who participate in development organizations are self-employed or own independent businesses (for example, farmers, people involved in cottage industries, and freelance laborers). These people can leave these organizations without causing serious impacts to their personal economies. In these types of environments, organizations' inside rules do not strongly regulate members' behaviors. Thus, social mechanisms that operate in surrounding societies must be mobilized to administer development organizations.

Indeed, local societies matter. One of the authors identified contrasting differences between microfinance organizations that operated in the rural Philippines and Thailand, in their forms as well as their methods of organizing people (Shigetomi 2011). One popular type of microfinance organization in Thailand is a savings group in which members pool their money and lend it to other members. Usually, a group forms at the village level and the village administration works as an agent to organize local people. In contrast, in the Philippines, one popular form of microfinance organization is the Grameen Bank type, in which money is contributed by outside agencies. The money is placed under peer control and managed by a small group that generally contains five people. In this case, outside agencies, rather than village administrators, are the main actors who organize local people.

Although these organizations' purposes are the same (that is, the provision of low-interest loans to rural people), their organizational forms and methods used in both countries differ significantly. This suggests that different mechanisms are used to make organizations in different local societies. Consequently, we must identify the mechanisms used to make organizations in local societies.

COMMUNITY DEVELOPMENT STUDIES THAT LACK COMMUNITY ANALYSES

These types of mechanisms that operate in local societies have rarely been the focus of studies that emphasize the importance of community in development. Advocates of participatory rural development have emphasized the importance of providing suggestions to rural development practitioners related to the attitudes they should adopt and methodologies they should use to approach rural societies (Chambers 2005; Burkey 1993; Korten 1980). Many studies in this field have discussed methods used for participatory rural appraisals. However, only a limited number of studies have discussed local mechanisms that could be used to ensure community participation. Even though the recently promoted approach of local community-driven development (LCDD) states that development programs should be designed based on local contexts to create projects that will be more applicable to wider areas, the LCDD approach fails to discuss how local contexts should be understood (Binswanger and Aiyar 2003; Binswanger-Mkhize et al. 2009). Dongier et al. (n.d.) assert that community-driven development should consist of institutional arrangements that combine the efforts of community-based organizations (CBOs), non-governmental organizations (NGOs), private firms, local and municipal governments, and central governments. However, in their framework, local communities were not considered as an element of institutional arrangements. CBOs serve as development organizations, rather than the communities themselves. These studies believe that communities are just geographical areas or units (Midgley 1986, p. 24). As a result, they fail to study the social functions of local societies.

The social aspects of community have been more seriously discussed by scholars of common-pool resource management. Some emphasize that the community functions as a social unit, rather than as a simple geographical unit (Agrawal and Gibson 1999). Communities are often assumed to contain attributes such as small geographical units, homogenous membership, and shared norms (ibid., p. 630). Singleton and Taylor (1992) define a community of mutually vulnerable actors as a group that possesses relevant collective capacities. McCay (2002, p. 385) state that the functions of a community can be evaluated as a whole by the "degree of community," and by relying on some criteria, such as the strength of shared beliefs, stability in membership, expectations of future interactions, and the existence of direct and multiple kinds of relationships among members. Community is often regarded as a culture, rather than an actual entity (Ostrom et al. 1994, p. 37; McCay 2002; Ostrom 1992). If the community is assumed to be a group of people that maintains a culture of mutual assistance, then the community can be considered a suitable social unit for collective actions, such as common-pool resource conservation. When the community is predetermined to be a unified, organic whole that contains certain cultures, these studies offer limited incentives to study the reality of social mechanisms' operations in the actual community (Agrawal and Gibson 1999, p. 633).

Many scholars who focus on common-pool resource management have taken reductionist approaches, rather than holistic ones. They reduce the community into elements that affect the collective actions of local people with respect to resources (Ostrom 2002; Agrawal 2002). They focus on the attributes of people in local societies, such as population size, face-to-face relationships, mutual understanding of common rules and penalties, leadership, and experiences in organizations (Ostrom 2002). These approaches assume that these attributes can be calculated to determine if the net benefits of the collective administration of resources can surpass the benefits of individual resource procurement. This is based on the idea that by setting collective resource management as the dependent variable, and by setting the attributes of resources and resource users as the independent variables, the correlation coefficients can be calculated to determine whether each attribute significantly affects the collective action.

Some scholars apply social capital theory to their analyses (Ostrom and Ahn 2010). According to Putnam (1993, p. 167), social capital can be defined as the "features of a social organization, such as trust, norms, and networks, that can improve the efficiency of society by facilitating coordinated actions." Social capital serves as an important tool that can be used to understand factors that contribute to successful collective actions for development at local levels (Woolcock and Narayan 2000). Since social capital itself cannot be measured quantitatively, researchers tend to make proxies of elements such as trust, networks, norms, and rules that they assume might represent social capital. Then, they examine the correlations that exist between each element (independent variable) and the performance of collective actions (dependent variable). In some rural development studies, social capital indicators are measured by the number of local groups, meeting attendance frequency, orientation towards and actual participation in group and village activities, trust in neighbors, inclinations towards mutual assistance, and cooperative spirit (Isham and Kähkönen 2002; Krishna 2002).

Esman and Uphoff (1984) applied the same idea in a comprehensive study that focused on local organizations that perform rural development projects. They selected 150 development organizations from 48 countries to determine whether organizations' structures, functions, and environments affected those organizations' performance. The authors assigned numerical points to each organization's performance (dependent variables) and assigned several indicators that they assumed would represent independent variables. Then, they examined those correlations by performing a regression analysis. Local society served as one of several environmental conditions represented by 18 indicators, such as physical-economic conditions (topography, resource endowment, infrastructure, economic diversification, income level, income distribution pattern), social-societal conditions (settlement pattern, social heterogeneity, social stratification, sex discrimination, social discrimination, literacy), and political-administrative conditions (partisanship, group patterns, community norms, societal norms, political support, administrative support) (ibid., pp. 105–106).

The regression analysis failed to discover any environmental indicators that correlated with organizational performance. Esman and Uphoff suggested the following possible causes for this result (ibid., pp. 124–127). First, the interactions among environmental variables in the microenvironments were so complex that the model was unable to find correlations. Second, the variables were not as linear as those required for proper analysis. Third, the variables might have worked in either positive or negative directions. Esman and Uphoff saw that the possibility existed that people might respond to their difficult environments to ensure the enhancement of organizational performance.

These reasons suggest that unobserved variables may have affected these correlations (Greif 2006, pp. 20–21). For example, the existence of a caste system represents a factional division or heterogeneity in a community. However, in some village communities, caste councils represent caste groups. Consultation mechanisms operate between caste leaders. Thus, caste systems serve as channels for consensus building for village-level collective actions.[4] This means that factional divisions or heterogeneity may cause positive or negative effects based on other factors that operate in local societies.

In the reductionist approach, each element that might affect the performance of collective actions in a local society is examined independently. The mutual relationships that exist between these elements are neglected. In other words, the local context is omitted from the examination. However, as suggested by Esman and Uphoff's analysis, social capital or other environmental elements may be interrelated and affect the performance of collective actions as a set. An additional approach, which would identify the set of elements that interrelate to facilitate rural people's collective action, is required. This perspective rests on the understanding that a local society operates as a system.

LOCAL SOCIETY AS A SYSTEM

Margaret Stacey is a pioneer who first questioned the feasibility of "community" as a concept used to understand social relations in a locality. Instead, she proposed the idea of the "local social system" (Stacey 1969). She defined the "social system" as "a set of inter-related social institutions covering all aspects of social life, familial, religious, juridical, etc., and the associated belief systems of each" (ibid., p.140). She continued: a "local social system occurs when such a set of inter-relations exists in a geographically defined locality" (ibid.). The focal components of Stacey's "local social system" are institutions. However, she did not specify the kinds of institutions that comprise local social systems and how they are interrelated, because she concentrated on determining the conditions that facilitate the development of local social systems.

Agrawal and Gibson (1999, p.638) stated that the attributes of community result in collective actions aimed at natural resource conservation because of interactions that occur between multiple actors and institutional arrangements. Although they did not use the word "system," they emphasized the interrelationships that exist between elements in local societies. In particular, they emphasized the importance of institutions when attempts are made to understand the ability of local communities to manage common-pool resources, because multiple and overlapping rules can affect resource management outcomes.

Toshihiro Yogo applies a systems approach to gain a better understanding of local societies. He assumes that local development is realized by the interactions of four elements (that is, households, markets, states, and local communities). He refers to the interactions of these elements as a "local system" (Yogo 1996). Organizations develop out of the interactions that occur among these elements. Households form social organizations when they interact with local communities. Yogo describes local communities that unite with households as internal systems that operate within local systems. These internal systems are identical to Stacey's description of local social systems. They also represent the focus of this volume.[5]

Yogo understands that social organizations that emerged from internal systems coordinate social relations among people and accumulate their experiences within each locality. Then, different types of collective actions emerge based on the functions of social organizations (ibid., pp.12–14). He states that each of the five types of social organizations (that is, mutual aid, resource pool, asset management, business management, and self-governance) is supported by different principles and rules that operate in local societies.

To simplify Yogo's framework: the interactions that occur between households and local communities give birth to social organizations whose functions determine particular types of collective actions. This framework offers an advantage because it links local social systems to the formation of collective actions aimed at development. However, in this framework, local communities remain intact. We must specify their contents to determine the elements that comprise local social systems or, in Yogo's terminology, internal systems that operate within local systems.

During a review of prior studies, we discovered that institutions were considered the primary components of social systems that operate in localities. We adopted this concept because institutions attempt to regulate human interactions in societies. We added resources as an additional component of social systems because they, as well as institutions, are mobilized to achieve organizational activities. Both institutions and resources can be used effectively in local people's collective actions only when they can be mobilized by certain groups of people. Therefore, we include actors as groups of people that serve as components of local social systems. By observing the actors who function within local social systems, we understand that social organizations, as Yogo stated, as well as local administrative organizations, should be examined. Thus, during the following discussion, for the sake of convenience, we will combine social organizations and local administrative organizations under the heading of locality groups.

In summary, we understand that local societies are systems in which actors (locality groups), institutions, and resources interrelate with one another. These systems differ because the characteristics of each component in these systems, as well as their compositions, also differ. We assume that the mechanisms involved in organizing people operate based on these social systems.

ORGANIZATIONAL PROCESS APPROACH TO LOCAL SOCIETIES

However, the identification of local social systems is not an easy task. Each system is quite multifaceted and complicated. Thus, it can be difficult to single out mechanisms used to make development organizations in entire social systems. Moreover, systems used to make organizations may be undetectable when no organizational activities occur. Therefore, we must first carefully observe the salient features of self-organizational activities conducted among local people, and attempt to discover how local factors function in these organizational processes. We must pay special attention to determine which locality groups become hosts for organizational activities, the forms these organization take, and how local people build and manage these organizations. Based on these salient features of organizational processes, we expect to discover local social systems that function in the making and managing of development organizations. Therefore we refer to this approach, which is based on observations of local societies through their organizational activities, as the organizational process approach.

The actual process involved in organizational activities includes the following four stages: (1) proposal and consensus building to make an organization; (2) coordination and control among local people; (3) resource mobilization and acquisition to make the organization; (4) outcome distribution and accumulation of organizational activities. We will explain below how the actors, institutions, and resources might possibly interrelate with one another during each stage.

Proposal and Consensus Building

The organizing process begins when a proposal is made by local leaders who recognize the need for an organizational activity. To ensure the call for organizing is considered a common matter by local people, one group of people must assume that they belong to the same group as the leaders. This group will become the foundation when they create the organization. Then, the proposal must be combined into the consensus-building process that develops among this group.

The processes inherent in proposal and consensus building require some institutional arrangements that involve the formal positions of local people who will be expected to call a meeting (for example, a village headman and village executives). Village institutions, such as a village general assembly or a village council meeting, should be used to help build consensus.

Consensus building also occurs through the efforts of informal institutions that operate in the local society. Social relations among neighbors and relatives are often mobilized to encourage participation and convince individuals who oppose the proposal.

Coordination and Control

After the organization is formed, leaders must attempt to find consensus amid conflicts that occur between members. Leaders must sometimes coordinate efforts between members and non-member residents. They must encourage and, on occasion, forcefully encourage members to achieve organizational purposes. Some institutions in the local society will be mobilized during this organizing process.

The actions of these institutions include the exertion of social pressure by respected leaders of social organizations. Locally shared sanctions, such as warnings provided by respected social leaders, gossip, and even restrictions on social interactions, are other institutional processes that may be used to control local people. The authority provided to local administrative bodies by the government might also influence people's behaviors.

Resource Mobilization and Acquisition

A development organization may procure resources from each member, as well as from the local society and outside agencies. In some local societies, common resources may be utilized to perform organizational activities. In addition to material resources, such as land, facilities and money, members' experiences of other organizational activities within the local society are also important (Yogo 1996). Through their shared experiences in the locality, people gain a common understanding of how organizational activities should proceed. They do not require discussions of organizing methods. This reduces organizing costs.

In situations in which outside agencies provide resources for organizational activities, such as money, equipment, information, and technical assistance, local administrative organizations may serve as receiving mechanisms (Oakley et al. 1991).

Outcome Distribution and Accumulation

Organizational activities for development occasionally produce economic surpluses. In the case of membership-based organizations, these surpluses should be distributed to members and stored within organizations. Sometimes, a locality group may receive some portion of the surplus and accumulate it for other communal purposes, especially when this group hosts or provides key resources for the development organization.

Members gain organizational experience by participating in organizational activities. Individuals who participate in the organizing process accumulate experience. For the length of time these individuals remain in the locality, their experience also remains, even after the organization disappears. This experience can be shared by groups of local people and passed on from generation to generation. In this way, the experience of organizing is accumulated in a local society.

OUTLINE OF CASE STUDIES

In this volume, we applied the organizational process approach to a variety of cases. The authors of each chapter selected particular development organizations in their fields and identified salient features of their forms, the locality groups on which they relied, as well as the ways these organizations were made and managed. Then, they attempted to discover local social systems that yielded these salient features of development organizations. We expect that these case studies will endorse the applicability of the approach we have presented in this introductory chapter. They will also reveal local mechanisms that operated in each locality. Based on these cases, field researchers and workers may discover appropriate types of local social systems most applicable to their own projects.

Summaries of each case study are provided below. The chapters are categorized into two parts based on their main focus. Part I consists of country studies that primarily examine the composition of locality groups and their roles as host organizations for development organizations. Part II presents case studies that focus on the forms of development organizations and the ways in which organizations are formed and managed. These case studies demonstrate how local social systems reflect salient organizational forms and responses. A synthesis of these case studies is presented in the concluding chapter of this volume, Chapter 9 in Part III.

Chapter 2 (Shinichi Shigetomi) demonstrates how each set of locality groups, institutions, and resources in a local society can affect the appearances of organizational processes. The chapter provides comparisons of two local societies located in different regions of northeastern and lower central Thailand. They involve similar types of locality groups: administrative villages, indigenous villages, and temple supporter groups. However, the compositions of locality groups are quite different. In the northeastern region, because of an overlap that occurred among the three locality groups, the administrative village fostered collective identities and accumulated experience. Therefore, it was able to mobilize institutions and their resources. In contrast, in the lower central region, the administrative village faced difficulties when it attempted to utilize the functions of other locality groups because the locality groups did not necessarily overlap. In this case, social organizations, such as a temple supporter group and a kin group, became the primary foundations for collective activities.

In Chapter 3, Misaki Iwai describes a case that demonstrates how the composition of social organizations can support a development project's performance. The Vietnamese case is unique because some social organizations, such as the Women's Union, were installed by the central government and designated to serve simultaneously as development organizations. These organizations played central roles in the management of a government-sponsored microfinance program that successfully achieved a high repayment rate. These formal organizations overlapped with the indigenous village, an indigenous social organization. The village coordinated interests among the different stakeholders within its domain. It also made decisions, mobilized resources, and exerted social pressure on the villagers. By fully utilizing these features of the local social system, exogenously formed social organizations can serve as mediators, as well as administrators of government programs.

In Chapter 4, Ikuko Okamoto demonstrates how a local society might function as a host organization for development organizations. Okamoto analyzed how a community forestry program was introduced in three different areas in Myanmar: the dry zone, the mountainous area, and the delta area. She discovered that villages played key roles in organizing people for the project. Further, she explored why the villages played key roles, rather than other locality groups. The villages maintained their informal mechanisms of consensus building, resource mobilization, and enforcement. Efforts were led by the village core leaders – village headman, ten-house heads, and village elders. Simultaneously, when any need arose for collective actions, the villages created informal committees or groups to provide detailed management. Because the villages accumulated different degrees of organizational experience, this mechanism had a stronger effect in the dry zone, as well as in villages located in the mountainous area, rather than in the delta area villages. This caused differences in organizational patterns between the three regions: the two former regions mobilized all villagers; the latter region relied on villagers' partial participation.

In Chapter 5, Motoko Shimagami discovered that microfinance groups formed under the same national poverty alleviation program showed contrasting responses with respect to members' repayment failures based on each region. A village located in Yogyakarta managed repayments by utilizing village assets. In Banten, the village head paid dues from his private earnings. A Torajanese village located in South Sulawesi repaid loans by utilizing kinship groups' funds. Finally, in a village located in Central Sulawesi, an unpaid loan was settled within the group by utilizing members' savings. A closer examination of the cases of Yogyakarta and South Sulawesi reveals the different natures of local social systems. In Yogyakarta, some of the local administrative organizations overlapped with locality-based social organizations. This enabled the entire village to take responsibility for their acceptance and management of the government project. In contrast, in South Sulawesi, a "ritual community" formed by a Torajanese kinship group overlapped with an administrative unit and functioned as the recipient of the government project.

Chapter 6, in which Atsuko Hayama focuses on the Philippines, also provides insightful evidence that local social systems may determine the possible forms of collective actions. Based on her observations of the failure of a community-based forest management project that was long promoted by the government and international development agencies, she inquires about the types of social mechanisms used to organize people in the rural Philippines. She explores several development organizations, both exogenously introduced and indigenously formed, and divides them into three categories. One type is organizations that pool resources for short periods by relying on strong dyadic relationships among a small group of people. This is the dominant form of the rural organizations in the country. The second type is also small and based on informal relationships among members but deals with long-term resources. This type is generally diffi- cult to create since members cannot wait long to receive benefits from the organization while the cost of maintaining it increases. The last category manages a long-term resource pool with a large membership with formal rules. However, in most cases, this type of organization is difficult to be materialized fully in the rural Philippines because of the nonexistence of a social system that supports large-scale organizations.

Each local society maintains its own pattern of collective action. The case studies of villages located in Southern India (Chapter 7 by Akina Venkateswarlu and Shinichi Shigetomi) clearly demonstrate this fact. The salient features of collective actions that occurred in the studied vil- lages relied on the possibility of obtaining rent from individual economic activities conducted by both villagers and outsiders. The rent was pooled into a common fund that was utilized for the entire village. To develop these collective actions, the leaders had to create an institution that could make collective decisions that would convince villagers to cooperate. However, the habitations (natural villages) that served as the hosts for these collective actions did not have any formal institutions that performed self-administration. Therefore, some habitations developed new institu- tions (for example, the Village Development Council) to administer rural development projects. Alternatively, some habitations utilized traditional institutions (for example, village councils) to achieve consensus building and to implement rural development.

Chapter 8 describes another salient pattern of collective actions that occurred in rural China. Even though this society has generally been characterized as a mere aggregation of individuals connected by economic motivation, Nanae Yamada discovered the existence of communal resource management in some villages. Collective administration is necessary because resources are communally owned and villagers expect to receive economic benefits from those resources. However, villagers' participation was limited, based on each individual's evaluation of the leader's manage- ment skill and economic viability. Resource administration methods differ, based on local social systems in Northern villages and Southern villages. In Northern China, the administrative village was equipped with ownership, strong decision-making skills, and enforcement power. It took the lead and managed shareholding co-operatives by encouraging villagers' individual investments. In contrast, in Southern China, because of more complicated village structures, the administrative village played a limited role: it pro- vided monitoring and authorization. Instead, village groups, which had stronger ownership of resources, served as brokers or coordinators for the management of resources and promoted bilateral contracts between the entrusted manager and villagers.

NOTES

1. Esman and Uphoff (1984, p. 18) define local organizations as organizations classified under the first category. However, we can see that the second category should not be neglected when we attempt to understand the local mechanisms involved in organizational activities, as discussed later.
2. Yogo (1996) defines development organizations as organizations formed by households to secure resources from the government and the market. However, borrowing Yogo's terminology, this term is used more generally in this volume than Yogo's definition.
3. According to Luhmann (1992), a formal organization is an organization in which the expectations for members' behaviors are formalized. This means that, in a formal organization, members can expect other members to behave in accordance with the formal system. Although members of a formal organization are involved in an expectation structure that operates outside the organization, they are obliged to follow formalized expectations inside the organization.
4. Chapter 7 of this volume provides a case study of Pindiprolu Village in which each caste council sent its representative to the Village Development Council, a body that implemented village-level development projects.
5. Yogo uses the term "local social system" in several other places. Even though they use the same words, Yogo and Stacey imply different meanings for this concept. The former describes it as a (total) system that operates in local societies. The latter describes it as a social system that operates in localities.

REFERENCES

Agrawal, Arun (2002), "Common resources and institutional sustainability," in Elinor Ostrom, Thomas Dietz, Nives Dolšak, Paul C. Stern, Susan Stonich, and Elke U. Weber (eds), *The Drama of the Commons*, Washington, DC: National Academy Press, pp. 41–85.
Agrawal, Arun and Clark C. Gibson (1999), "Enchantment and disenchantment: The role of community in natural resource conservation," *World Development*, **27**(4), 629–649.
Binswanger, Hans P. and Swaminathan S. Aiyar (2003), "Scaling up community-driven development: Theoretical underpinnings and program design implications," Policy Research Working Paper, Washington, DC: World Bank.
Binswanger-Mkhize, Hans P., Jacomina P. de Regt, and Stephen Spector (eds) (2009), *Scaling Up Local and Community Driven Development (LCDD): A Real World Guide to Its Theory and Practice*, Washington, DC: World Bank.
Blau, Peter M. and W. Richard Scott (1963), *Formal Organizations: A Comparative Approach*, London: Routledge & Kegan Paul.
Burkey, Stan (1993), *People First: A Guide to Self-Reliant Participatory Rural Development*, London, UK and Atlantic Highlands, NJ: Zed Books.
Chambers, Robert (2005), *Ideas for Development*, London: Earthscan.

Chaskin, Robert J., Prudence Brown, Sudhir Venkatesh, and Avis Vidal (2001), *Building Community Capacity*, New York: Aldine de Gruyter.

Dongier, Philippe, Julie Van Domelen, Elinor Ostrom, Andrea Rizvi, Wendy Wakeman, Anthony Bebbington, Sabina Alkire, Talib Esmail, and Margaret Polski (n.d.), "Community-driven development," World Bank, PRSP Sourcebook, available at http://siteresources.worldbank.org (accessed June 25, 2012).

Esman, Milton J. and Norman T. Uphoff (1984), *Local Organizations: Intermediaries in Rural Development*, Ithaca, NY: Cornell University Press.

Galjart, Benno (1981), "Participatory development projects: Some reasons from research," *Sociologia Ruralis* (*Journal of the European Society for Rural Sociology*), **2**(2), 142–159.

Greif, Avner (2006), *Institutions and the Path to the Modern Economy: Lessons from Medieval Trade*. New York: Cambridge University Press.

Isham, Jonathan and Satu Kähkönen (2002), "How do participation and social capital affect community-based water projects? Evidence from Central Java, Indonesia," in Christiaan Grootaert and Thierry van Bastelaer (eds), *The Role of Social Capital in Development: An Empirical Assessment*, Cambridge: Cambridge University Press, pp. 155–187.

Korten, David C. (1980), "Community organization and rural development: A learning process approach," *Public Administration Review*, **40**(5), 480–511.

Krishna, Anirudh (2002), *Active Social Capital: Tracing the Roots of Development and Democracy*, New York: Columbia University Press.

Luhmann, Niklas (1992), *Funktionen und Folgen formaler Organisation*, Japanese trans. by Yutaka Sawaya, Mitsuharu Sekiguchi, and Koichi Hasegawa, Berlin: Duncker & Humblot.

McCay, Bonnie J. (2002), "Emergence of institutions for the commons: Context, situations, and events," in Elinor Ostrom, Thomas Dietz, Nives Dolšak, Paul C. Stern, Susan Stonich, and Elke U. Weber (eds), *The Drama of the Commons*, Washington, DC: National Academy Press, pp. 361–402.

Midgley, James (1986), "Community participation: History, concepts and controversies," in James Midgley, Anthony Hall, Margaret Hardiman, and Dhanpaul Narine (eds), *Community Participation, Social Development, and the State*, London, UK and New York, USA: Methuen, pp. 13–44.

Oakley, Peter et al. (1991), *Projects with People: The Practice of Participation in Rural Development*, Geneva, International Labour Office.

Ostrom, Elinor (1992), "The rudiments of a theory of the origins, survival, and performance of common-property institutions," in Daniel W. Bromley (ed.), *Making the Commons Work: Theory, Practice, and Policy*, San Francisco, CA: ICS Press, pp. 293–318.

Ostrom, Elinor (2002), "Common-pool resources and institutions: Toward a revised theory," in Bruce L. Gardner and Gordon C. Rausser (eds), *Handbook of Agricultural Economics, Volume 2A: Agriculture and its External Linkages*, Amsterdam: Elsevier, pp. 1315–1339.

Ostrom, Elinor and T.K. Alm (2010), "The meaning of social capital and its link to collective action," in Gert Tinggaard Svendsen and Gunner Lind Haase Svendsen (eds), *Handbook of Social Capital: The Troika of Sociology, Political Science and Economics*, Cheltenham, UK and Northampton, MA, USA: Edward Elgar, pp. 17–35.

Ostrom, Elinor, Roy Gardner, James Walker (with Arun Agrawal, William

Blimquist, Edella Schlager, and Shui Tan Tang) (1994), *Rules, Games, and Common-Pool Resources*, Ann Abor, MI: University of Michigan Press.

Putnam, Robert O. (1993), *Making Democracy Work: Civic Traditions in Modern Italy*, Princeton, NJ: Princeton University Press.

Shigetomi, Shinichi (2011), "Organizational capability of local societies in rural development," *Social Development Issues*, **33**(1), 24–31.

Singleton, Sara and Michael Taylor (1992), "Common property, collective action and community," *Journal of Theoretical Politics*, **4**(3), 309–324.

Stacey, Margaret (1969), "The myth of community studies," *British Journal of Sociology*, **20**(2), 134–147.

Yogo, Toshihiro (1996), "An analytical framework of local social systems in development," Discussion Paper No. 49, Nagoya, Graduate School of International Development, Nagoya University.

Woolcock, Michael and Deepa Narayan (2000), "Social capital: Implications for development theory, research, and policy," *World Bank Research Observer*, **15**(2), 225–249.

World Bank (2003), *Reaching the Rural Poor: A Renewed Strategy for Rural Development*, Washington, DC: World Bank.

Zamora, Mario D. (1990), *The Panchayat Tradition: A North Indian Village Council in Transition 1947–1962*, New Delhi: Reliance Publishing House.

PART I

Locality Groups and Host Organizations in Local Society

2. Composition of locality groups as the basis of local social systems: the case of rural Thailand

Shinichi Shigetomi

INTRODUCTION

The introductory chapter presented a local social system as a set of locality groups, institutions, and resources in a local society. There must be a variety of locality groups, such as social organizations and local administrative organizations, each of which has a different capacity for mobilizing institutions and resources, including organizational experiences, into the local people's collective actions for rural development. The differences in the composition of these groups were assumed to matter in the ways local people structure their organizations. This chapter examines this assumption by looking at case studies from rural Thailand.

In Thailand, new types of development organizations have been created by the local people themselves and introduced by development agencies during the past several decades. Rural people have responded to the environmental changes stemming from the rapid economic growth after the 1960s. However, the way people organized themselves appeared to differ by region, especially in the lower central region compared to the north and northeast regions. In the north and northeast, the organizational activities for development usually occurred at the administrative village level. On the contrary, in the lower central region, the local people were more often organized in social groups other than local administrative units.

Focusing on this difference between the regions, I here examine how local institutions and resources affect the process of organizing, which locality group facilitates these institutions and resources, and how the locality groups are composed in each local society.

The organizational activities of rural people have been well reported and studied by non-governmental organizations (NGOs) and scholars in Thailand. However, these analyses are dominated by a communitarian idea, the so-called "community culture thoughts" (Kitahara 1996). The authors have asserted that rural people got together because they had a traditional culture of cooperation (Seri 1989; Chatthip and Pornpilai 1994). Because this cultural perspective places importance on the consciousness of local people rather than on environmental elements, it cannot explain why the spirit of cooperation takes a certain form of cooperative action. Even though this concept emphasizes the importance of community, it does not reveal the reason for the various structures in local society.

Other scholars focus on socio-economic and political conditions in discussing the participation of local people in rural development projects (Turton 1987; Hirsch 1990). Hirsch observed that local people have been more and more influenced by external control, so he regarded villagers' organizations as a response against such control. Hirsch is correct in stating that people organize themselves to respond to environmental change. However, how can we explain the fact that local people are able to resist collectively against external control rather than simply submitting to being controlled? This is a question to which Hirsch did not give a convincing answer (Shigetomi 1998). In order to discover an answer, we need to identify the institutions and resources that local people can mobilize for their organizational responses, and that is the topic of this chapter.

In the following sections, I first describe how the environmental changes of rural society during macroeconomic growth give rise to economic needs for new types of organizational activities. After a brief explanation about the form of the new development organizations, I contrast how organizations are formed in the two regions. I present differences in the data collected through field surveys from dozens of villages and from an in-depth survey of the organizational processes in two case study villages. The conclusion summarizes the composition of locality groups, institutions, and resources in each local society of rural Thailand, and advances some general propositions about how to understand the local social system.

The data on the local situations presented in this chapter were collected from my extensive rural survey, during the late 1980s and the early 1990s, of more than 50 administrative villages in the northeast region and 17 sub-districts in the lower central region. An intensive survey of the two case sites was implemented in the early 1990s and has already been reported in detail (Shigetomi 1994, 1995, 1998).

ENVIRONMENTAL CONDITIONS AND PROGRAMS OF PARTICIPATORY RURAL DEVELOPMENT IN THAILAND

Traditional Form of Cooperative Actions

Traditionally, the form of cooperation among rural Thai people has been predominantly dyadic (Shigetomi 1992). One of the popular manifestations of this form was cooperative labor exchange, which was called *ao raeng, kho raeng,* and *long khaek* in local Thai. When a farm household needed some extra help, its members would ask someone else to help with the farm task. Those who helped the household did not expect any monetary payment; rather, payment would be made via returned help in the future. The amount of labor exchanged might not be exactly equal. The trust and love between the two households allowed for such non-market mutual exchange (Hanks 1962). This logic of cooperation was applied to other occasions, such as funerals, when a household needed assistance from other families. Those who had a good relationship with the deceased or the bereaved might offer assistance to the household hosting the funeral. Various kinds of resources – money, fuel, and labor – were voluntarily brought to the host. Such assistance was important for the economic survival of a household because some rituals needed more resources than the household could afford. Even though such cooperation appeared to be collective work, those who gathered for the work came to help because of dyadic relationships with the individual or individual household that needed the help. The mutual assistance happened sometimes even in securing money. Andrews (1935) reported that many rural people relied on their relatives and neighbors for monetary help rather than moneylenders. No interest or nominal rate was applied between these villagers. Research by the Thai government found a similar situation in the early 1950s (OUSS 1955).

By way of contrast, cooperative economic activities by collective consent among villagers were rarely seen in traditional rural Thailand. Collective actions for administering natural resources, for example, were not common except for traditional irrigation in the northern villages, even though the rural people deeply relied on the resources from nearby forests, grasslands, swamps, and ponds for their economic productivity. The village did not have any common fund for its activities. Collective activities among villagers were limited mostly to religious and traditional cult activities. Thus, villagers might mobilize resources for building a Buddhist temple and maintaining it. In the northern and northeastern regions, villagers held rituals for worshipping the guardian spirit of their village.

The environmental conditions of rural Thailand in the old days partly explain the dominance of dyadic cooperation rather than collective action. There was plenty of unclaimed forest land in Thailand, and people could individually claim a part of it by merely marking the border and clearing it for farmland (Ingram 1971; Leffers 1974). There were also plenty of natural resources – such as woods, wild animals, and edible wild plants – around the settlements, so the residents did not feel the need of collective agreements before taking them individually from nature. In this environment, a household could have farmland through inheritance or even by individually claiming forest land. The resource in which rural households did occasionally face a shortage was labor for farm work. Relying on dyadic social relations rather than on a group, farmers could flexibly procure the labor according to the changing needs of their households in terms of the amount of labor needed and the occasion. Thus, it is easy to see why traditional cooperation was dominated by the dyadic type based on personal social relations.

The Changing Environment and the Response of Local People

The traditional environment changed as the market economy intruded more deeply and widely into rural Thailand. The first impact came when rice became a cash crop for farmers, starting in the Chao Phraya Delta in the middle of the nineteenth century and expanding into other regions that had transport access to the Bangkok port. The second impact came after some upland crops, such as kenaf, maize, cassava, and sugarcane, were disseminated after the 1960s into areas where the rice cultivation was still for self-consumption. Farmers responded immediately and rapidly to expand the area for these cash crops by turning forest into upland farms. In the same period, Thailand experienced rapid economic growth through industrialization, which affected the rural economy deeply. Rural people found opportunities to earn wages from the non-farm sectors, and such non-farm income became indispensable in their farm economy. In this way, the market economy intruded into the agricultural economy, both production and the farmers' livelihood. Cash income became necessary for purchasing farm inputs and daily expenses. More and more farmers had to rely on moneylenders to secure funds by paying interest at a high rate. The government agency loan supply for farmers was limited until the early 1990s and was not applicable to daily and short-term expenses.

The expansion of cash crops drastically changed the ecological environment for rural people. With the forest land rapidly turning into farmland, the villagers could find hardly any unclaimed land for their farming. As the farmland was divided and passed on to children by way of inheritance, farm sizes rapidly became smaller. For example, in Si Phon Thong Village, which I later discuss in detail concerning its organizational activities, the first settlers around 1900 found large areas of forest land to occupy. However, by the early 1980s, around half of the households did not have large enough paddy fields to meet their own consumption needs (Shigetomi 1996).

As the environmental conditions of rural areas changed, the rural people observed that traditional dyadic cooperation no longer worked well in various situations. Mutual labor exchange, for example, had been replaced by labor for hire, which meant that labor could now rarely be secured through dyadic cooperation. A similar situation arose with the traditional methods of cooperation for managing funerals: host households could not acquire enough resources, such as money and firewood, from their neighbors, even though the cost of funerals had increased.

In response to the changing conditions, the villagers began to create new forms of cooperation in their own way. As one example, they established funeral associations in their villages and collected a certain amount of money and materials from the members. This new cooperation relied on collective agreement and enforcement among the membership, not dyadic relations and voluntary contributions among well-wishers. My field survey revealed that the first such funeral association was formed in the northern region in the 1960s, and they later disseminated widely into the other regions. In some villages, farmers agreed to form a labor exchange group with several households instead of calling for help individually. Members made agreements concerning the amount of offered labor and the food served to the helpers, and then offered their labor to each member in turn. It is not clear exactly when this type of response occurred; however, I discovered some cases in the late 1980s.

The collective actions at the village level were also changing by that time. When the forest land surrounding the village had been turned into farmland, the villagers found that they had little land left for public use, such as collecting natural resources and grazing their cows. In response to the need they felt for conservation, some of the remaining forest was claimed as community forest by the villagers in the northern and northeastern regions. The swamps and ponds near the settlements also came to be considered as village property and were administered through the villagers' collective consent.

Projects for Creating Development Organizations

The rural development policies of the Thai government were initiated in the late 1950s when rapid economic growth was taking place. From the very beginning, organizing local people was one of the major tasks for rural development agencies, such as the Community Development Department (CDD) of the Interior Ministry. It guided the local leaders, namely the village headmen, to establish groups of villagers, such as women's groups and youth groups. However, because the local people had no reason to organize themselves in such groups, these organizations were used mainly when the government needed to mobilize local people for official events.

The government had to reconsider its rural development policies when it faced serious challenges in the 1970s from the students, farmers, and communists, who claimed that rural poverty remained a serious problem despite decades of rapid economic growth after the early 1960s. The United Nations published influential reports in the 1970s to promote community participation (Midgley et al. 1986). Such an emphasis on popular participation in the international society also influenced Thai government officials (NESDB, c.1982). In the late 1970s, the CDD first started promoting a new type of development organization that was expected to be managed by and yield benefits for the local people. In the 1980s, the government prioritized rural development as the main topic of the fifth national development plan, having understood the importance of local initiative in development projects. Savings groups, rice banks, and co-operative shops were among the projects that the government promoted in the 1980s, and these are still in existence today.

The savings group is a microfinance organization for supplying loans with low interest rates. The members pool their savings in the group once a month for purposes of lending money to the members, and borrowers pay back the loans with interest to the group. With the accumulation of savings and interests, the pooled fund is expected to grow and provide more benefits to the members. The members are required to save an amount to which they agree, usually 20 baht (about $1 before the 1997 Asian financial crisis) each month, a practice that promotes the good habit of saving among the villagers.

The rice bank is meant to provide rice for farmers who are experiencing a shortage of rice for self-consumption. Each member provides a certain amount of unhusked rice after the harvest and stores it in a common granary. The members are entitled to borrow some rice, and return it, with a certain additional amount as interest, after the next harvest. The granaries are built either by the local people themselves or with some assistance from outside agencies.

The co-operative shop is a small retail shop for selling goods for the daily use of the local people, who in turn provide the capital and human resources for running the shop. The shop is sometimes a part of private premises or perhaps a detached small building once the shop has successfully accumulated enough capital. The local people benefit from the shop, by both receiving dividends as shareholders and purchasing goods at reasonable prices as customers.

These organizations are something of a contrast to the traditional form of co-operative activities and earlier development organizations, in two ways. First, the basic resources for co-operative activities are pooled and managed by the local people themselves. The money for savings groups, the rice for rice banks, and the initial capital for co-operative shops are procured from the private resources of local people, although in some cases the organizations use common local resources and ask for assistance from outside agencies for some facilities, such as granaries or shop buildings. The pooled resources are lent out for the members or spent on purchasing merchandise, through the decision of the local people. The outside agencies leave the decision-making to local people, and the field workers play a modest role as advisers rather than organizers. In this sense, these organizations are owned and managed by the local people.

Second, they are formed through collective agreements rather than by means of dyadic personal relations. Participants are obliged to follow certain rules, regardless of their personal relations with the other members. The resources are provided through collective agreement, not through amicable personal relations; thus, personal relationships in the organization do not dictate who can borrow, how much they can borrow, or when the money should be returned.

These organizations are assisted by both the government and NGOs. The savings groups were promoted by an NGO before the government started the project, and rice banks were an innovation by a local teacher. The pioneering role of rural development NGOs should not be neglected, but it has been the government that has disseminated them all over the country. Though government agencies tend to use the same procedures for introducing these projects in various places, the self-organizing process among local people can differ according to the region, especially between the northeast and the lower central region. Rice banks, for example, tend not to be popular in the lower central region because farmers are accustomed to selling all their crops after the harvest. However, microfinance and retail shops are still needed in this region. Through visiting dozens of villages, I found that the local conditions were quite different between the two regions, and attributed these differences to the various ways of organizing among local peoples, even though the kinds of development organizations were the same. I will confirm this difference in the next section by examining the actual process of organization in the case villages.

THE ORGANIZING PROCESS OF THE LOCAL PEOPLE IN TWO CASE VILLAGES

Si Phon Thong Village in the Northeast Region

Si Phon Thong (SP) Village is an administrative village of Roi Et Province that is located in about the center of the northeast region. The village was established in 1980 through a division of Phon Thong (PT) Village, which was formerly a cluster-type settlement, formed by a few settlers who had migrated from other places in about 1900 (Figure 2.1). This pattern and history of settlement is typical in the northeastern region. The two villages shared a Buddhist temple and a guardian shrine, which is assumed to protect the entire settlement. Near the settlement, there are two swamps, one of which, Phon Thong Swamp, is located near the residential area of SP Village and was regarded as under the supervision of SP Village. In 1993, SP Village had 60 households while PT Village had around 90.

The organizational activities of SP Village started with its young, active village headman, who was elected after the village was administratively separated from PT Village. The first organizational project was creating the rice bank in 1982. The headman introduced this project after observing a successful case in a neighboring village, proposing that his villagers deposit 50 kilograms of rice for mutual lending at 20 percent interest until the next harvest. Farmers with middle-sized farms were the main participants in this project. The bank was managed by the village executive committee members. If someone failed to return the rice with interest, the issue was discussed at the village meeting. The bank used a private granary at first, but in 1983 the village headman was able to build a new one by means of a government subsidy and donations from the villagers. Therefore, the granary and its site became the common property of the village.

In 1983, the village headman established a savings group, following the recommendation of the CDD, by collecting savings every month from the members. He soon faced difficulty in collecting the savings and gave up the group activity. However, he was able to convince the members to keep the pooled money in a local bank branch, indicating the possibility of using the money for some village development activities in the future.

In 1984, the villagers agreed to set up a co-operative shop. Nearly every household in the village became a shareholder in this shop, and the members took turns at shopkeeping. In the first two years, the shop performed very well, yielding a high rate of dividend to the shareholders. However, after the third year, the shop management faced a serious problem: the members did not pay proper attention to tending the shop, and shoplifting and bookkeeping mistakes became rampant, whereupon

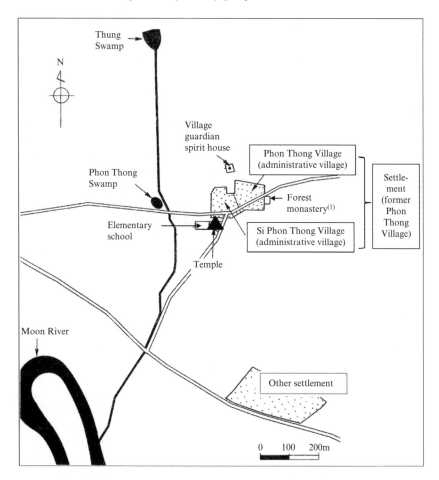

Note: (1) A religious facility formed by a Buddhist monk for practising meditation.

Source: Prepared by the author from NS3K Land Cadastral Map.

Figure 2.1 Settlement map of Si Phon Thong Village and its vicinity

the profits dropped to zero in the fourth year. The village leaders called the villagers responsible for the misconduct to a village committee meeting, in order to convince them to follow the group regulations. Senior villagers who were respected by their kinspeople were also invited to the meeting, and the village headman tried to mobilize their informal influence over the village administration. However, these measures did not eradicate the problems, and at last the leaders decided to hire a shopkeeper instead of relying on the members' voluntary services. Even so, the shop was never free from trouble. When a member committed a serious offense at the shop, the village leaders would call him to the village committee meeting and convince him in front of dozens of villagers to sign his name on a document, stating that he regretted his conduct and swearing to keep to the rules in future.

The village started some economic activities for itself after it overcame the troubles related to the voluntary group activities mentioned above. In 1987, the village headman proposed that members of the rice bank give the opportunity of borrowing rice to poor villagers who were too poor to provide the initial deposit. The amount of stored rice had increased enough for the members' needs, and the granary was already a village asset. The call from the village headman to help the other villagers was accepted. Now that the village owned all the resources of the rice bank, it could provide benefits to all the villagers and accumulate rice for future use.

Another economic activity of the village was a fish farming project in Phon Thong Swamp. The swamp had formerly been an open-access resource that everyone, not just the SP and PT villagers, could use for private needs. At the time the administrative village was divided, the swamp was regarded as belonging to SP Village because of its location. In 1988, the SP villagers agreed to prohibit private fishing, brought fingerlings and animal droppings to feed into the swamp, and caught fish for sale. The revenue from the project and the deposited money from the defunct savings group was used to lend out to farmers so that they could purchase rice husks for making compost. This rice husk fund helped the farmers to increase rice productivity considerably. Once, a villager broke the rule against private fishing and poached fish at night. When the leaders were informed about it, they summoned the person to the village meeting. The leader mentioned this incident repeatedly in the following meetings to remind the other villagers to abide by the rules.

The organizational activities described above originally limited both their membership and the beneficiaries to SP Village. However, one development organization that originally formed in the village, a savings group of village women organized in 1988, developed a membership that eventually was extended beyond the village boundaries. This group of 39 village women members, unlike the first savings group that had malfunctioned, lent out all of its pooled savings to the members every month. This helped the members to feel the benefit of the organization and motivated them to continue the activity. Their accounting practices were also improved when they solicited advice from an NGO. As a result, the group successfully increased its members to 148 by 1992. Until 1993, the group accepted members only from within the village, and its activities were reported to the village meetings. Then, the group decided to register itself legally as a co-operative, upon which it was required to open the membership beyond the village jurisdiction. Based on its experience and good performance during its village-level operation, it was able to expand its business rapidly to 433 members and savings of 3.2 million baht by the end of 2003 (Si Phon Thong Credit Cooperative 2004).

The organizing process in SP Village shows that the administrative village played the role of making and managing organizations. The village leader raised the idea of organizational activities and brought the idea to the villagers. The village leaders, in turn, tried to coordinate and sometimes to guide the behavior of villagers to achieve the organizational goals. They mobilized such social organizations as kin groups for village activities, and applied rules and sanctions in their activities. The village had resources, such as a natural swamp and the assets from the rice bank. It used the swamp to produce another form of common resource, money, which was used as a fund for the joint purchase of rice husks. In sum, the village worked as a mechanism for accumulating resources and transferring the resources from one activity to another.

Huai Rong Settlement in the Lower Central Region

Huai Rong (HR) was a small settlement of 84 households in 1994 when I surveyed it. Administratively, it is a part of Village No.1 of the Huai Khan Laen Sub-district, Wiset Chaichan District, Ang Thong Province. It is located in the middle of the lower Chao Phraya Delta. In a map showing the settlement pattern of this area about 1880, it can be seen that local people at that time lived in small clusters of houses along the rivers and canals (Figure 2.2). HR was one such cluster that became larger as the population increased. Nonetheless, the settlement pattern, in which various sizes of settlements are dispersed among the fields, has not changed except that roads instead of canals connect these settlements nowadays. Rice is the main crop in this area, and in the early 1990s, the rice could be planted twice a year when the rainfall brought enough water to the canal. There is no significant manufacturing around HR, and Bangkok, about 100 kilometers southward, is too far to commute daily for work. Therefore, villagers rely on agriculture as their main source of income, with some additional income through cottage industries, construction work, and remittances from household members who have migrated to Bangkok.

As shown in Figure 2.3, there are three settlements in the territory of Village No.1. An important factor in the establishment of new social systems proved to be the Huai Rong Buddhist Temple, which, although it is right beside the HR settlement, receives local worshippers not only from

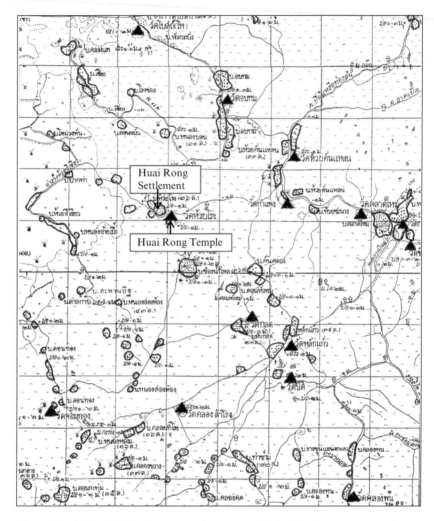

Note: The circles with dots represent settlements, and black triangles represent temples.
The grid is one kilometre square.

Source: Map produced by Army Mapping Department (based on a survey from 1881 and
printed in 1956).

*Figure 2.2   Settlement pattern around Huai Rong Settlement in the late
          nineteenth century*

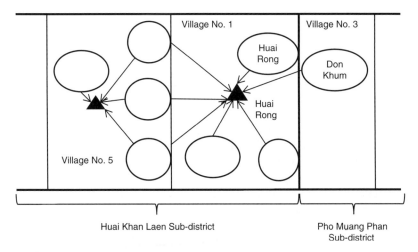

Notes:
The circles represent settlements. Triangles represent temples.
The arrows indicate the temple attended by the villagers.
The thick lines represent boundaries between sub-districts while the thin lines represent
boundaries between administrative villages.

Source: Prepared by the author.

Figure 2.3   *The pattern of settlements, temples, and local administrative*
   units in Huai Rong area

these three settlements but also from three other settlements of Village
No. 5 in the Huai Khan Laen Sub-district and one settlement (Don Khum
Settlement) from Village No. 3 in another sub-district. Some residents in
the three settlements of Village No. 5 do visit another temple, because
people consider the convenience of daily visits in supporting the temple.

Before 1983, collective action for development was rarely seen in the HR
area. Most of the development projects were implemented through such
local administrative organizations as the administrative village and the
sub-district. The headman of Village No.1 was conscious of the need for
development in his area, and he persuaded local people to contribute some
money and labor for infrastructure improvement work. When there were
some law-and-order problems around the village, the headman organized
a village guard. However, these activities ended within a short period of
time.

In 1983, the CDD suggested that the headman form a women's group
in the village. The headman, instead of organizing people himself at the
administrative village level, handed the task to a woman named Bupha

who lived in HR Settlement and was a respected member of the Srisuwan kin group, the largest kin group in the settlement.

The leader of the women's group started persuading her relatives and neighbors to join the group, relying on her dyadic personal relationships. Soon after the establishment of the women's group, the CDD proposed that the group participate in a savings group that had already been formed at the sub-district level by the instruction of the CDD. The women's group accepted the proposal, and 37 members, including children of the group members, also became members of the savings group. Thirty-five members lived in HR Settlement while 18 of the HR resident members were relatives of Srisuwan kin. Bupha collected savings every month from her group members and brought it to the sub-district leader, who was the wife of the sub-district headman.

However, the sub-district was a local administrative unit with several administrative villages. The Huai Khan Laen Sub-district, for example, contained five administrative villages in those years. The local people had no sense of belonging to such a large and administratively demarcated unit, nor did the HR members personally know the members outside of their settlement. Because they were not sure about leadership from a sub-district-level organization, the number of members did not increase.

Bupha also began to feel unsure about the management of the sub-district organization and proposed that the CDD separate their group from the sub-district organization. Thus, in 1985, the Huai Rong Savings Group was established as an independent organization, and the membership immediately increased to 70. Residents who were not Srisuwan kin members and who did not live in the HR Settlement started to join the group. The existing temple network previously mentioned played an important role in this development, as the geographical distribution was limited to the settlements in which residents regularly paid respect to the HR Temple. In particular, many people from Don Khum Settlement, which did not belong to the same administrative unit as HR, became members. Thus, when the membership expanded beyond the kin group, people regarded the sphere of temple visitors as the social basis of organization.

Even though the group had its basis in members' knowledge of each other, Bupha did not allow the pooled money to be lent out because she was not sure about the trustworthiness of the members. Therefore, because the monthly savings were simply pooled and deposited in a bank, the members received benefits only in the form of interest for their savings. Subsequently, the interest rate was never higher than the rate offered by the bank. Finally, in the fourth year, the leader decided to start lending out among the members, and after that the membership rapidly increased because the people clearly saw the economic benefits of the organization.

However, the group allowed the members to borrow money only insofar as the amount did not exceed the total amount of savings of the borrower, and with two underwriters or the provision of their land as collateral.

The formal representative of the HR Savings Group was the headman of Village No. 1. However, Bupha was the actual manager. As seen in the organization process, the administrative village merely played the role of receiver for the project from the outside, and the headman was only a nominal leader in this case. According to group records, it had 225 members in 1994, more than triple the number of initial members, and loaned out more than 170 000 baht to the members.

In 1986, the CDD brought in another project, establishing a cooperative shop. The CDD expected that the savings group would persuade its members to provide funds for the new organization. However, the person who actually took initiative was the abbot of the HR Temple. The abbot provided the largest share of funds and allowed the shop to use a building on the temple grounds. He was also a member of the Srisuwan kin group, so he called some reliable kinswomen to become the shopkeepers. At the beginning, the abbot instructed the shopkeepers about how to keep accounts and checked the account books until the shop was proving to be successful. Fair accounting and shopkeeping are definitively important for the success of this organization. Shop profits were shared by the members according to the amount of their shareholding and purchases, and by the shopkeepers and management staff as rewards, with some held for the shop as internal reserves. In the fiscal year of 1992–1993, the shop had 184 shareholders and the rate of dividend was as high as 20 baht for a 100 baht share.

LOCAL SOCIAL SYSTEMS BEHIND THE ORGANIZATIONAL ACTIVITIES

Locality Groups, Institutions, and Resources

The roles of the administrative village in the two cases show a clear contrast. In SP Village, the village was the unit of organizational activities, and the village leaders fulfilled most of the functions in the process of forming and managing organizational activities. On the contrary, the administrative village in the HR case played a limited role, merely receiving information and instruction from the government agency and delegating it to suitable social groups for implementation.

The administrative village is a governmentally installed locality unit, so it has the same institutions – the village headman, the village committee and committee meeting, and the village meeting – regardless of its region. Their roles, obligations, and authority are also formally defined by the government.

However, the performance of the village in the HR case suggests that these formal institutions, which are the tools for proposing, consulting, and making collective decisions, do not necessarily work because the local people do not regard the administrative village as the suitable body for implementing these functions. In other words, a collective identity of local people is necessary for mobilizing such institutions effectively. The difference between the two cases indicates that the administrative village does not automatically secure a collective identity among the villagers.

Indigenous settlements, especially those in a cluster, visually demarcate the same group of people, as is the case in most settlements in the northeast region. The early settlers set up a small shrine for worshipping their guardian spirit, which they believe protects their entire residential area (Shigetomi 1998, pp. 55–57). The villagers thus regard themselves as belonging to the same social group because they are protected by the same spirit. They confirm the belief by means of an annual ritual and on occasions when, because of such unhappy events as sickness or drought, they fear that the guardian spirit might stop its protection. The villagers of SP and PT Villages perform such rituals together as the members of an indigenous village.

The settlement pattern in the lower central region, on the other hand, is quite different from that of the northeast region. The houses originally stood along the rivers and canals in a line, or were gathered into small clusters scattered in the fields (Sternstein 1965). Even in cases where the houses form a cluster, it is difficult to find any social institutions that require the residents to form a social unity. The village shrine is rarely to be seen in this region because each household sets up a small guardian shrine in its compound. Although some settlements, like HR, hold a ritual for worshipping a guardian spirit and people believe that every participant, even non-residents of the settlement, will be rewarded by the spirit if they join in the ritual, there is no collective sense among the residents that the settlement as a whole is protected by the guardian spirit.

People respond to the call of organizing if they share the experience of organizing. As mentioned earlier, collective types of cooperation were not common in Thai rural society, with the exception of temple affairs. The facilities of rural temples are constructed from the contributions of local people in the form of money, materials, and labor, and they also manage the annual festivals. In the construction and festival events, local people share the work, assign the tasks, and collaborate to accomplish the events.

As the events occur repeatedly, however, they accumulate the experience of collective actions.

In the northeast region, the temple events had been carried out as events involving the entire village (Tambiah 1970). It is often the case that every household is obliged to provide a certain amount of resources for the events. In the lower central region, however, the temple events are usually carried out through voluntary contributions from the local people, and some devout Buddhists may form a temple committee to manage the events. On this point, the HR Temple had an exceptional feature as the abbot persuaded the local people to organize themselves for carrying out temple affairs. In a temple event in 1990, the temple assigned more than 500 local people to 20 tasks, a large organizational event indeed. The abbot organized people into small groups for delivering food to the temple during the Lenten period. In addition, he formed a funeral association among the temple visitors in 1983 (Shigetomi 1995, pp. 57–59).

As for the resources mobilized for organizational activities, we found other clear contrasts between the two cases. SP Village as an administrative village had some common natural resources that were used for organizational activities, and the villagers accumulated other common resources, such as rice and money, through their organizational activities. As an official unit of local administration, the village sometimes received resources from the outside agencies of both the government and NGOs. SP Village, for example, received a subsidy to build a granary for its rice bank.

An indigenous village also has the capacity to administer some common-pool natural resources under its control, especially those covering wide areas, even after it is divided into plural administrative villages. For example, of the 14 community forests that I surveyed in the northeast region in 2000, four were under the administration of an indigenous village (Shigetomi 2012). The density of common-pool natural resources at the administrative and indigenous village level also differs between the two regions. According to my extensive rural survey, more than 80 percent of 38 villages in the northeast region had wetlands, and more than 50 percent had uplands, including forests, under the collective administration (Shigetomi 1998, p. 86). In contrast, the figures were 35 and 9 percent, respectively, for the 46 villages surveyed in the lower central region.

The temple may be the institution that collects the most resources in rural Thailand. It receives donations both regularly and occasionally from local people and well-wishers outside of the locality. Although these resources are assumed to be consumed for temple affairs, it is often the case that the temple shares some of them for the secular activities of the local people. One example is the case of the HR Temple, which offered a building for the co-operative shop.

Composition of Locality Groups

The composition of the three locality groups in the two cases also presented a contrast. In SP Village, the three groups covered the same area until SP Village was separated from the former PT Village. This was the commonly observed pattern for locality group composition in the northeast region. Almost all the cases surveyed in the 1980s and the 1990s were instances in which one indigenous village overlapped one administrative village, or in which one indigenous village had been divided into plural administrative villages (Table 2.1). The numbers of each type of case were nearly equal. Even though one indigenous village might be divided administratively, most indigenous villages still had just one temple.

When the three locality groups exactly overlap each other, the administrative village becomes a unit that has the "we-feeling" of the villagers, and that shares experiences in collective action with relation to temple events. With the institution of the administrative village for consensus building, the sense of belonging to the same social group, and the shared experiences of collective actions, the villagers take it for granted that the village is the unit for collective actions.

Even in a case like SP Village, in which the administrative village does

Table 2.1   Number of villages by the overlapping pattern of locality groups

Relation between locality groups	Patterns	Region			
		Northeast		Lower Central	
			%		%
Number of administrative villages by the relationship with indigenous village	Exactly overlapping	23	47	16	42
	An indigenous village exactly separated into multiple administrative villages	25	51	10	26
	Others	1	2	12	32
	Total	49	100	38	100
Number of indigenous villages by the relationship with temple	An indigenous village with a single temple	30	75	1	2
	Residents from other indigenous villages attend the same temple	4	10	50	85
	Others	6	15	8	14
	Total	40	100	59	100

Source: Surveys by the author.

not coincide with an indigenous village, the sense of unity and organizational experience is not divided within the administrative village. The village leaders can use the institutions of self-administration, the sense of unity, and the experiences of the local people for collective action. The villagers may face difficulty, however, when they need to organize certain collective actions, such as administering common-pool resources at the indigenous village level, because they have to coordinate the leaders of different administrative villages.

In the lower central region, the three locality groups do not often coincide with each other. Table 2.1 shows that one-third of the surveyed administrative villages do not coincide with an indigenous village or do not exactly form an indigenous village with other administrative villages. The relations between the indigenous village and temple are not simple as in the northeast region. Indeed, as we see in the case of HR in Figure 2.3, the administrative boundaries were drawn without regard for the indigenous settlements and social organizations. In this pattern of composition, an indigenous village or a temple supporter group, even if it has some sense of social unity and experience of collective action, cannot use the institutions of the administrative villages. Government agencies like the CDD do not see the administrative village as a suitable unit for organizing local people, so they tend to bring their projects to the sub-district administration. The result does not seem to be positive, because the sub-district is never based on an existing social unity. The savings group of the sub-district to which the HR people used to belong had only 16 members in 1994, whereas the independent HR Savings Group increased its members to 225.

In other words, if any conditions are present that serve as a suitable substitute for locality groups, the local people in the region seem able to organize themselves successfully. The case of HR demonstrates some special conditions. First, it had a group of kinspeople large enough to be the core of the savings group, and a kin leader was present to manage the group. Second, its abbot was eager to guide collective actions among the local people. Thus, the people visiting the temple were more accustomed to organizational activities than the population that visited other temples in the area (Shigetomi 1995).

CONCLUSION

In Thailand, rural people have begun to organize themselves in new forms of organizations over the past several decades. Traditionally, they relied on dyadic personal relationships to cooperate with each other. When rapid economic growth began to make such a mutual exchange of resources difficult, people formed membership organizations and started collective administration of natural resources. Outside agencies, both government agencies and NGOs, also promoted such organizational activities. These organizations, especially those promoted by the government agencies, consisted of the same repertoire regardless of the project sites. However, the processes by which these organizations were set up differed between the northeast region and the lower central region. In the northeast, the administrative village took charge of organization, whereas other social organizations often spearheaded such efforts in the lower central region. Focusing on this contrast, I have examined the local factors that may have caused such a difference. The findings are summarized below.

There are three locality groups in rural Thailand, in effect: the administrative village, the indigenous village, and the temple supporter group. In the case of the northeast regions, I found that each locality group has its own institutional identity: proposing and consensus building on the part of the administrative village, providing a collective identity by the indigenous village, and accumulating experience for collective action by the temple supporter group. Each group also has some common resources. These groups overlap with each other geographically. Because of this local setting, the people could mobilize all of these institutions and resources for organizational activities.

On the contrary, in the lower central region, the collective identity at the indigenous group level may be weaker than that in the northeast region, and their way of mobilizing collective action for temple affairs may not be the same as that of the northeast region. More importantly, the members of each group do not necessarily overlap with each other, making it difficult for the administrative village to rely on a sense of belonging, and experiences accumulated through collective actions. Organizational activities for development were possible where there were already fortunate conditions, such as having a person who could lead secular activities among the temple supporter group, and having kin groups that can serve as a basis for organizing people.

The case of Thailand can be generalized in the following propositions: (1) Each rural local society is composed of plural locality groups. (2) Each locality group has its own institutions and resources, which may be mobilized for organizational activities among the local people. (3) The function of a local society in the organizational process is determined by the combination of the locality groups. (4) Because the characteristics of each locality group and the combination of groups may differ from place to place, the method of structuring organizations differs among local people.

REFERENCES

Andrews, James (1935), *Siam 2nd Rural Economic Survey, 1934–1935*, Bangkok: Bangkok Times Press.

Chatthip Natsupha and Pornpilai Lertwicha (1994), *Watthanatham muban thai (Thai Village Culture)*, Bangkok: Sathaban phatthana chumchon, Munnithi muban, Samnak phim sangsan.

Hanks, Lucian (1962), "Merit and power in the Thai social order," *American Anthropologist*, **64**(6), 1247–1261.

Hirsch, Philip (1990), *Development Dilemmas in Rural Thailand*, Singapore: Oxford University Press.

Ingram, James C. (1971), *Economic Change in Thailand, 1850–1970*, Stanford, CA: Stanford University Press.

Kitahara, Atsushi (1996), *The Thai Rural Community Reconsidered: Historical Community Formation and Contemporary Development Movements*, Bangkok: Chulalongkorn University, Faculty of Economics, Political Economy Centre.

Leffers, Horace L., Jr (1974), "Baan Dong Phong: Land tenure and social organization in a northeastern Thai village," PhD Dissertation, Boulder, CO: University of Colorado.

Midgley, James, Anthony Hall, Margaret Hardiman, and Dhanpaul Narine (1986), *Community Participation, Social Development, and the State*, London and New York: Methuen.

National Economic and Social Development Board (NESDB) (*c*. 1982), "Phaen phatthana chonnabot yakchon nai raya khong phaen phatthanakan sethakit lae sangkhom haeng chat chabap thi 5 2525–2529" ("Development plan of poor rural area in the Fifth National Economic and Social Development Plan, 1982–1986"), Bangkok.

Office of Under-Secretary of State (OUSS), Ministry of Agriculture, Thailand (1955), *Thailand Farm Economic Survey, 1953*, Bangkok: OUSS.

Seri Phonphit (1989), "Development paradigm: Strategy, activities and reflection," *RUDOC News*, **4**(3–4).

Shigetomi, Shinichi (1992), "From 'loosely' to 'tightly' structured social organization: The changing aspects of cooperation and village community in rural Thailand," *Developing Economies*, **30**(2), 154–178.

Shigetomi, Shinichi (1994), "The experience of Si Phon Thong (SP) in Thailand," Nagoya: United Nations Centre for Regional Development Expert Group Meeting on Self-Organizing Activities of a Local Community.

Shigetomi, Shinichi (1995), "Formation and management of development organizations in the 'loosely structured' society: Case studies in Ang Thong Province," in Shinichi Shigetomi, Chantana Banpasirichote, and Surichai Wungaeo (eds), *People's Self-organizing Activities for Rural Development in Central Thailand*, Tokyo: Institute of Developing Economies, pp. 43–108.

Shigetomi, Shinichi (1996), *Tai noson no kaihatsu to jumin soshiki (Rural Development and Local Organizations in Thai Rural Society)*, Tokyo: Institute of Developing Economies.

Shigetomi, Shinichi (1998), *Cooperation and Community in Rural Thailand: An Organizational Analysis of Participatory Rural Development*, Tokyo: Institute of Developing Economies.

Shigetomi, Shinichi (2012), "Komonzu to chiiki shakai – tai noson ni okeru tochi

no chiiki kyodo kanri" ("Commons and local society: Communal land administration in rural Thailand"), in Haruka Yanagisawa and Yoshiko Kurita (eds), *Ajia Chuto: Kyodotai kankyo gendai no hinkon*, Tokyo: Keiso shobo, pp. 59–78.
Si Phon Thong Credit Cooperative (2004), "Ekasan prakop kan prachum yai saman pracham pi 2547" (Document for the annual meeting of 2004), Roi Et.
Sternstein, L. (1965), "Settlement patterns in Thailand", *The Journal of Tropical Geography*, **21**, 30–43.
Tambiah, Stanley J. (1970), *Buddhism and the Spirit Cults in North-east Thailand*, Cambridge: Cambridge University Press.
Turton, Andrew (1987), *Production, Power and Participation in Rural Thailand: Experiences of Poor Farmers' Groups*, Geneva: United Nations Research Institute for Social Development.

3. Rural development in a multi-layered local system: a poverty reduction program case in Central Vietnam

Misaki Iwai

INTRODUCTION

Similarly to other developing countries, the rural poverty in Vietnam has still been one of the social and economic problems to be urgently solved. The National Program for Hunger Eradication and Poverty Reduction (HEPR, *xoa doi giam ngheo*) was launched by the central government in 1998 and has strengthened under the national policy for Comprehensive Poverty Reduction and Growth Strategy since 2002 (Bo Lao Dong – Thuong Binh va Xa Hoi va UNDP 2004). Microfinance has the most important role to play in fostering sustainable development in the HEPR. Microfinance managed by a state-owned bank, or the Vietnam Bank for Social Policies (VBSP, *ngan hang chinh sach xa hoi*), which provides low-interest credit without collateral, is the main scheme of this program and has successfully provided credit to the poor and other social policy beneficiaries. The VBSP provides six programs of credit loan with the following objectives: (1) loans for poor households; (2) scholarships for poor students; (3) employment for the disabled; (4) loans for guest workers; (5) loans for living conditions[1] improvement; and (6) housing for poor households.

Microfinance in rural Vietnam has succeeded in achieving very high loan repayment rates. According to the VBSP's website, the overdue rate among total outstanding loans to poor households was only 1.39 percent in August 2012, and at the end of that year total credit amounts for ten years rose to 113 921 billion VN dong. At the same time, the impact of the recent "decentralization," which has been in progress especially since 2004, on rural development also cannot be disregarded in promoting the microfinance program nationwide (Mai et al. 2012). As a result, this microfinance has become available to all people in rural areas of the country. Many international development donors, including the World Bank and the Asian Development Bank, financially support the HEPR. Since 2007, the Japanese government has provided official development assistance for this program as well.

Various types of microfinance organizations, such as the well-known non-governmental organization Grameen Bank of Bangladesh, have no prior connection with local communities and institutions. This is due to the situations in which these organizations find themselves, such as, for example, when certain local groups with no real interest in social and economic change dominate local communities (Uphoff 2004, p. 1). Therefore the Bank has to organize local people by itself from the beginning. The Grameen Bank sends fieldworkers to the project's villages and lets them organize and supervise the local groups. The local administrative organizations are usually bypassed by the donor agencies. This is the successful approach of participatory development.

In contrast, microfinance organizations within Vietnam rely heavily on local institutions. The VBSP, which has no branches under the district level and only 9000 employees with which to reach an estimated 7 million borrowers, entrusts financing to local organizations – these being mass organizations (*doan the xa hoi*) such as the Women's Union (WU) and the Farmers' Association (FA) (USAID 2011). They are national organizations with their own system of local organizations operating at lower levels to establish Saving and Credit Groups (SCG, *to vay von va tiet kiem*) at the village level. This is, in fact, the development organization for providing loans to each borrower. The reason for this excellent performance is suggested to be the efficient management of mass organizations, and their application of group lending (*tin chap*) schemes. According to USAID, this type of microfinance has enhanced VBSP's capabilities by leveraging the manpower of local institutions as a resource (USAID 2011, p. 10).

Why is VBSP's microfinance introduced and entrusted to mass organizations in rural Vietnam? In spite of outstanding results, the actual performance process of the VBSP's microfinance at the local level has not been analyzed enough. The purpose of this chapter is to examine how the development organization is accepted by the local society and then how it performs for poverty reduction in rural Vietnam.

REVIEWING LOCAL INSTITUTIONS FOR RURAL DEVELOPMENT

There is some literature on effective roles of the local institutions for rural development in Vietnam. According to Uphoff, three levels should be regarded as local: (1) the locality level – a set of communities; (2) the community level – a relatively self-contained socio-economic residential unit; and (3) the group level – a self-identified set of persons with some common interest (Uphoff 1992, p. 3). In general, when applied in a Vietnamese context, localities – the level at which local government is established – are regarded as communes (*xa*); communities are regarded as villages (*lang* or *thon*); and groups are regarded as hamlets (*xom* or *ap*). The word for 'village' differs from region to region. It is commonly called *lang* in the Red River Delta (the northern area) and *thon* in the central area, but no name exists in the Mekong Delta (the southern area). The village is the basic local unit which coincides with a geographical unit and circle of kin people. Each mass organization is composed at the commune level, and its branches are the lowest organization at the village level.

Previous studies of the relationship between rural development and local institutions focused on local institutions in order to examine their potential for rural development. However, these studies did not satisfactorily take into consideration the mechanism of how these developmental organizations work. One reason for this oversight is that the functions of mass organizations such as the WU and FA at the three aforementioned local levels had not been accurately understood and analyzed.

Okae (2009) studied the relations between rural microfinance and the mass organization in the northern rural area.[2] He focused on the FA branch in two hamlets and asserts that the monitoring function of the community is helpful in preventing defaults by borrowers. Nevertheless, the two hamlets indicated by Okae do not demonstrate or prove that collective action was organized by mass organizations. In fact, certain groups take power – that is, decision-making is concentrated among key individuals holding posts in the Communist Party and the agricultural co-operative. The FA branch's primary functions are performed by an agricultural co-operative that also controls the irrigation system. Rather than being a mass organization, the FA branch seems to be an extension of the co-operative (Okae 2009, p. 13) that exclusively controls common resources such as water. Okae argues that good repayment performance is the result of maintaining a sense of solidarity; however, the fact that borrowers who defaulted would lose access to the irrigation service demonstrates that using limited access to resources as a simple form of compulsion ensures repayment. He has misread the reason for the success of microfinance at the research site.

Meanwhile, concerning the implementation of rural development in general, Onda draws attention to the functions of the mass organizations at commune or locality level in northern Vietnam (Onda 2001, p. 260). He introduces one of the WU's collective activities: microfinance by managing the common fund of members. However, it is unfortunate that he makes no distinction between the terms "village" and "hamlet," since there are four villages and 11 hamlets in the research commune. He could not put the social mechanism that mobilized and managed resources among WU members into perspective, but instead dealt exclusively with the WU's formal and legal activities in the research commune.

Consequently, the two scholars mentioned above were unable to successfully analyze the relationship between local society and rural development – for instance, microfinance – in rural Vietnam. The existing literature seems to be dominated by an a priori assumption of the cohesive local community in the Red River Delta region, which has been suggested by Rambo (1973). However, Rambo's study does not examine how the community works in terms of development practices. It is vitally important to define the local society in order to prove its potential by analyzing the process of rural development management.

In this chapter, I will examine effective instances of microfinance organization working with local societies in rural Vietnam. In other words, I will discuss which level of local institutions microfinance organizations may most effectively work with for rural development in Vietnam.

THE RESEARCH SITES AND METHODOLOGY

Outline of the Research Sites

The research sites are three villages (*thon*): Kim Doi, Thanh Trung, and Thuy Dien, which are located about 12 kilometers from Hue City. The villages are parts of Quang Thanh commune, Quang Dien district, Thua Thien Hue Province of Central Vietnam. The Quang Thanh commune has nine villages with a total population of 11 862 people and 2625 households. Agriculture is the main economic activity of the three villages.

In the case of the research villages, *thon* is the natural village, and the population is about 2700 (420 households) in Kim Doi, about 2000 (350 households) in Thanh Trung, and 368 (81 households) in Thuy Dien. Below the villages, there are several hamlets along the main road. Kim Doi has 16 hamlets, and Thanh Trung has 21 hamlets. Thuy Dien has no hamlets because its scale is so small.

The residents in the Kim Doi and Thanh Trung villages are descendants of the pioneers who moved together from the same villages in the north of Vietnam, including Thanh Hoa Province and Ha Tay Province, between the sixteenth and eighteenth centuries. The residents' history is thus characterized by long-term migration and a strong sense of nostalgia for their common remote home (Nishimura et al. 2012). In addition, the area is prone to severe natural disasters such as typhoons and heavy rain, which greatly affect agricultural production almost every year and also create a strong sense of social unity for risk-avoiding among the residents in these villages (UBND Xa Quang Thanh 2012a).

Field Research Time and Methodology

This chapter is based on the field research that I conducted over two weeks, from late August to early September 2012, and from late December 2012 to early January 2013. The main materials and data collected are the annual reports of the commune and mass organizations and some documents related to the VBSP's credit loans to borrowers in the three villages. In addition, I interviewed some political and administrative cadres of the commune, the chairpersons of mass organizations (such as the WU and FA), the branch heads of mass organizations at the village level who directly manage credit services as SCG leaders, and the borrowers. I also interviewed three village chiefs and such cadres of the Kim Thanh Co-operative as the chairman, the vice-chairman and production team leaders.

LOCAL INSTITUTIONS AND ORGANIZATIONS IN CENTRAL VIETNAM

As mentioned in Chapter 1 in this volume, a development organization is distinguished from a social organization. By "development organization," I mean one which is formed to achieve specified targets, for example, economic growth and improved living standards. In rural areas, this type of organization may include microfinance organizations which aim at providing low-interest loans, and better market access through joint marketing groups. On the contrary, social organizations are not formed to achieve specified goals. Rather, they play the role of coordinating social relations and activities of their members and facilitating members' mutual help. They may include voluntary organizations, and in some cases they are based on kinship groups, religious groups, and a natural or indigenously formed village. In the following, I will examine functions of the two types of organization in the three villages.

Local Institutions and the Leadership

Vietnam's political system consists of three components: the Communist Party, the State, and the society (Sakata 2006). The Communist Party tries to control the society through both the state institutions and the mass organizations.

The commune is the lowest administrative level, and all formal organizations exist at the various administrative levels from the central to the three local levels (that is, province, district, and commune). The People's Committee (*Uy ban nhan dan*) is the administrative body. The chairperson of the People's Committee is elected from among the People's Council (*Hoi dong nhan dan*) members, holds office for five years, and is responsible for administrative matters. The general secretary of the Communist Party at the commune level is the position of a leader. In many cases, the general secretary also holds a formal position on the People's Committee or the People's Council at the commune level.

Below the commune are the villages. The village chief (*truong thon*), which is not a formal position, is elected by the villagers who participate in the village meeting, to which the entire village is invited. The village chief holds office for two and a half years and works on behalf of the local government, dealing with everyday local matters such as maintaining public order or arbitrating disputes among villagers. The three village chiefs are not currently Communist Party members. Each hamlet head (*xom truong*) is in charge of daily life in a particular residential area.

There are two agricultural co-operatives in the Quang Thanh commune, and the three villages belong to the Kim Thanh Co-operative. Kim Doi has two production teams, Thanh Trung has two, and Thuy Dien has one. The co-operative not only manages agricultural production services such as irrigation and dike patrol, but also raises some funds to provide microcredit to the members.

Meanwhile, major mass organizations such as the FA, WU, Ho Chi Minh Youth Union (YU, *Doan thanh nien cong san Ho Chi Minh*) and Veteran's Associations (VA, *Hoi cuu chien binh*) are the members of the Vietnam Fatherland Front (FF, *Mat tran to quoc*) and are approved as the formal social institutions by the State. Therefore, the chairpersons of mass organizations at the commune level are treated in the same way as other government cadres; for example, they receive a monthly salary, and so on. Apart from the political and administrative channels, various directions and policies come down to the local level through these mass organizations to mobilize the common people. Mass organization branches form a social channel connecting the commune (the State) and the village (the society) and take the initiative to implement various social, economic, and cultural policies, campaigns, and programs in the villages.

Self-Governing Functions of the Village

The village seems to be a self-governing institution that consists of some social organizations such as patrilineal kinship groups (*dong ho*) and religious groups. For example, Kim Doi village was founded by three patrilineal kinship groups, named Duong, Truong, and Nguyen, that migrated from the same villages in Thanh Hoa Province 22 generations ago. According to one elderly prestigious man of the Truong family who was interviewed in this study,[3] the Kim Doi villagers had managed the cultivated land as collective property, and they used to allocate a plot of land to every male person aged 18 years and over. This method of allocating plots of land continued until the fall of the Republic of Vietnam in 1975.

The village has its own code that clearly stipulates the obligations and rights of villagers. For example, the Thanh Trung village code, which was drawn up in 2003, consists of five chapters and 26 articles in all (Thanh Trung 2003). The main obligations of the villagers are to participate in the collective activities such as organizing rituals,[4] and to observe the rules and norms formulated in the code.

All important matters concerning village management are submitted to the full village meetings (*hop dan toan thon*) that form the highest level of decision-making. In 2012, there were 12 full village meetings in Thanh Trung. The executive committee of the village consists of the village chief, the security police, the secretary of the Communist Party, branch leaders of mass organizations including the FF, WU, FA, YU, VA, and 24 hamlet heads. For example, a village meeting was held on November 4, 2012 in order to deliberate on the annual settlement of accounts in 2012 by an accounts council (*hoi dong thanh quyet toan*) consisting of one chairperson, one secretary, and three members. The chairperson is a man who also holds the other positions of vice-president of the Kim Thanh co-operative and branch leader of the FA and FF. According to the minutes of the account balance, Thanh Trung village pooled 4785 kg of rice, equivalent to about 26 million dong, as the village fund. Total revenue amounted to about 77 million dong, and about 25 million dong were reserved as the fund for the next year after paying annual expenditures of 52 million dong. According to the village chief, almost all of the expenditures went to the repair and maintenance of public facilities and infrastructure: communal house (*dinh*), temple, hamlet gates and community center, and various activities and recreations such as a boat race and village festival. The agenda of the full village meeting was passed, and the minutes were signed by seven persons: the chairperson, the secretary, three members, the village chief, and the cashier.

Women's Union as a Social Organization

Mass organizations, as discussed in this section, are the branches of the WU and the FA that are mainly in charge of the management of the VBSP's credit loans. Among the mass organizations, besides the two above-mentioned organizations, the VA and the YU also have the right to manage the VBSP's credit loans.

Here I will examine the activities of the social organizations by taking the example of the WU. In Vietnam, the WU has two functions: first, to present and defend women's interests and egalitarian rights; and second, to unify, propagandize, educate, and mobilize women to implement the Communist State's policies (Trung uong Hoi lien hiep phu nu Viet Nam 2011, p. 10).

According to the chairperson of the WU of the Quang Thanh commune, its members include 2014 women of the 3052 local women who are aged over 18 and who are registered as residents. In other words, 66 percent of the total number of women who live in this area, and who qualify, participate in the WU. Table 3.1 shows the number of members of three WU branches.[5] The rest of the women belong to one of the three following categories: women aged over 60 years, unmarried young women aged over 18, and middle-aged women who have left home to work as migrant workers in big cities like Ho Chi Minh City.

The central committee of the WU has set a target to recruit 85 percent of eligible women to become members, but if only the married women who are living in the villages are counted, then the percentage of the WU numbers (except women in the three above-mentioned categories) rises to nearly 90 percent.[6] In other words, most of the able-bodied women are members of the WU.

The WU in the Quang Thanh commune achieves good results for various activities and has been awarded certificates of merit and the honorary flag by the central WU headquarters as the "outstanding unit" for five years successively. As the chairperson states, "Nothing is much more important

Table 3.1   The number of members in three WU branches

	Women aged over 18 years old	Members	%
Thanh Trung	418	275	66
Thuy Dien	112	74	66
Kim Doi	509	336	66

Source: Information provided by the chairperson of the WU in the commune.

than honor." This means that external evaluation is extremely important in establishing both social and economic merit. As an honorable mass organization, the WU in the commune has been given priority to obtain far more additional loans from the VBSP than the other WUs in the same district. Members feel that "honor" or "prestige" is important to increase the WU's social capital. At the same time, this sense of 'honor" becomes a motive for the women to mobilize and put pressure on all members to accomplish common tasks together.

For example, each member is evaluated according to three criteria: whether they study hard, demonstrate innovation at work, and maintain a happy family. Members are assigned one of four grades, depending on the extent of their accomplishment of the tasks: (1) excellent members; (2) good members; (3) ordinary members; and (4) bad members. One who fulfills all three tasks could be qualified as grade 1, that is, an excellent member. However, in practice, the WU pays attention to grades 1 and 4 only, and grades 2 and 3 exist only nominally. The evaluation for 2012 shows that 1751 women or 87 percent of total members were grade 1, while 263 women or 13 percent were grade 4 or "bad members." Total evaluation of the members makes a mass organization "excellent" or "bad" due to the extent of the contribution of every member who joins in the WU's everyday activities.

In a general meeting that is held at the end of the year, every member participates in a mutual evaluation of each member. No one has ever opposed an evaluation made by the other members. For instance, in the case of the criterion for studying hard, in 2012 there are records for the members who have attended each of the 12 courses about household economy, including information about kitchen gardening, vegetable growing, and livestock care. Therefore, no one can complain about the evaluation.

The WU committee recommends about 20 women who are qualified as the most excellent members to the People's Committee of the commune that gives the award certificates every year. At the same time, some women are regarded as "bad members" in the open discussions.

The WU has a large number of members, and it performs effectively. As a result, it attracted the attention and sponsorship of Bread for the World (a German non-governmental church-based organization)[7] in 2004.

Farmers' Association as a Social Organization

There are many voluntary activities organized by the branches of mass organizations (such as the WU and the FA) that are based on the villages. All of the members pay a membership fee twice a year after the rice harvest: once after the winter–spring crop and once after the summer–fall crop.

In this section, I will introduce the activities of the Kim Doi FA branch, which consists of 387 members who mainly engage in agricultural production. Two FA branch committee cadres also hold the positions of production team leaders. The FA branch in the Kim Doi village organizes many courses specializing in the introduction of new agricultural techniques and investment for rice production.

This FA branch holds a general meeting each year[8] where all of the members gather to reassess and evaluate the activities carried out in that year. According to the FA local resolution, the membership fee is fixed at 10 kg of rice after the harvest.[9] The membership fee is collected by the production team leaders together with other service fees such as the irrigation fee and contributions made to the government. The production team leaders collect 10 kg of rice from each member, who can pay 55 000 dong per person in cash instead of the rice. In this case, obviously the production teams work as village organizations. The main reason the production team works on behalf of the FA branch is that for the most part the members of the FA branch and the production teams overlap, and the villagers regard these farmers' organizations as a part of the communal activities of their village.

The membership fee per person paid up to the commune-level organization is only 6000 dong due to a decision of the central FA headquarters. This means that to make up the 55 000 dong, the villagers pay an extra 49 000 dong a year. However, no one feels dissatisfied about this because they prefer to keep some money for a fund (about 2 million dong per year) for their own social welfare. For example, a local resolution stipulates that: (1) when a member dies, a sum of 300 000 dong will be withdrawn from the fund to pay respects to them; (2) when a member gets sick, 100 000 dong is offered to them; and (3) when their parent dies, 100 000 dong is given to help them. The rest of the money is turned over to a mutual financing association with a low monthly interest of 0.35 percent. Moreover, the members are invited to a feast after the annual general meeting.[10]

The FA branch cadres emphasize that "if the villagers do not participate in the mass organization, they would be entirely isolated from the local society because they will receive no information about important issues and will have no cooperation from their fellow villagers for a long time." Consequently, to avoid social isolation, they pay much more attention to their social behavior.

LINKING MICROFINANCE AND THE LOCAL SOCIAL SYSTEM IN CENTRAL VIETNAM

In this section, I would like to examine how the VBSP's microfinance works on the local society. As mentioned above, the VBSP provides low-interest microcredit without collateral to poor households and has contributed to widely promoting social welfare in rural Vietnam. Four major mass organizations (such as the WU, FA, VA and YU) have rights to access the VBSP's loans through a group lending scheme. In the three villages, two main mass organizations (that is, the WU and FA) actually deal with the VBSP's credit loans.

The Loan Application Procedure

Applicants need to prepare an application form signed by both the SCG leader and the village chief at the village level. They then submit it through the WU or the FA at the commune level to the People's Committee, in which the Poverty Reduction Board consists of chairpersons of the WU and the FA and some cadres in the People's Committee.[11] As shown in Figure 3.1, the Poverty Reduction Board at the commune is composed of ten cadres of the commune and 11 village chiefs. After getting approval from the People's Committee, the SCG leader submits the application forms directly to the VBSP banker. In the Quang Thanh commune, on the 20th of every month (even holidays), all the SCG leaders and the Poverty

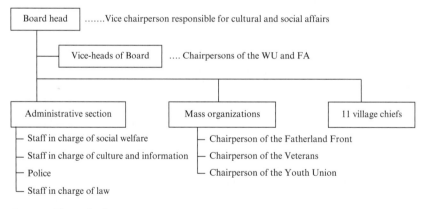

Source: The author's survey.

Figure 3.1   The structure of the Poverty Reduction Board in the Quang Thanh Commune

Reduction Board members meet together and work with the district-level banker of the VBSP. Applicants do not need to visit the branch office of the VBSP in the district town. When they apply for the loans, they are guaranteed by mass organizations through group lending in the scheme.

The VBSP issues an account book for the credit loan to each borrower after examination. This book is called the "green book" due to its green cover (*so vay von ngan hang chinh sach xa hoi* or *so xanh*). The SCG leaders distribute an account book to each borrower. The borrowers and the banker do not meet except when the banker distributes the loan directly to the borrower at the commune office.

The Flow of the VBSP's Finance

The borrowers form SCGs in the same village. The SCGs are formed from fewer than 50 members; if the size were to exceed 50, a new SCG would be formed. SCG leaders do not necessarily all live in the same hamlet inside the village. For example, the WU branch head in Kim Doi said that in the beginning, they divided the SCGs based on some of the hamlets. In spite of this division, they found it difficult to manage the work, especially when a new SCG was set up, due to the increase in the number of borrowers. On account of these difficulties, they now form SCGs independent of residency. Figure 3.2 shows the organizational channels at the local society. Because they have three levels, they are multi-layered local organizations.

The SCG leaders are not assigned by the VBSP but are selected by the mass organization. In the three villages, all of the SCG leaders of the WU branches are the heads and vice-heads of the branch, while the SCG leaders of the FA branches are the production team leaders (Kim Doi), the FA accountant (Thanh Trung), and the head of the FA branch-cum-production team leader (Thuy Dien).

As shown in Table 3.2, in 2012, there were ten SCGs, consisting of the following: four groups in Kim Doi (WU, 3; FA, 1), four groups in Thanh Trung (WU, 2; FA, 2), and two groups in Thuy Dien (WU, 1; FA, 1). The number of borrowers of the VBSP credit loans rose to 281, amounting to over 3 billion dong.

When a family wants to borrow some money for rearing livestock, the husband (who joins the FA branch) and the wife (who joins the WU branch) should consult each other and then decide which organization they should apply to for the loan. In the three villages, the number of the WU branch members is bigger than that of the FA branch members. The WU branch cadres in Kim Doi emphasized that SCGs in the WU work with honor and that the women in general take great care with the money so that they can spend it on their families.

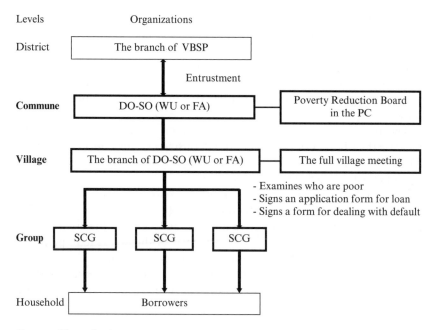

Source: The author's survey.

Figure 3.2   Organizational channels for the three levels at the local society

Table 3.2   The outstanding loans of the SCGs in the research villages (VN dong)

SCG names	WU	Amounts	FA	Amounts
SCG Kim Doi 1	23	140 300 000	35	360 044 000
SCG Kim Doi 2	33	378 536 000	–	–
SCG Kim Doi 3	33	520 418 667	–	–
SCG Thuy Dien	23	344 905 000	24	231 600 000
SCG Thanh Trung 1	20	234 237 000	30	422 200 000
SCG Thanh Trung 2	35	436 871 000	25	307 000 000
Total	167	2 055 267 667	114	1 320 844 000

Note: WU and FA unit = households.

Source: Documents of VBSP, October 2012.

In early 2004, the VBSP had financed all of the members who applied for a loan from the VBSP, not distinguishing between the poor households and the others. However, at present, only poor households can make a new application for a loan. The other members are not permitted to apply for new loans, although they can continue to borrow money. The reason is that it is difficult to enlarge the scope of banking due to the limitation of credit lines.

The borrowers could be loaned 15 million dong for three years to increase their household income through raising livestock, growing vegetables, processing food, and so on. Then they start to repay the interest and the principal regularly through their SCGs.

The borrowers repay the principal twice a year, amounting to six times for three years, so they repay only the interest (0.65 percent per month, 7.8 percent per year) for the first five months, and then on the sixth month they repay both the interest and the principal. A three-year loan period is divided into six terms. For example, a borrower who is loaned 15 million dong repays 97 500 dong every month plus 2.5 million dong for the first term. As mentioned before, the VBSP banker visits the commune on the 20th of every month to collect the money.

The Mass Organizations as Development cum Social Organizations (DO-SO)

The SCG leaders mainly play the two following roles:

1. Visiting all borrowers at their homes to collect the interest and the principal two or three days before the settlement date every month.
2. Finding a solution for members who need a loan rescheduling, or temporary payment of the interest on behalf of the members whom the leaders could not meet before the setting date.

In addition, the SCG leaders hold a group meeting once every three months at the village communal hall.

The leader receives a meager commission of only 1.2 percent of the interest. This is too little to reward the leader's labors and time. The sole incentive for the leader is that new SCG leaders can also apply for the VBSP credit loans. However, when interviewed, they said that they fulfill their duties not for the sake of economic benefit, but for the sake of "social responsibility" and "our village." The SCG leaders can monitor all borrowers' economic situations and livelihood every time they visit the members' homes to collect money. Each year, there are two or three cases of rescheduling, but there have been no defaults. The SCG leaders "urge" members to repay the loans regularly because the SCG's group lending scheme does not extend to bailing out defaulting members.

According to the WU 2012 report of the Quang Thanh commune, the VBSP credit loan is a contract activity of mass organizations. The WU audited the management of 26 SCGs and 347 members, and found that all the SCGs were well managed and there was no defalcation. In addition, the WU cooperated with the VBSP to organize two training courses of asset management for SCG leaders; 75 leaders attended the course. These kinds of collaborative activities are so effective that the SCG leaders are able to maintain high morale to prevent wrongdoing in the village.

The SCG leaders are actually the leaders of mass organizations, namely the WU and the FA branches at the village level. The mass organizations are social organizations that connect the external authorities and the fund providers (such as the VBSP) with internal relations and activities among members in order to achieve improved living standards and to promote mutual assistance of their members. This means that the mass organizations work as development organizations. In other words, the mass organizations can be characterized as development-cum-social organizations (DO-SO).

Meanwhile the borrowers try to repay the credit loans in order to continuously receive the social and economic benefits of being members of the mass organizations. The credit loans are recognized by the borrowers not as the individual contract with the VBSP, but as their responsibilities for the fellow members who belong to the same organizations. At the same time, there is a sense of keeping the honor and prestige of mass organizations among the members. This also works as an incentive among the members to prevent default on the loan.

Microfinance and the Self-Governing Function of the Village

According to the VBSP's guideline, a "poor household" that could apply for the VBSP's credit loans must have an income per capita of below 400000 dong per month. The guideline defines a "fairly poor household" as one whose income per capita falls below 520000 dong in rural areas.[12] However, this standard is insignificant and exists only on paper because, in rural areas, the calculation of income of the poor households is not based on the amount of cash but on the property they own, including the rice fields, garden, and livestock, which can be turned into cash if they are sold on the market.

So, how are the poor households defined? Actually, the village is authorized to define and choose the poor households (UBND Xa Quang Thanh 2012b). First, the village executive committee examines and lists candidates for poor households. Then it submits the list to a full village meeting. The discussion and decision are recorded in the minutes. Thuy Dien village has a larger number of poor households than the other villages, and the meeting to determine entitled households is usually long. The village meeting for this purpose is held in November every year. The village chief signs his name on the application form for the VBSP credit loans as the representative of the village consensus.

The screening of poor households for microfinance is an extremely important collective action of the village. It guarantees fairness and prevents discontent and complaints from other villagers. For the "screened" poor households, repayment is not only an individual duty but also a chance for participation in the village. They are not isolated, but independent socially inside the village, despite getting preferential support from the government. The village promotes their active participation in various collective activities by giving them priority access to social welfare. This participation has prompted a favorable response from other villagers. Consequently, they realize the potential to contribute to the village through their own roles. This feeling motivates them to participate in the village as formal members.

The screening of poor households is necessary because, according to the Thanh Trung village chief, earlier in 2012 the village had made a list of 38 poor households, but later they heard about a quota set by the district authorities, according to which the number of poor households had to be reduced. Therefore, they had to reduce the list from 38 to 33. This meant that five poor households had to be excluded and reassessed as "fairly poor" households.

After examining the candidates for poor households, the executive committee submits the draft list of candidates to the full village meeting for deliberation. Contents of the deliberation and decision are recorded in the minutes of the meetings.

Moreover, mass organizations are expected to achieve full payment to the VBSP, in which moral hazard among the borrowers needs to be avoided to maintain social order and a mutual relationship of trust. Indeed, the WU successfully manages microfinance. As shown in Table 3.3, the rate of overdue repayment is extremely low: 1.4 percent average at the commune level, 0.9 percent in Kim Doi, 0.7 percent in Thanh Trung, and 0.2 percent in Thuy Dien (Hoi lien hiep phu nu xa Quang Thanh 2012).

In coordination with the Poverty Reduction Board in 2012, the People's Committee always monitors and checks the management of microfinance by those mass organizations. Default is the most serious situation in which the risk of moral hazard rises.

Table 3.3   *The situation of delayed repayment in the research villages,*
            December 20, 2012 (VN dong)

Village	Loan amounts	Delayed repayment	%
Kim Doi	1039254334	9416667	0.9
Thanh Trung	671108000	4983000	0.7
Thuy Dien	344905000	805000	0.2
Total	2055267334	15204667	0.7

Source: Hoi lien hiep phu nu xa Quang Thanh (2012).

How does the mass organization deal with "bad debt" (*no xau*) or default?
There are three suggested solutions:

1.   Rescheduling (*gia han no*).
2.   Turning a loan into an interest-free one (*khoanh no*).
3.   Writing off debt (*xoa no*).

Rescheduling is the most popular measure to avoid overdue repayment.
Turning a loan into an interest-free one means that debtors have to pay the
capital, but for a certain period do not have to pay the interest, due to their
business failure or natural disasters. Writing off debt is applicable only to
the cases when the debtor dies but has no heir, no able-bodied laborers,
and no relatives. These cases are examined at an SCG meeting which is
attended by the SCG leader, the branch head of the mass organization, the
village chief, and a policeman. After discussing the size and the cause of
default case by case, and building up a consensus with the SCG members,
the village executive committee writes a proposal and submits it to the
VBSP through the People's Committee at the commune. This series of procedures means that the village does not take over the borrowers' debts but
legally deals with the default problems on behalf of the debtors.

How Does the Scheme Help the Poor?

This section will examine two cases of poor households which are borrowing via VBSP credit loans through the WU and the FA branches in the
Kim Doi village. The first case features NTL, a woman who was born in
1974 and lives with her husband and three children. She has been issued a
"poor household" certificate and has borrowed 10 million dong from 2007
to 2010 to raise livestock.[13] The family does not have their own house, so
they reside temporarily inside the grounds of the communal house of the

Truong Huu patrilineal kinship group. After borrowing from the VBSP to breed pigs through the WU branch for several years, she was able to save money little by little. She is now preparing to build a new house[14] in the next year, so is planning to borrow 15 million dong under the VBSP's program 6: housing for poor households.

Replying to the question, "How do you feel when you are approved as a poor household by villagers?" NTL said, "When we are extremely miserable and they put us on the list, the only thing I can do is thank them." She had not been able to get access to the VBSP's microfinance until the village gave her the certificate of "poor household."

Moreover, she feels happy when participating in everyday activities with the WU branch members. She especially enjoys the two parties that are held on the anniversary of the Women's Days. She also enjoys mutual helping. She reported, "In a rural area, when engaging in farming, some anniversaries are joyful opportunities for us. All members have tea and cakes, sing songs, and chat together. When I need some help, I ask the neighbors, the village, and the WU fellow members."

In this way, she does not feel as though she is dealing with the VBSP, but she has a strong sense of belonging to the WU branch (the same as the SCG) and feels that she has to fulfill her responsibility for her own village. In the same way as the SCG members she feels that the scheme consists of two main merits: 1) the members have a chance to meet each other and receive the VBSP's credit loans, 2) they can consult with one another about the repayment. Therefore they reinforce the partnership among the SCGs.

The second case is a man named NHV, who was born in 1965 and lives with his wife and two children.[15] He has been issued with a "poor household" certificate for ten years now. He had earlier borrowed from the VBSP through the FA branch, but he could not repay the debts within the specified time limit because his wife was hospitalized and his children were also sick. Thanks to relatives, neighbors, and friends who helped, all of whom "gave in dribbles," he was finally able to repay his debts to the VBSP.

Since 1993, the family has resided temporarily as caretakers inside the grounds of the Kim Doi communal house and community center. He plans to build a house if he can borrow the money from the VBSP in the next year.[16]

He was asked how he felt when he was approved as a poor household. He said, "When being issued the certificate of the poor household, I feel at ease because all members of our family are exempted from medical expenses."

He was asked what he felt was the main benefit of the FA. He said, "Borrowing credit loans, participating in common activities, and studying how to make a living. If I did not become a member of the FA branch, I would not know anything." In other words the scheme can clearly help him to see himself as a member of the SCG and strengthen a sense of belonging to his own community.

These extracts from in-depth interviews with local residents have shown their emotions and high evaluations of the mass organizations such as the DO-SOs and their home village. The VBSP's scheme which links to the government program effectively works to guarantee the poor's "normal" living in their own village. Clearly, they are not socially isolated, because social capital accumulated by the DO-SOs and the village is a safety net for them. The government support is promoting their social participation and a sense of solidarity with fellow members through the activities of the DO-SOs in the village level.

CONCLUSION

Why does microfinance with a group lending scheme through mass organizations work well in Vietnam? There are two salient features in the relationship between the development organization and the local society of the research villages that are able to answer this question.

First, the relationship between the development organization for the microfinance program and social organizations as mass organizations mattered in the program's performance. The mass organizations (such as the WU and the FA) are entrusted by the VBSP to manage the loans within the village. This allows the leaders to mobilize the functions of a social organization for monitoring the members of a development organization. The development cum social organization (DO-SO) regards the group lending scheme not as its exogenously appointed task, but as its entrusted mission. In other words, to outsiders the DO-SOs may look like development organizations, but to the villagers they are also their social organizations.

Meanwhile, the double function as DO-SO is useful for the VBSP. It reduces the cost of management drastically. Indeed, the VBSP bankers do not have to screen and monitor every borrower in rural areas. I would like to emphasize that in order to lower the management costs the VBSP has no office at the commune level. Instead, it has relied on and made full use of the existing mass organizations. Through the SCG's leaders, who are local and know all the borrowers well, the VBSP has managed not only to reduce its staff (an economic benefit) but also to create good cooperation and solidarity between the SCG's members (a social benefit).

Second, the relationship between the mass organizations and the village matters in the program's performance. The mass organizations are attached to the indigenous village that has an institution for creating consensus through the full village meeting and the village executive committee for collective activities. Therefore they have become a part of the social system which the indigenous village has long implemented. The sense of retaining the honor and prestige of mass organizations comes from the sense of unity as an indigenous village.

This local system, therefore, has a three-layered structure as a mass organization (DO-SO) at the commune level, a branch of DO-SO at the village level, and an SCG at the group level. The system as a whole works positively for the implementation of rural development projects. Since the development program is hosted by a part of the village (that is, the mass organizations), it has some flexibility and sustainability. The local institutions continually apply social pressures and supply incentives in order to maintain the members' motivation within the DO-SOs. It seems that the raising of the villagers' living standards increases confidence in the DO-SOs, resulting in the villagers holding the DO-SOs in high regard as part of the village social capital. Accordingly the village has the ability to mobilize its inhabitants at will as the need arises, depending on the purposes of the tasks assigned by the government (such as national development policies of the HEPR). Then the SCGs work on the basis of members' partnership voluntarily emerging through everyday cooperation. This multifunctioning of the DO-SOs makes it easy to respond to any purpose. Moreover, social organizations are to be maintained, not dismantled. Consequently this means they can continue to take on the task of development, regardless of whether one development project ends or not.

Compared with the Grameen Bank system, which forms a group lending scheme with joint liability and bypasses the village-based organizations, the Vietnam system uses the DO-SOs to manage group lending without joint liability, on the basis of the self-governing functions of the village. It is inclusive towards the poor rural population, compared with Grameen Bank-type microfinance organizations in which individual "risky fellows" are excluded from the SCGs due to relying on the dyadic peer liability. This explains why microfinance organization works effectively with local societies in rural Vietnam.

NOTES

1. This means the supply of clean water and a hygienic environment in rural areas.
2. Wolz (1997), Dufhues et al. (2002), and Sakata (2006) review the VBSP's (former VBP) microfinance as one of the poverty reduction programs and examine its relations with mass organizations. However, they offer no explanation as to why the VBSP is entrusted to the mass organizations.
3. Interview was held on December 25, 2012.

4. There are three village rituals in Thanh Trung. The first one is organized on the Lunar New Year day to pray for public peace. The second one is held in the seventh month to celebrate the village gods. The last one is organized on the 16th of the tenth month to remember the ancestors. According to the Village Code, "rituals and festivals are the collective responsibility of all villagers," with the Elders Association and the organizing committee in charge together.
5. According to three WU branches' leaders, the number of active members is smaller than that of the members registered: it ranges between 63 percent and 76 percent.
6. Besides the conditions of age and marital status, requirements for membership in the WU in Quang Thanh commune exclude three types of people: (a) a person who has been previously convicted; (b) a person whose children dropped out before graduation from the junior high school; and (c) a person whose children suffer from malnutrition. However, in fact there is no case in which any member could be expelled from the WU, and almost all members participated in the WU after marriage when they were still young.
7. Bread for the World was founded in 1959 and has been working in Vietnam since 1996 in the sectors of rural development, ethnic minorities, food security, overcoming violence, and HIV/AIDS (http://www.ngocentre.org.vn/jobs/advisor-impact-orientation-0).
8. Since 2012, the FA branch in Kim Doi village has established a new regulation that the general meeting will be held once every two years.
9. According to the local resolution, the membership fee of the WU is also 10 kg of rice, while membership in the Ho Chi Minh Youth Union is 5 kg, the Veterans' Association is 10 kg, and the Elders Association is 5 kg, respectively.
10. In the case of the WU branch, every year all of the members organize a party to celebrate the Women's Days on March 8 and October 20. They cook together and have a banquet in the community hall of the village.
11. According to the HEPR, there is a structure that organizes the committees from the central level to the local levels. Below the committee for the HEPR at the commune level, HEPR groups are organized at the village level, in which the village chiefs are responsible for the program (Bo Lao Dong – Thuong Binh va Xa Hoi 2004).
12. The criterion for designation of a poor household and a fairly poor household in urban areas is much higher than for those in rural areas, whose income per capita falls below 500 000 dong, and 650 000 dong, respectively.
13. She stopped attending school in the fourth grade of elementary school, and her husband has never attended school. Due to the lack of money, she cannot afford to support her oldest daughter's wish to continue studying, and she plans to remove her from school from the eighth grade and send her to work in a factory in suburban Ho Chi Minh City.
14. The land for housing was allocated by the commune, which grants 20 million dong in addition to the land.
15. He completed elementary school, and his wife went to school for only one year.
16. NHV estimates the total cost of construction at about 70–80 million dong. Besides the funding of 20 million dong given by the commune, he has to manage to raise money somehow through the VBSP credit loans and private moneylenders. In this area, according to NHV, the interest rate on private loans comes to 1.2 percent (about twice that of the VBSP). Private moneylenders do not require collateral.

REFERENCES

Bo Lao Dong – Thuong Binh va Xa Hoi va UNDP (2004), "Danh gia chuong trinh Muc Tieu Quoc gia ve Xoa doi Giam ngheo (CT MTQG XĐGN) va Chuong trinh 135" ("Evaluation of National Hunger Eradication and Poverty Reduction Program and Program 135"), http://www.undp. org.vn/digitalAs sets/3/3971_Report__v_.pdf.

Dufhues, T.B., P.T.M. Dung, H.T. Hanh, and G. Buchenrierder (2002), "Information and targeting policies and their principal–agent relationships – the case of the Vietnam Bank for the poor," *Quarterly Journal of International Agriculture*, **41**, 335–362.

Hoi lien hiep phu nu xa Quang Thanh (2012), "Bao cao tinh hinh hoat dong vay von uy thac giua Ngan hang chinh sach xa hoi voi Hoi lien hiep phu nu xa Quang Thanh nam 2012 va phuong huong nhiem vu nam 2013" ("Situation of credit scheme entrusted by the Bank for Social Policies to the Quang Thanh commune's Women Union in 2012 and Some Planned Directions for the 2013"), unpublished report.

Mai Lan Phuong, Nguyen Mau Dung, and Philippe Lebailly (2012), "Phan cap quan ly va Chuong trinh Xoa đoi giam ngheo – Truong hop nghien cuu tai tinh Hoa Binh" ("Decentralization of management and Hunger Eradication and Poverty Reduction Program – The case study of Hoa Binh province"), http://orbi.ulg.ac.be/bitstream/modernisation.pdf.

Nishimura, M., Nguyen Quang Trung Tien, H. Noma, and K. Kumano (eds) (2012), *Hue chiiki no rekishi to bunka* (*History and Culture in Hue Region*), Kansai Daigaku.

Okae, T. (2009), "Rural credit and community relationships in a northern Vietnamese village," *Southeast Asian Studies*, **47**(1), 3–30.

Onda, M. (2001), *Kaihatsu Syakaigaku-Riron to Jissen* (*Sociology of Development: Theory and Practice*), Kyoto: Minerva Shyobo.

Rambo, T. (1973), *Peasant Social Systems in Northern and Southern Vietnam*, Monograph Series III, Carbondale, IL: Center for Vietnamese Studies of Southern Illinois University.

Sakata, S. (2006), "Changing roles of mass organizations in poverty reduction in Vietnam," in V.T. Anh and S. Sakata (eds), *Actors for Poverty Reduction in Vietnam*, IDE ASEDP Series No. 13, Chiba: Institute of Developing Economics (IDE), pp. 49–79.

Thanh Trung (2003), "Quy uoc lang van hoa Thanh Trung, xa Quang Thanh, huyen Quang Dien, tinh Thua thien Hue" ("Code of Thanh Trung cultural village"), unpublished document.

Uphoff, N. (1992), *Local Institutions and Participation for Sustainable Development*, Gatekeeper Series No. 31, London: International Institute for Environment and Development.

Uphoff, N. (2004), "Local communities and institutions: Realizing their potential for integrated rural development," in C.M. Wijayaratna (ed.), *Role of Local Communities and Institutions in Integrated Rural Development*, Tokyo: Asian Productivity Organization, pp. 63–84.

UBND Xa Quang Thanh (2012a), "Ke hoach giam nhe rui ro va thich ung bien doi khi hau" ("Plans of risk reduction and adaptation to climate change"), unpublished document.

UBND Xa Quang Thanh (2012b), "Bao cao tinh hinh thuc hien cua Ban xoa doi giam ngheo o xa Quang Thanh sau thang dau nam 2012" ("How did the Poverty Reduction Board of Quang Thanh commune perform in the first half of 2012?"), unpublished report.

USAID (2011), "Promoting sustainable, market-based microfinance: Viet Nam case study and lessons learned for APEC economies", paper presented at APEC Workshop on Microfinance Best Practices, Hanoi, April 7–8.

Wolz, A. (1997), "The transformation of rural finance systems in Vietnam," Discussion Paper 60, Heidelberg: FIA.

4. Organizing community forestry in rural Myanmar: capability and functions of villages

Ikuko Okamoto

INTRODUCTION

How do the Myanmar rural communities organize for collective action? This is the key question that this chapter attempts to answer. With increased emphasis on community-based and participatory approaches in rural development, as explained in Chapter 1, an understanding of the specific mechanisms for organizing in each local society is critical for creating local organizations that are "spontaneous, sustainable, and transferrable."

To better grasp the features of local mechanisms for organizing collective actions in rural Myanmar, this chapter focuses on a community forestry program that was introduced to the country in the mid-1990s. As is well known, community forestry programs are methods of forest management that involve local people's active participation. By examining details of the organizing process, including who takes the lead, how local people are mobilized, how ideas are implemented, and how activities are monitored, I attempt to identify the local social mechanisms at work in the community forestry program in present-day rural Myanmar.

There are two main reasons that this analysis focuses on the case of community forestry. First, the community forestry program is the first ever program in which the Myanmar government has explicitly emphasized "local people's participation." Over the past 50 years, under both the socialist regime (1962–1988) and the military regime (1988–2011), policy and decision-making processes in Myanmar have generally been top-down. In this context, this community forestry program stands out as unique and is the sole officially endorsed program suitable for the examination of local people's organization-making processes in Myanmar.

Second, the local context is likely to have influence over the forms of organization that have emerged among community forestry programs in Myanmar. The institutional framework of this program provides some room allowing local people to adjust the program to suit their own conditions. The Community Forestry Instruction (CFI), issued in 1995, is the legal framework that has been applied uniformly throughout the country, and it is backed by the 1992 Forest Law and the 1995 Forest Policy that clearly promote the participation of local people in forest management. However, the actual structure of an effective organization is defined only vaguely. Kyaw Tint et al. (2011, p. 42) note that "the FUG (that is, forest user group) membership selection process for members is a lacuna in the CFI. The CFI does not mandate whether the whole village should be included or indeed all the current users of the forest, even those beyond the village [*sic*]."[1] Therefore, the CIF provides room to allow various organizing patterns with regard to community forestry.[2]

To identify how the local social system influences the community forestry organization, I have paid special attention to how the program takes shape in different areas. Furthermore, related investigations were undertaken to answer the following two questions: (1) What are the organizing patterns, including the basic unit of organization? (2) What factors in the local social system influence these organizing patterns?

Previous research on Myanmar's local social systems is limited compared with that conducted in neighboring countries. However, differences in local regional conditions are well understood, especially the differences between Upper Burma (dry zone)[3] and Lower Burma (including delta area). Before colonization by the British in the nineteenth century, Upper Burma was the heart of the Burmese dynasty and the local people were ruled under a semi-feudal system. In contrast, Lower Burma was a less populated area with a looser central authority. The differences in the cooperative nature of villages in each region are also reflected in how tax was collected. In Upper Burma, the tax (called the *tathameda* tax) was imposed on the village and the whole village was responsible for the payment, although this was allotted to each household according to economic capacity. In Lower Burma, the tax was collected individually as a capitation tax, and the village did not intervene in tax collection (Tinker 1954, pp. 23–24).

Both areas fell under direct British rule (Lower Burma in 1852, and Upper Burma in 1886) (Cady 1958; Furnivall 1948, 1957). British colonization, however, did not fundamentally change the differences between the two regions. In Upper Burma, although the British government attempted to weaken the existing rural local system by introducing a new local administrative system (that is, the village tract system), there was strong communal feeling there to some extent. The village and its residents still felt a certain cohesion. In Lower Burma, however, because of increasing population mobility in response to the economic boom caused by expanding rice exports followed by the severe recession, communal feeling and collective activities were not fully developed, and villages often did not even have a monastery, which would have served as a nucleus for the community (Furnivall 1948, p. 105; Saito 1975, p. 127). Relatively speaking, communal bonding remained stronger in the villages of Upper Burma than in those in Lower Burma during the colonial period. This general understanding about regional difference is adopted in this chapter.

Information on Myanmar's present-day local social systems is limited, mainly because of difficulties in conducting field research within the country in the past few decades. The most prevalent view to be found in Western literature is that the people were in a position of passive obedience to the country's authoritarian military regime from 1988 to 2011, which hints that there was no room for self-organizing based on the collective will. For example, Fink (2001) describes the nature of communities as disintegrated and divided under the military regime. She writes that "the regime considers all dynamic organizations to have the potential to rally people in opposition to the government. Thus, most have been crushed or absorbed, leaving people who want to do something good for their communities with few options" (Fink 2001, p. 135). In a similar fashion, Turnell (2009, p. 347) discusses the needs for trust among the people for successful microfinance schemes, which take the form of group lending; however, he questions the existence of trust in Myanmar's society. He states, "Burma is under a military dictatorship whose political control in many parts of the country is almost complete, and whose intrusion into everyday life is often shocking to those unfamiliar with the country." Turnell further explains that various arms of the state "have created in Burma an atmosphere of profound *mis*trust."

However, Japanese researcher Takahashi has put forward a contrasting view on Myanmar's rural society, arguing that Myanmar villages are freer and more self-reliant than often previously perceived (Takahashi 2012, p. 9). Takahashi (2012) describes several collective activities found in rural Myanmar, including the management of common resources, assets, and facilities. As his work compares the nature of Myanmar's rural society with that of Japan, Takahashi's emphasis is on the loose cohesion found in Myanmar's rural villages, compared to the stronger village cohesion in Japan. He finds that Myanmar villages cannot be the unit of collective activities for production, whereas Japanese villages can. He argues that whole-village participation is fundamentally difficult in Myanmar villages, and that common asset management is often successful only when the asset is entrusted to a single villager, to reduce the cost involved in possible conflict resolution among villagers. This chapter supports Takahashi's characterization of the nature of Myanmar's rural society as a more free and self-reliant one. However, as the various cases presented in this chapter show, other organizing patterns do also exist in Myanmar villages. This study attempts to provide a hypothetical perspective on the factors behind differences in organizing patterns, paying particular attention to local social systems.

The following three areas were chosen as study sites: (Southern) Shan State located in the country's mountainous area, the Magwe Region in the dry zone area, and the Ayeyarwady Region in the delta area. Myanmar's community forestry program has been promoted in these three areas, and each area has distinct ecological conditions, as well as historical and social backgrounds.

The field surveys were conducted at the following locations: Kalaw and Nyaung Shwe Townships in Shan State; Magwe and Mindon Townships in the Magwe Region; and Labutta, Pyapon, and Bogalay Townships in the Ayeyarwady Region (Figure 4.1).

The surveys were conducted during the period 2010–2012 (Shan in May 2010 and January 2011, Magwe in January 2011 and June 2012, and Ayeyarwady in November 2012). The numbers of surveyed community forestry program sites are 33 in total, 11 in Magwe (A1–A11), 10 in Shan (B1–B10), and 12 (C1–C12) in Ayeyarwady. Basic information regarding the community forestry programs and the villages where they are established are shown in Table 4.1. In terms of ethnicity, Magwe and Ayeyarwady villages are predominantly Burmese, while Shan villages consist of various ethnicities.

The community forestry sites were selected to support various locations within the respective townships, and the local Forest Department in each township was consulted for guidance in the selection process. I made efforts to visit as many program sites as possible to understand the variation in organizing patterns. In each location, interviews were conducted with the leaders and members of the community forestry user groups, and with the village headmen and village elders where the community forest sites were located. The interviews were conducted in the Burmese language by myself, using a pre-prepared questionnaire that covered basic information such as the village's number of households, its main means of livelihood, the details of the community forest program management, and the existence of collective actions and activities undertaken by the villagers.

The organization of this chapter is as follows. The next section provides the features of Myanmar's rural administration to provide readers with some basic knowledge about the local setting associated for the community forestry program. After a brief overview of Myanmar's community forestry program and its institutional framework, the following section extracts the organizing patterns of community forestry programs in the

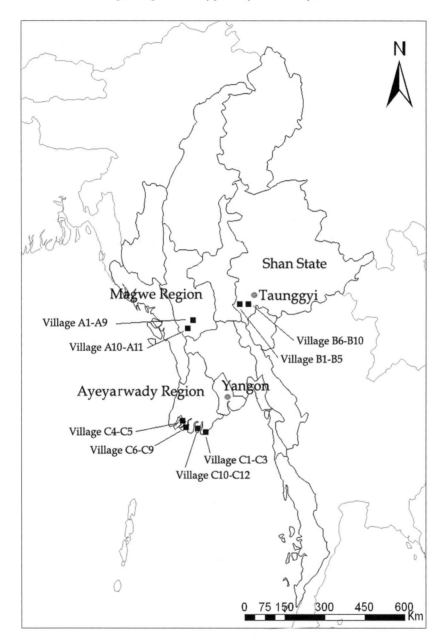

Figure 4.1   Location of villages studied

Table 4.1   Basic information regarding villages and community forestry

State & Region	Township	Village	Number of households	Ethnicity	CF area (acres)
Magwe	Magwe	A1	250	Burmese	50, 30, 15
		A2	226	Burmese	2.5, 1, 1, 0.5
		A3	243	Burmese	52.25
		A4	153	Burmese	50, 100
		A5	149	Burmese	50
		A6	280	Burmese	100, 5
		A7	323	Burmese	150, 120, 170, 40
		A8	278	Burmese	5, 12, 1.6
		A9	154	Burmese	50
	Mindon	A10	167	Burmese	482
		A11	150	Burmese	436, 600
Shan	Kalaw	B1	130	Danu&Taungyo	300
		B2	195	Palaung	40
		B3	80	Danu&Taungyo	13.7
		B4	77	Pa-O	16.5
		B5	52	Danu	1163
	Nyaung Shwe	B6	167	Intha	600
		B7	150	Intha	600
		B8	82	Intha	508
		B9	80	Pa-O	29
		B10	37	Intha	326
Ayeyarwady	Pyapon	C1	297	Burmese	157
		C2	256	Burmese	179
		C3	1400	Burmese	100, 150
	Labbuta	C4	156	Burmese	202
		C5	83	Burmese	200
		C6	110	Burmese	693
		C7	61	Burmese	850
		C8	206	Burmese	150
		C9	127	Burmese	1051
	Bogalay	C10	130	Burmese	50
		C11	93	Burmese	700
		C12	328	Burmese	40

Source: Author's field survey.

field, delving into one case from each of the three regions. The discussion is followed by the examination of the reasons why community forestry takes specific forms and exhibits regional differences relative to local social systems. The last section contains my conclusions.

RURAL ADMINISTRATION: VILLAGE TRACT AND VILLAGE

First, I examine the village administration of Myanmar to clarify its structure (Figure 4.2). Under the new government, the local administrative structure was reconstituted slightly, based on the constitution established in 2008. Currently, there are seven states, seven regions, and a union territory (*Nay pyi taw*). The administrative units within the states and regions are districts (*kayain*), townships (*myone*), and wards or village tracts. Generally, several villages (*kyayywa*) comprise a village tract (*kyayywa ouksu*).[4] The number of the villages in one village tract varies widely

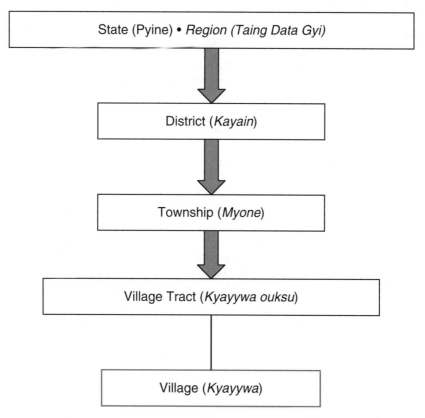

Note: The bold arrows indicate that the state, or region, maintains the highest level of official administrative authority and official authority does not extend beyond the village tract level, though there is an indirect link with the village through the village tract.

Figure 4.2   Local administrative structure

depending on the area. For example, in the study areas featured this chapter, there were 8–15 villages in a village tract in Shan, 3–5 in Magwe, and 7–40 in Ayeyarwady.

Village Tract

The village tract stands as the channel connecting the village and the township. This is reflected in the way a village tract head is selected, as well as in the nature of the meetings relating to the village tract.

The head of a village tract (called *ouk kyo hmu* under the new Ward and Village Administration Act 2012) is chosen from among the headmen of the villages (called *yar ein hmu*, or hundred-house heads, at the village tract level) within the same village tract. The way in which the village tract head is chosen varies widely.[5] In some cases, the headman of the "main"[6] village was automatically selected as the head of the village tract. In other cases, selection was done by all the residents of the village tract. However, most frequently the township selected a village tract head from the list submitted by the villages, so that township could exercise authority over the village tracts. This became especially apparent in 2007, when the government decided to limit the position of village-tract head only to those who were university graduates as well as Union Solidarity and Development Association (USDA) members, which was a mass organization established by the military government in 1993. The appointed person may retain the position for a long term if he manages to act according to the expectation of the township, in addition to maintaining his position as the headman of the village he lives in.

These village tract headmen are called to monthly or bi-weekly township meetings, for which government policies and instructions are the major agenda items. Headmen are expected to deliver instructions to each village in their respective village tracts by calling the headmen of the villages to the village tract meeting. Apart from these administrative issues for central and local government, it seems that there is little horizontal linkage between the villages, even if they belong to the same village tract.[7] The village tract, therefore, appears to be a rather loose unit.

Village

In contrast to the village tract, the village has more autonomous features and functions. The selection of village headman is done by the consensus of the whole village. Intervention by the township at this level is quite rare. In many cases, one person from each household would be called to a meeting and the headman is selected by their vote or show of hands.

In selecting the village headman, personal quality is important, as Nash pointed out more than 50 years ago (Nash 1963, p. 197). There are three major concepts of the personal qualities required from those who take on the village's most important roles: *pon* (power and glory), *gon* (virtue), and *awza* (the authority to command). In addition, since no official monetary reward is provided and no particular budget is allocated to manage village affairs, these headmen must have an economic base that will enable them to spend their time on village issues on a "voluntary" basis.[8] Since not many people meet these qualifications, a headman tends to retain his position for a considerable time as long as he has no problems, such as age, health issues, or losing popularity among the villagers. It is not rare to have a headman in the position for more than five years or to find that the same person is re-elected after a certain interval. For example, the headman of Village B2 was in the position for 40 years, though this may be an extreme case. In the case of Village A1, the headman was in the position during 1999–2000 and was re-elected ten years later, in 2011.

There are other actors who support the village headman in village affairs: that is, the ten-house heads (*se ein hmu*)[9] and the village elders (*yammi yappa*), and in some cases monks.[10]

The ten-house head is the leader of a group consisting of around ten households who live near each other.[11] The number of households in a group is not fixed to ten. Some groups may include 20–30 households, with an increasing number of households. In one contrasting case, a village headman intentionally reduced the size of the household group from ten to eight members, as he believed that this would help the system to work more efficiently. The ten-house head is responsible for the various issues related to the households in his group. If there is a dispute between the households, the ten-house head tries to settle it, and only when he finds that he cannot handle it is the issue brought to the village headman.

In addition to ten-house heads, some villages appoint hundred-house heads (*yar ein hmu*),[12] who act as coordinators for the ten-house heads. Generally, a village with a large number of households will have hundred-house heads to lessen the burden on village headmen.

The other influential actors, village elders, are generally senior male villagers who are knowledgeable, have the capacity to exercise certain influence over fellow villagers, and are respected by the villagers. Former village headmen often become village elders because of their perceived trustworthiness and their leadership experience. Normally there are three to ten village elders and they are consulted whenever important village issues arise.

In most cases, the agenda for a village meeting is more flexible than one for a village tract meeting. The issues discussed in village meetings are not limited to administrative concerns; instead, they cover a wide range of matters closely linked to the villagers' everyday lives, such as village development and social and religious affairs.

The subsequent sections will examine Myanmar's community forestry program and how it was introduced and organized in the local context.

BACKGROUND AND INSTITUTIONAL SET-UP OF COMMUNITY FORESTRY PROGRAM IN MYANMAR

Myanmar has the second-largest forest area in Southeast Asia (that is, 79 million acres in 2010) after Indonesia. However, this area is being depleted at a faster pace (0.9 percent per year) than the average pace for depletion in Southeast Asia (0.4 percent per year). The major reasons for depletion are the felling of timber for export, agricultural encroachment, and daily collection of firewood by rural residents. Considering the fact that 70 percent of Myanmar's population lives in rural areas, many of which still lack electricity, firewood usage can be quite destructive to forest resources (Kyaw Tint et al. 2011, pp. 11–12). Thus, to manage forest resources in Myanmar, it is imperative to meet the rural demand for firewood and to assist in improving rural living standards. This is the foundation of Myanmar's community forestry program.

The CFI defines community forestry as follows:

1. Establishment of woodlots where there is a lack of firewood and other wood products used by the community.
2. Planting trees and exploiting of forest products to obtain food supplies, consumer products, and incomes "at farmers' level."

The procedure for the establishment of community forestry is as follows. More than five village members who have a common interest in community forestry form a forest user group. The group does not necessarily have to be linked to the administrative unit. The user group members then set up a management committee. The chairman of the committee applies to the District Forest Department via the Township Forest Department for the establishment of a community forestry program. When the application is approved, the committee must draw up a management plan that includes information on plantation and silvicultural operations for the coming years. After this management plan is submitted, the District Forest Department will issue a community forestry certificate to the user group. The community forestry land is leased to the user group for 30 years.[13] This lease contract can be renewed with the approval of the District

Forest Department. If there are sales of products derived from the community forest, any revenue is to be deposited in the user group's joint bank account. The Township Forest Department helps with the preparation of documents and maps and, during the initial year of a community forestry program, it will also provide free seedlings for planting.

In 2010, the area under community forestry management was only 0.1 percent of all forest land (0.3 percent of the forest land under the Ministry of Forestry's jurisdiction) (FAO 2010, p. 10), thus, it is still marginal. In addition, no community forestry program has officially begun harvesting (Woods and Canby 2011, p. 19). As noted earlier, the three areas – Southern Shan (a mountainous area), Magwe (dry zone), and Ayeyarwady (delta area) – were designated as priority areas for community forestry during the initial stage of the program (Table 4.2).

Trees for planting are selected according to the ecological condition of each area.[14] It is necessary to pay special attention to those community forestry sites located in the delta area. These community forestry projects are located in the mangrove forests, that is, the very southern part of the delta. This area was severely affected by an unprecedented cyclone, which caused a tremendous number of casualties, in 2008.[15] Because of the damage caused by this cyclone, most of the community forest programs in this area had to be halted, at least temporarily. In fact, most of this area's existing community forest projects are either new or were restarted after 2009.

COMMUNITY FORESTRY PROGRAMS IN PRACTICE

Let us take a closer look at the actual community forestry program. Individual cases for the three areas – Magwe, Shan, and Ayeyarwady – will be discussed in detail, and the features of organizational patterns, including commonalities and differences according to area, will be identified.

Village A1 in Magwe Township, Magwe Region

A1 is a typical village in the dry zone. There were 250 households in the village and all are Burmese. The primary livelihood is upland cultivation, from which the main crops are sesame, peanuts, and pulses. But those who had land to cultivate[16] accounted for only 40 percent (111 households) of the total households, with the rest dependent on agricultural wage labor. The high rate of landlessness is a common feature of villages in the dry zone.

There were three community forestry sites allotted to this village. One site encompassed 50 acres; originally, it was a village firewood plantation

Table 4.2 *Distribution of community forestry area*

State & region	Community forestry area (acres)				Share in total community forestry area (%)			
	1996/97–2000/01	2001/02–2005/06	2006/07–2010/11	Total	1996/97–2000/01	2001/02–2005/06	2006/07–2010/11	Total
Southern Shan	**4957**	**44568**	**2012**	**51536**	**23.4**	**63.7**	**16.4**	**49.8**
Magwe	**6191**	**3297**	**1030**	**10517**	**29.2**	**4.7**	**8.4**	**10.2**
Mandalay	1500	8417	997	10914	7.1	12.0	8.1	10.6
Ayeyarwady	**1862**	**4344**	**0**	**6206**	**8.8**	**6.2**	**0.0**	**6.0**
Eastern Shan	5173	430	0	5603	24.4	0.6	0.0	5.4
Sagaing	618	3234	410	4262	2.9	4.6	3.4	4.1
Kachin	0	0	3387	3387	0.0	0.0	27.7	3.3
Rakhine	853	1805	680	3337	4.0	2.6	5.6	3.2
Chin	0	1220	1861	3081	0.0	1.7	15.2	3.0
Northern Shan	0	322	1060	1382	0.0	0.5	8.7	1.3
Kayin	0	1103	0	1103	0.0	1.6	0.0	1.1
Kaya	0	100	0	100	0.0	0.1	0.0	0.1
East Bago	0	20	265	285	0.0	0.0	2.2	0.3
West Bago	63	235	0	298	0.3	0.3	0.0	0.3
Yangon	0	675	90	765	0.0	1.0	0.7	0.7
Mon	0	165	0	165	0.0	0.2	0.0	0.2
Tanintaryi	0	0	445	445	0.0	0.0	3.6	0.4
Total	21215	69935	12236	103385				

Note: Bold type indicates the area where the study villages are located.

Source: Forest Department, Myanmar.

established in 1993 according to instructions of the Forest Department. Upon the commencement of the United Nations Development Programme (UNDP) community forestry project, this area was allocated as a community forest site, together with the other two sites (15 acres and 30 acres). The targeted land was almost barren before the start of the project but now planted eucalyptus is growing soundly in the 50-acre site (trees in the other two sites have not grown to an extent that can be utilized).

When initiating the project in 1995, the UNDP contacted the village directly (that is, the village headman) rather than dealing with the village tract. The UNDP had access to information regarding the village and had knowledge of some possible sites for the project, because the UNDP hired local Forest Department staff who had experience with the firewood plantation project there.

When the site was the Forest Department's firewood plantation site, the villagers regarded it as just another sort of government order, and did not show much interest. However, after the project fell under the UNDP's leadership, villagers started to regard it as beneficial. This may be partly due to the economic benefit of receiving a wage from the UNDP for planting seedlings.

The village decided that the then village headman would be the chairman of the community forestry management committee, and the ten-house heads of the village (21 persons) would be registered as the members of the user group. However, it should be emphasized that this framework was established just following official procedures; in reality, it did not have any practical meaning for the villagers. Villagers shared the idea that all the village households were the user group members of these community forests. As a reflection of this concept, requisite silvicultural operations for this community forest, such as fire protection and weeding, were done twice a year by one person from every household, until the trees grew to a certain size.[17] This is similar to the way they do other collective works (*loukar pei*) for the village, which will be discussed in detail later.

The logs taken from this community forestry site have been used for four major public facilities in the village. In 1999–2000, they were first utilized for the construction of a school. Then, the logs were used for constructing common livestock feeding facilities in 2001, the expansion of the school in 2004, and for electricity poles in 2005. They have not used the logs in recent years, although there was discussion over whether to use them again for school buildings at the time of the survey in 2012. All the decisions regarding the use of the logs were made at village meetings, irrespective of the official management plan. Neither the UNDP nor the Township Forest Department were involved in these decisions, although the village reported the decision to the Department as prescribed in the CFI. For smaller-scale utilization, such as the construction of a hut for the monastery, the village did not bother to inform the Township Forest Department.

One household lived in the 50-acre community forestry compound between 2004 and 2012. A villager asked the then village headman for permission to live in the compound, promising to guard the community forest in return. The village headmen called a meeting with the ten-house heads on this issue and decided to allow the man the right to harvest plums from the site and to sell them as a reward for his guarding duties. In fact, the CFI does not allow anyone to live in the community forestry site, but the village made this decision under its own discretion. However, as there was a warning from the township office in 2012, the village urged the household to move out of the compound and instead live on the homestead land of one of the village elders. This land was close enough to the forest so that the forest guard could continue his monitoring and thus retain his right to harvest plums.

Although Village A1 generally follows the CFI in order to proceed smoothly in line with support from its donor agency (the UNDP in this case), the village actually makes many of its own decisions. These are intended to meet the needs of the village and create a specific model of operations, for example, making the whole village the de facto user group and limiting the use of forest products to the facilities related to the public interest of all villagers.

Village B1 in Kalaw Township, Shan State

Village B1 is located in southern Shan State. As is often the case in Shan State, the village comprises various ethnicities. Both Danu and Taungyo people (the ratio is three to one) live in Village B1. The village has 130 households. Upland cropping (upland rice, ginger, potatoes, and so on) is the major income source, but unlike the case of villages in the dry zone, the proportion of landless households is low (only five households).

B1's community forestry area is rather extensive and encompasses 300 acres. This community forestry was approved in 2001 and is one of the oldest in the Kalaw Township. The area consists of the degraded natural forest (70 percent) and plantation forest (30 percent).

The Township Forest Department contacted the village and urged it to apply for the community forestry program. The targeted forest area included a Forest Department plantation, potentially threatened by illegal logging because of its proximity to Kalaw town. Thus, the Township Forest Department intended to encourage the village to monitor the plantation forest by making it a part of community forest. The area also covers the water source forest (about 50 acres), which the village had been keeping in good condition for quite a long time. Thus, the village also had an incentive to agree to the plan. What made it easier for the village to accept and initiate the program was that the official procedure (including paperwork) was supported by a Kalaw-based non-governmental organization (NGO), the Rural Development Society (RDS).

For the sake of the application procedure, a representative from the NGO became the user-group chairman and 16 villagers were registered as the members of the user group. However, similar to the case of A1, this registration was only a nominal one, and it was understood that all village households were responsible for maintenance of the forest. Planting, enacting fire prevention measures (once a year), and weeding (twice a year) were to be performed by a family member from each of the village's households. Again, this strategy resembled existing labor mobilization (*loukar pei*) by the village.

Since the conservation of water source forest was the most critical issue for the village, the village decided to prohibit the collection of firewood from this community forest. However, if the poorest households needed some firewood, the village headman might grant them the right to collect it in exceptional cases. As this forest faced a higher incidence of illegal logging due to its proximity to the town, two guards were hired with financial assistance from the RDS for a year and three months in 2004. Although this arrangement was only for a limited period, cases of illegal logging have decreased since then and the village has decided to shift the responsibility for monitoring to the whole village. Therefore, each villager is required to pay attention to the forest while they are working in the fields (they can hear sounds if someone is cutting the trees). If an illegal logger were to be arrested by villagers, the village would levy a fine and any firewood that the logger had collected would be seized. The seized firewood would be donated to the monastery in the village, as this arrangement would never face any objection from villagers.

Village C1 in Pyapon Township, Ayeyarwady Region

Village C1 is a remote Burmese village, located in the very southern part of Pyapon Township. The village was established in 1965 by a few people who sought good fishing grounds. People continued to flow in, and at one point, there were 700 households in the village. However, an increase in shrimp aquaculture that reclaimed the surrounding mangrove forest changed the tidal patterns, and the natural catch of fish has decreased dramatically since the early 2000s. Because most of the villagers depend on fishing wage labor for their livelihood, many have since suffered from reduced incomes. Furthermore, this village was severely affected by the cyclone in 2008 and many of its households moved to other places. Consequently, the number of households declined from 378 to 297 in the aftermath of the cyclone. Probably because of decreasing employment opportunities locally, there were about 40–50 villagers working in the industrial zones in Yangon at the time of the survey.

In this village, the community forestry program was instigated in 2009 after the cyclone, with the support of the Japan International Cooperation Agency (JICA). The community forestry area is 157 acres. To organize the user group, the village headman called a meeting. At the meeting, the village headman asked for those who were keen about participating in the community forestry program. Those who showed interest at that time became the user group, comprising 63 members. The primary motivation for participation was the likely availability of firewood. However, unlike the two cases above, the village authorities did not attempt to persuade every household in the village to participate in the community forestry program.

Thus this community forestry program did not attract whole-village participation; instead, the community forestry site is managed collectively by user-group members, who are involved in planting and other silvicultural operations. The user group is divided into six groups and a leader is appointed for each group. These subgroups make arrangements for silvicultural operations (yearly planting, weeding, and so on) and promote smooth communication among the user group members. The idea of subgrouping was adopted by the user group themselves, seemingly as an analogy to the ten-household groups I described earlier. The user group expects to harvest firewood in 2015 and their plan is that all user-group members will harvest it collectively, and distribute it equally between the members. If a new member wishes to join the user group, the committee has decided to levy an entrance fee of 50 000 kyat, in order to compensate the efforts of the existing members. There are some written criteria for membership, and one condition particularly worth noting is that the member must live "in the village permanently," suggesting that there is high mobility of the population in the area.

COMMONALITIES OF ORGANIZING PATTERNS IN THREE AREAS

From the cases described above, it is clear that the village is the basic hosting organizational unit for community forestry programs, regardless of region. It is not the administrative unit, that is, the village tract or other unit. In other words, the organization of user groups never extends beyond the villages, though the CFI gives flexibility for forest user groups to take various forms. In practice, the user group consists only of those who belong to the same village. In fact, this is all true for the 33 cases studied in all three areas.

According to one of the foresters in charge of the community forestry program in Kalaw, new donors were inclined to contact the village tract headman, as the village tract is the lowest unit in the official administrative structure, and there are fewer difficulties in obtaining information and data at the village tract level compared to the village level. In fact, the lists of villages are rarely available to outsiders. When the headman of the village tract is contacted, he tends to introduce the proposed program to his village first; he does not make special efforts to expand it to the entire village tract unless requested to do so by donors or authorities. If the same donors want to expand the community forestry program later, he might hand over the responsibility to the village headman to introduce it to other villages in the village tract. Thus, even if the village tract is the initial contact point, the village often becomes the actual base for collective action (such as community forestry).

What, then, are the reasons why the village can function as the unit for implementation of the community forestry program? In response to this question: the village has sufficient capacity for organizing collective action and sustaining it. Some relevant features of the village are elaborated below.

Decision-Making Mechanisms

Decisions and rules concerning village affairs can be made at the village level. The village headman, ten-house heads, and village elders are important decision-makers regarding village affairs, such as village development and social and religious affairs.

Decisions are made in the village meetings, which are called whenever issues arise. The villagers – represented by one member from each household – are called to a meeting if the village headman believes it is important. Otherwise, only the village headman and the ten-house heads (along with the hundred-house heads, if they exist) will discuss important matters with the village elders and make decisions. Then, the ten-house heads will deliver news regarding decisions to the households in their respective groups.

Each village usually has some informal rules intended to keep village social life stable and peaceful. Typical examples include prohibitions on making loud noises after a certain time, prohibitions on drinking alcohol or fighting publicly, keeping good control over livestock and preventing damage to others' fields or crops, prohibitions on working during villagers' funerals, and seeking help from the village headman and/or ten-house heads in solving difficult disputes. Some villages write these rules down (for example, B1 and B2) but others retain them only orally (these are sometimes affirmed at village meetings).

With this practice of making decisions and rules at the village level, it is relatively easy to make arrangements when a program such as community forestry comes to the village. The village headman calls a village meeting as usual, and discussions ensue.

Creating and Maintaining Village-Based Organizations

While village governance lies mainly in the hands of the village headman and ten-house heads, supported by the village elders, what is quite distinct about villages in Myanmar is that they do have several small groups, or committees, which manage specific village activities (Figure 4.3).

For example, if the village has its own monastery,[18] it normally will have a religious committee.[19] The committee takes responsibility for maintaining the monastery and village pagodas and for organizing various religious festivals. Some religious committees also manage the village's common funds. The members of the religious committee are generally senior persons who have detailed knowledge of religious affairs (thus, these committees often include village elders).

The other example is the educational committee. This committee will be responsible for managing the school located in the village. Sometimes, if there is an insufficient number of government-dispatched teachers relative to the number of students, or if teaching of high grades is not yet officially approved by the government, the village will make arrangements to hire a teacher or teachers locally (often certain villagers). The committee collects money either from parents or from all the households in the village to pay the teacher's salary. Some villages manage this money in the form of common funds.

For social affairs such as funerals, the "youth group" (*kalathar apwe*) in the village plays an important role. Normally there are male and female groups and they are responsible for assisting in the weddings and funerals[20] of villagers, preparing meals, and attending to guests.

The organizations described above exist in almost all of the villages that were surveyed. Furthermore, villages act quickly to establish new committees or groups if there is a need.[21] For example, Village A1 has established a committee to manage the lease of the mechanized well that supplies water to the villagers. Village B1 formed an electricity committee to install a transformer in the village by negotiating with local authorities and collecting money from village households.

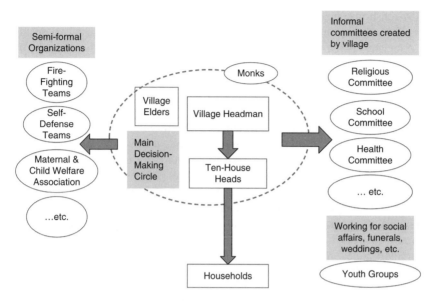

Notes:
1. Dotted line shows the main decision-making circle of the village.
2. Arrows shows governance positions.
3. Semi-formal organizations (left) are those initiated by government instruction, while informal organizations are initiated by villages (right).

Source: Author's survey.

Figure 4.3   Village internal structure and organizations

Again, the village provides the foundation upon which the community forestry user group can be formed, analogous to these committees or groups already existing in the village, while the village governance body plays the role of monitoring its activities, as was evident in the case of Villages A1 and B1.

Resource Mobilization Mechanisms

Once an organization is established, or when initiatives are set to begin, the village must mobilize the resources for implementing related activities. The main actor in this process is the ten-house head. If any village-wide collective actions are being decided upon, under the guidance of the village headman, the ten-house head will pass on the relevant information to the households in his group and will monitor their participation and work. In similar vein, if the village decides to collect money for certain activities, the ten-house head will often take the responsibility of collecting it from each household in his group. Thus, it was natural for Village A1 to decide to register its ten-house heads as members of a user group for the sake of making an official application for a community forestry project.

If laborers must be mobilized for a public purpose, villages are likely to practice labor mobilization (*loukar pei*) regardless of location.[22] One member from each household is called on to provide labor for free. Labor mobilization is often used for village road maintenance and the cleaning of the village monastery, ponds, schools, and so on. Normally, one member per household is expected to participate in this collective work. Villages may vary in the number of the days per year during which they will mobilize such labor, averaging four to ten days. If the village starts some large-scale collective work, such as road construction or school construction, each person may end up devoting a considerable number of hours to working on the project. For example, in the case of Village B5 in Shan, a new road was constructed linking the village to the main road; each household devoted their labour amounting to some 30 days per year. When Village C10 in Ayeyarwady constructed a school on its own, each household was required to provide as much as 45 days' worth of labor. A household may be exempt from this obligation if the householder best able to contribute is out of the village (either for personal travel or for work) or is ill. In some cases, those who cannot participate in these collective works must hire another laborer to meet their obligations. Village B7 has a rule stating that if anyone does not meet their labor obligation without legitimate reason, they will face a penalty, such as transporting one bullock cart of sand without assistance for public purposes.

There is another common type of labor mobilization: night guards for the village. This used to be quite common in villages in the dry zone, as these villages are typically equipped with village gates at their entrance points. It seems that the gates are no longer in use in most of the villages in the dry zone, as security conditions have improved, and villagers began to feel safe without gates or night guards by the early 2000s. However, it is likely that the arrangement could be started up again, if the need arises. On the other hand, labor mobilization of night guards is still in place in the delta region. Typically, the villages in this region are located along a river bank and do not have gates. As the waterways are the main means of transportation, the night guards are placed at the village jetties. One or two households take turns checking on anyone entering the village, as well as watching out for the theft of boats.

Therefore, the village has the capacity to mobilize the laborers required for a public purpose; further, it is capable of adjusting the form of mobilization most suitable for the objective. As shown in Table 4.3, the actual

Table 4.3   Actual utilization of community forestry

Utilization	Magwe	Shan	Ayeyarwady
Public purpose	6	2	0
Annual quota to villagers	3	3	0
Individual usage	1	2	2
Conservation	0	1	1
Not ready	1	2	9

Source: Author's field survey.

utilization of community forestry is geared mostly to the public; otherwise, villagers receive equal shares in the annual quota of firewood collected. Thus, for the silvicultural operations of community forestry, it is relatively easy to mobilize labor in a similar way, if the village judges it as leading to the public interest of the villagers.

Reflecting the general economic level of the villagers, households experience cash collections less frequently than they do labor mobilization. Nonetheless, villages have the capacity to collect cash for various purposes, especially for purposes that satisfy the villagers' common interests.

Some villages even keep common funds for various purposes, such as general development, religious affairs, education, or health (Table 4.4). These common funds can be either started with the villagers' money or can stem from outside donations. Their common feature is that they are exclusively managed within the village; that is, the only people who can borrow from the fund are villagers, over whom the village has enforcement

Table 4.4   Common funds in villages studied

	Magwe	Shan	Ayeyarwady
Religion	8	2	2
Education	4	4	3
Health	5	–	4
General	2	2	2
Other	3	3	–

Notes:
1.   Number of cases is on a gross basis. A village can have several common funds.
2.   "Other" includes the fund for youth group, management of the mechanized well, and support for elders.
3.   – indicates no cases reported.

Source: Author's field survey.

power, as well as sufficient information regarding credibility. The reasons for this are quite simple, and are to reduce the transaction costs in managing the fund.

Let us take the example of the religious common fund for Village B6 to illustrate the capacity of a village to manage certain funds independently. There is an annual occasion (*kathein*) during which robes and other necessary goods are donated to the village monks. To pay for that ceremony, the village (in fact, the religious committee described earlier) started a common fund in 2007, collecting donations from the villagers. As these are donations and not obligatory payments, each household provides only what it can afford. The committee decided to lend any unused monies to villagers, with monthly interest of 5 percent. In 2011, the loan amount was 30 000 kyat per household and, in principle, all households are expected to borrow. If some households are unwilling to borrow the money for any reason, such as fear of failing to meet repayments, the ten-house heads are responsible for borrowing the money on behalf of the particular household. This means that a ten-house head might have to borrow up to 300 000 kyats if his group consists of ten households.

The CFI requires the user group to keep and manage funds if they have some cash income from selling the produce from the community forestry. However, as most of the community forestry has not reached the stage of selling products, I did not find a case in the villages surveyed where a common fund for community forestry was maintained. However, given the prevalence of various types of common funds at the village level, it is highly likely that a village has the capacity to manage a common fund for community forestry if benefit can be found in doing so.

Enforcement Power

Even if certain consensus-building, decision-making, or resource-mobilization mechanisms are built into the village, these will not be effective unless accompanied by sufficient enforcement power. As described earlier, the village headman is generally selected based on his personal qualities, including the power to exercise authority over villagers. Village elders and ten-house heads should have similar personal qualities as well, although the extent to which they possess them may vary. Thus, it is highly likely that the decisions made by these leaders, with the agreement of the villagers, are basically respected.

A village keeps its own informal rules. If these rules are broken, there will be some sort of informal punishment. Some villages use fines to penalize villagers who break these rules. However, the penalty is not always monetary. In the case of Village A1, it was decided that rule-breakers would be compelled to donate 6 feet of corrugated iron for use in the roof of a library that the village was constructing. A more common form of punishment is the labor penalty, as it can be imposed easily, even on the poorest villagers. Labor punishments include repairing the village road, weeding the school and monastery compound, or cleaning the monastery.

With these features of enforcement, the village often enforces penalties for illegal logging of the community forestry, either by seizing the logs or firewood and donating them to the monastery, or levying fines, or making perpetrators plant new seedlings.

The features described above demonstrate that, generally, the village is equipped with organizing capability and enforcement power. The headman, ten-house heads, and village elders are the main drivers of these activities. However, if it is determined that a new organization (for example, a committee) should be formed, the village will quickly establish one. If the specific collective activity requires mobilizing labor, thanks to the existence of the labor-provision practice a village can do so with relative ease, especially if the objective is for the general benefit of all villagers. With this basic function and organizational mechanism, the village can be the hosting organization for a program like community forestry without many difficulties.

DIFFERENCES IN ORGANIZING PATTERNS IN THE THREE AREAS

Despite the common village governance features, differences were found in the organizing patterns of user groups at the village level, depending on the area. The first difference involves the extent of participation by the villagers. In 20 out of the 21 cases examined in Magwe and Shan, the user group consists of all the households in the village (Table 4.5). However, this does not mean that all villagers are registered officially as FUG members. As was found in the cases of villages A1 and B1, some villages applied using the names of only a few villagers, to make the procedure easier. However, in actual implementation, the village perceives its community forestry program as a village-wide activity and mobilizes the whole village whenever necessary. At the same time, as this is a village-wide activity, the products from the community forestry are utilized for public purposes, benefiting every villager almost equally (Table 4.5)

There was one case in which a community forestry program did not follow this line (Village B2). However, this particular village had another "village forest" that had been maintained through the establishment of a village forestry committee, which was pretty much in line with Myanmar's

Table 4.5   Organizational patterns of community forestry

FUG	Management type	Magwe	Shan	Ayeyarwady
All villagers	Jointly	11	9	
Partial number of	Jointly	0	0	5
villagers	Individually	0	1	4
	Jointly & individually	0	0	3
Number of community forestry projects		11	10	12

Source: Author's field survey.

official concept of community forestry. Since the proposed area for the community forest was somewhat distant from the village itself, the village headman decided to allocate it to an individual household, allowing them to live there and to earn income from some commercial trees and bushes (such as orange and tea) so that the area could be managed more effectively.

In contrast, among community forestry programs in the delta area, there were no cases where entire villages were mobilized as user groups as in Magwe and Shan. Only a portion of the village's households form the user group, and actual implementation and utilization are also limited to these members. The number of user groups range from 3.2 percent to 81.5 percent, for which 29.4 percent represents the average for the total number of households in each village. There are also variations in how the user groups manage community forestry sites. Some manage it collectively (five cases, including C1), while others divided the plot to be managed individually (four cases), and some chose a combination of both (three cases).

The second difference was found in the extent of the role played by the village in organizing the user group. In the case of Village A1 in Magwe and Village B1 in Shan, the villages took the lead in organizing the whole village's involvement in this program, by modifying it according to the village's and villagers' needs and the availability of the resources they could mobilize for their purposes. On the other hand, Village C1 in Ayeyarwady did not involve all of the village households in the program. Rather, the village acted as a sort of mediator or entry point for the introduction of the program into the village, and did not take the lead in organizing all the villagers. This feature was also found in other cases in the delta.

Why do these differences in organizing patterns emerge? Some might think that this is due to differences in motivation or in the objectives of the community forestry program. However, as can be seen in Table 4.6, the motivations for introducing the programs are not distinctively different among the areas surveyed. The main motives for initiating such programs

Table 4.6   Motivation for introducing community forestry

Motivation	Magwe	Shan	Ayeyarwady
Firewood	9	7	9
Logs	7	0	0
Prevention of encroachment	0	1	2
Conservation	1	4	3
Water availability	3	2	0
Disaster prevention	0	0	2
Income (agroforestry, crab catching)	0	1	2

Note: There can be multiple motivation depending on the FUG.

Source: Author's field survey.

seem to be meeting the demand for firewood, and for conservation (this can be either to maintain the water source, preventing outsiders' encroachment, or disaster prevention). It is natural to expect that the extent of the demand for the community forestry program could vary depending on the location and surrounding environment of the village. However, variations were found within each area, and they were not distinct according to region.

The other possible reason may be the influence of donors. However, as Table 4.7 shows, organizing patterns are the same within each area regardless of donors. The same donors operate in different regions (for example, the Forest Resource Environment Development and Conservation Association, FREDA in Shan, Magwe and the delta; and the UNDP in Magwe and the delta), but the organizational patterns are different depending on the region. Thus, we may say that the influence of a donor is not very evident in the organizational aspect of program implementation.

What may be inferred is that this is probably due to differences in the accumulated capacity and experiences of the villages regarding the organization of collective activities. Among the surveyed villages in the delta region, these differences have presumably arisen due to these villages' shorter histories, together with their populations' higher mobility.

The villages in Magwe and Shan are mostly more than 100 years old. Although seasonal migration can be observed in the dry zone, the mobility of the population is rather low in both areas, especially with respect to population inflow.

In contrast, the surveyed villages in Ayeyarwady are relatively new, established only around the 1960s. These villages are located within the reserved forest area, although in legal terms no village should be sited

Table 4.7   Donors of community forestry program

Donor	Magwe	Shan	Ayeyarwady
UNDP	9	1	1
JICA	–	–	5
FREDA	2	3	1
RDS	–	1	–
BANCA	–	–	1
EcoDev	–	–	3
None	–	5	1

Notes:
1. UNDP – the United Nations Development Programme;
     FREDA – Forest Resource Environment Development and Conservation Association;
     EcoDev – Economically Progressive Ecosystem Development;
     RDS – Rural Development Society;
     JICA – Japan International Cooperation Agency;
     BANCA – Biodiversity and Nature Conservation Association.
2. – indicates 0.

Source: Author's field survey.

there. However, people continued to flow in from the upper part of the delta (Ayeyarwady), searching for farmland or good fishing grounds. A village may not consist only of people with the same origin, as seen in the case of Village C1. Because of the nature of the area, population mobility seems to be much higher there than in other areas – in terms of both inflow and outflow – up until the present. In fact, some villages were established as recently as the early 1990s. The damage caused by the 2008 cyclone seemed to accelerate this process. Thus, in villages with higher population mobility and shorter histories, it may be more difficult to take a strong initiative. Consequently, there may be fewer opportunities for accumulating experiences of village-wide collective activity.

Table 4.8 lists the observed collective activities in three areas, excluding those common to almost every village, such as religious affairs and labor provision for cleaning the roads or schools. The number and variety of collective activities is greater and more diverse in Magwe and Shan than in Ayeyarwady.

For example, there are three cases where the village has kept forest land as a village forest in Shan, one of which is Village B2, mentioned earlier. The village established a forest committee to monitor illegal logging by both villagers and outsiders. On the other hand, in Ayeyarwady, Village C7 used to have a forest (30–40 acres) managed by the village. However, it was turned into paddy fields by 1996–1997. It was not clear whether the forest

Table 4.8   Collective activities in the surveyed village

Activities	Magwe	Shan	Ayeyarwady
	11 villages	10 villages	12 villages
(1) Supporting school teachers	7	6	6
(2) Managing common funds	11	6	8
(3) Constructing school, clinic, road and pagoda	2	6	2
(4) Conserving traditional village forest*	0	3	0
(5) Organizing village-wide supplies of electricity	2	2	0
(6) Managing mechanized wells for water supply	4	0	0
(7) Forming a fire fighting team**	1	2	0

Notes:
*   This excludes community forestry.
**   Not government initiated fire brigades.

Source: Author's field survey.

was cut down by the villagers or by outsiders, but this indicates that there was less power to mobilize the villagers to protect the common resource.

To explore the difference in the village capability for mobilizing resources and leading collective actions, let us take a closer look at the case of common funds. In terms of numbers, it does not appear that there is any distinct difference between the areas surveyed. However, what is critically different is that villages in Magwe and Shan manage a greater number of common funds that have been initiated by mobilizing money from within the village, as shown in Table 4.9.

Let us take a look at the case of Village A1 in Magwe and its internal mobilized common fund for management of the mechanized well. The village has a mechanized well, which was donated by the United Nations International Children's (Emergency) Fund (UNICEF) in the early 1980s. It is now leased to a villager at the cost of 700 000 kyat per annum. In fact, the lessee is the former village headman and an expert in mechanical engineering. The lessee sells the water to villagers at a prescribed price during a fixed daily time (14:00–18:00 in the rainy season, 6:00–18:00 in the dry season). The price of water changes according to fluctuations in the price of diesel, and with the endorsement of the village. To manage this lease income, the village decided to establish a committee of five members,

Table 4.9 Shares of internally mobilized common funding in all common fund cases (%)

Type of Fund	Magwe		Shan		Ayeyarwady	
	Total Cases	%	Total Cases	%	Total Cases	%
Religion	8	87.5	2	100.0	2	0.0
Education	4	50.0	4	25.0	3	33.3
Health	5	40.0	–	–	4	25.0
General	2	50.0	2	50.0	2	0.0
Other	3	66.7	3	100.0	–	–

Notes:
1. Number of cases are on gross basis. A village can have several common funds.
2. Other includes the fund for youth group, management of mechanized well, and support for elders.
3. – indicates no cases reported.

Source: Author's field survey.

which I touched upon earlier. In 2011, the committee lent 100 000 kyat each to seven villagers at a monthly interest of 4 percent. The usage of this common fund was not yet decided at the time of survey, but it is very likely that it will be used for maintenance of the mechanized well in future. It will not be used for other purposes, such as education for example.

In the case of Village B1, a common fund was started based on the consensus of villagers to install electrical substation equipment in the village. The village electricity committee was established in 2007 and negotiated with the electricity authority of the township. Typically, if the government does not have a sufficient budget to meet all these needs at the village level, the village is to bear the cost. B1 decided that each household should contribute 400 000 to 800 000 kyat to the project over three years. The amount was decided according to each household's economic level. If the households were not able to pay in time, the village allowed them to pay over a longer term. After the installation, the committee collected an electricity utilization fee from each household, the rate of which had been decided at a village meeting, and after paying the bill to the electricity authority, the committee kept the rest as an electricity common fund to be utilized in future for maintenance. At the time of the survey, the committee had available funds of 100 000 kyat.

On the other hand, this type of fund is found in only one village (C12) in Ayeyarwady. The rest were mostly initiated with resources provided by various external donors, as a part of the reconstruction assistance after the cyclone. This was also the case for Village C1, which started a health common fund in 2010, with the support of the World Health Organization (WHO). In other words, if the area had not been disaster-stricken, prompting the inflow of external assistance, it is not certain whether as many common fund activities would have been found in villages in this area.

This evidence suggests that in Magwe and Shan the villages are more active in establishing their own initiatives according to the village needs, and can successfully mobilize the required resources. On the other hand, in Ayeyarwady, collective activities remain at a minimum level (mainly for education) and are rather passive. Thus, unsurprisingly, the villagers themselves have less opportunity to perceive any benefit from village-wide collective activities.

Given these pronounced differences in village capability, the villages studied in the dry zone and mountainous area were more inclined to engage in community forestry as a village-wide activity, fully utilizing their existing organizing mechanisms. The villages in these two areas have the capacity to make programs, such as community forestry, a regular part of village activities. However, the villages studied in the delta accepted the program more passively, allowing those villagers who were motivated to form the community forestry user group. Even though these villages have similar basic organizing mechanisms, their weaker capacity for making decisions and for enforcement means that the cost of making community forestry a whole-village activity may be too high at present, partly because of these villages' high population mobility. The criterion for user-group membership required by Village C1 – that is, permanent residency in the village – presumably reflects the fact that it needed to confirm potential members' attachment to the village before allowing them to join the group.

It should be remembered, however, that this difference exists only in relative terms at the time of comparison. In fact, such contrasts also existed in the past, as described in the Introduction, between Upper Burma and Lower Burma in the colonial period. This difference shrunk during the socialist period, when the villages in Lower Burma developed some sense of unity and social bonding similar to those in Upper Burma (Saito 1986, pp. 123–128). This may also be the case with the villages in the southern part of the delta, and they may also come to have a similar capability for village-based collective activities in time.

CONCLUSION

This chapter aimed to explore the organizing mechanism in rural Myanmar by comparing how the community forestry program has developed in different areas within the country. Findings of this analysis follow.

First, the village, rather than the village tract, is the most important hosting organization for collective action associated with a specific
purpose, such as community forestry. It is rare for any voluntary collective
actions to be organized beyond the village level, regardless of the area in
which the village is located or its ethnic background.

Second, in organizing collective activities, the village governance body
is key to initiation. The village headman, with the help of the ten-house
heads and the advice and support of the village elders, is able to initiate new organizations and groups. The ten-house heads, with their close
relationship to each household, can mobilize resources such as labor or
money. Whenever the need arises, the village organizes committees or
groups for detailed management of specific issues, while the village leaders
monitor their activities. In this sense, Myanmar villages are equipped with
a well-functioning mobilization mechanism that relates to the welfare of
the villagers.

Third, however, this organizing mechanism built into villages appears
to vary depending on area with regard to the resources it can mobilize.
This chapter has demonstrated the different organizing patterns of community forestry according to area. Villages in Magwe and Shan used the
full organizational mechanism discussed above, adopting the program in
the same way that they carry out other collective activities. Those villages
have the will and capacity to make community forestry a part of their
village-wide activities, and to create community forestry committees that
are under close village control. The benefit of such collective activity is
fine-tuned to meet the public needs of the village. Thanks to their previous
experience of collective mobilization, villagers seem to accept such programs without any sense of strangeness.

On the other hand, villages in Ayeyarwady may mediate the program
but their responses are rather passive, and they do not attempt to mobilize whole-village participation in the program. The village may create a
committee or a group but this will possess a weaker capacity to mobilize
the resources necessary for initiating village-wide activities. The delta villages' shorter history and higher population mobility may mean that their
residents have fewer positive experiences of past collective activity, thus
weakening the villages' capacity for collective mobilization. At least for
now, the arena in which the village can play a role seems to be smaller in
the southern part of the delta, compared to the stronger village influence
found in the other two areas.

ACKNOWLEDGEMENTS

This research was possible with the valuable support of the Forest Department and the Forest Research Institute of the Ministry of Environmental Conservation and Forestry, Myanmar. I am especially grateful to Dr Nyi Nyi Kyaw and Dr Thaung Naing Oo from the Forest Department, who encouraged me to conduct research on Myanmar's community forestry programs. Additionally, I would like to thank Daw Myint Myint San from the Forest Research Institute, who provided me with considerable assistance in administering the surveys, and Mr Tomohiro Shibayama, the chief advisor for the FD/JICA's Mangrove Project in Delta who provided me with valuable information and suggestions. The research was funded partly by a Grant-in-Aid for Scientific Research (JSPS KAKENHI Grant Number 23510337).

NOTES

1. This CFI was drafted taking Nepal's community forestry as its model (as per an interview with Dr Kyaw Tint in January 2012, then Director-General of the Forest Department, who drafted the CFI). In the case of Nepal's community forestry, the user group does not necessarily match administrative categories, and non-resident forest users can also be members of the group. At the same time, a household can be a member of several user groups (Springate-Banginski et al. 2003, pp. 14–15).
2. By taking advantage of this flexibility, there are cases where the community forestry scheme is utilized by non-local people, that is, those who do not live in the area, for investing in the land to grow trees as cash crops. I found those types in Pin Oo Lwin and some in Kalaw. This is not what the community forestry was originally designed for.
3. "Burma" is used in the historical description included in this chapter.
4. The village tract system was originally introduced by the British government. It was formalized with the enactment of the Village Act 1907, which was valid until 2012. In February 2012, the Ward and Village Administration Act was enacted.
5. Village tract heads will henceforth be selected through a uniform process under the new law. However, the elections had not been held at the time of the survey (December 2012).
6. In some village tracts, in parallel to population increases and decreases in available residential areas, a proportion of villagers will move out of the existing village and form new villages. In this case, the original village is regarded as the 'main' village (*ywa ma*).
7. The exceptions are when the village shares a monastery. Among the surveyed villages, this was observed in Shan State (B3, B5, B9).
8. According to the Ward and Village Administration Act 2012, there will be a salary paid to the headman of the village tract, together with a budget for village tract administration. However, there is no specific mention of any salary or reward for the village headman.
9. These ten-house heads are mentioned in an eighteenth-century poem: 'In early days . . . people of the same kindred, living in a group of household, would choose the most suitable to be their leaders' (U Tin 2001, p. 206). The system continues to exist, although the ten-house heads' roles and functions may have changed with time. Under the current administrative system, lists of these ten-house heads are submitted to the township office; thus being a ten-house head is not an entirely informal position.

10. Some villages will punish a villager if they break a village rule, by taking them to the monk to be admonished by him.

11. There were two exceptional cases among the surveyed villages. Village B4 intentionally groups households that are not physically close to one another, in order to avoid hesitation in mobilizing resources. Village B8 groups the household according to the house list, without any consideration of the proximity of households. In these cases, the ten-house heads are nominated by the village head.

12. It is a little confusing as the head of the village is also called *yar ein hmu* at the village tract level. The idea is that the village headman is one of the *yar ein hmu* (if these are plural) of the specific village.

13. In legal terms, there are no strict restrictions on the land type where the community forestry can be established. The CFI states that community forestry programs can be established on: (a) reserved forest; (b) public protected forest; (c) land at the disposal of the state; and (d) with the permission of the owner on privately owned land or land owned by government organizations or non-government organizations. Thus, it includes almost all land except agricultural land. However, in reality, because of the relative ease in applying for the community forest program, the Forest Department tends to put priority on firstly public forest land and secondly reserved forest land, both of which are under its jurisdiction.

14. The most common trees planted in each area are as follows: *sha* and eucalyptus in the dry zone and mountainous area and *thame, byu,* and *kambala* in the delta area.

15. It is reported there were at least 140 000 fatalities, and 2.4 million people were affected by this cyclone. Labutta, Bogalay, and Pyapon, in the studied area, were among the severely damaged areas.

16. Until the enactment of the new farmland law in April 2012, the state held the ownership of farmland and farmers merely had tillage rights which they cannot dispose of. Under the new law, farmers gained the right to sell, buy, and mortgage their tillage rights.

17. For planting seedlings, the UNDP paid wages for the labor provided, so there was a type of economic incentive involved.

18. In some cases, a monastery is supported by multiple villages, especially when the number of households is small. It can also be the same with schools. In these cases, committees will consist of members representing all the villages involved. However, it seems that this is a sort of transitional process and there is a tendency for villages to desire their own monasteries or schools. The example of B10 village may be illustrative. It does not have a village monastery and its residents support various monasteries (not necessarily fixed). However, Buddhist events such as *Kathein* take place in their own village, for which ten-house heads take responsibility.

19. It is called *gobaka apwe*. Translated literally, it means "pagoda trustee group." However, it is not limited to the maintenance of pagodas; thus, I refer to it here as a religious committee.

20. Some villages may have a special association for helping with funerals (*narye athin*). Among the surveyed villages, C3 had such an association, which was established with the support of the Red Cross in 2011.

21. In the same manner, some groups or committees are organized by government instruction (Figure 4.3). It is often the case that these organizations remain nominal.

22. This term is also used for forced labor, which was practiced under Myanmar's military regime. The existence of these forced labor practices is one of the main reasons for international criticism of Myanmar, especially by the ILO. However, what is described here is different from those practices. This type of labor mobilization is arranged by the village itself.

REFERENCES

Cady, John F. (1958), *A History of Modern Burma*, Ithaca, NY: Cornell University Press.

Fink, Christina (2001), *Living Silence: Burma under Military Rule*, New York: Zed Books.

Forest Department, Food and Agriculture Organization (FAO) (2010), *Global Forest Resources Assessment 2010 Country Report: Myanmar*, http://www.fao.org/docrep/013/al576E/al576E.pdf.

Furnivall, John S. (1948), *Colonial Policy and Practice*, New York: New York University Press.

Furnivall, John S. (1957), *An Introduction to the Political Economy of Burma*, 3rd edn, Rangoon: People's Literature Committee & Houses.

Kyaw Tint, Oliver Springate-Baginski, and Mehm Ko Ko Gyi (2011), *Community Forestry in Myanmar: Progress & Potentials*, Yangon: Ecosystem Conservation and Community Development Initiative (ECCDI).

Nash, Manning (1963), "Party building in Upper Burma," *Asian Survey*, **3**(4), 197–202.

Springate-Baginski, Oliver, Om Prakash Dev, Nagendra Prasad Yadav, and Hoohn Soussan (2003), "Community forest management in the middle hills of Nepal: The changing context," *Journal of Forest and Livelihood*, **3**(1), 5–20.

Takahashi, Akio (2012), *Myanmar no Kuni to Tami* (*State and People in Myanmar*), Tokyo: Akashi Syoten.

Tinker, Hugh (1954), *The Foundations of Local Self-Government in India, Pakistan and Burma*, London: Athlone Press.

Turnell, Sean (2009), *Fiery Dragons: Banks, Moneylenders and Microfinance in Burma*, Copenhagen: NIAS Press.

Saito, Teruko (1975), "Dentouteki nouson syakai no kaitai to noumin hanran" ("Resolution of traditional rural society and farmer revolt"), in Toru Ono, Minoru Kiryu, and Teruko Saito, *Biruma: Sono Syakai to Kachikan* (*Burma: Its Society and Concept of Values*), Tokyo: Gendai Ajia Syuppankai, pp. 93–156.

Saito, Teruko (1986), "Biruma shiki syakai shyugi ka no nouson shyakai" ("Rural society under the Burmese way to socialism"), Ajia Teikaihatsu, Chiiki Nougyou and Mondai Kenkyuukai (eds), *Daisansekai Nogyo no Henbou* (*Transformation of Agriculture in the Third World*), Tokyo: Keiso Syobo, pp. 123–151.

U Tin (2001), *The Royal Administration of Burma*, transl. Euan Bagshawe, Bangkok: Ava House.

Woods, Kevin and Kerstin Canby (2011), "Baseline Study 4, Myanmar: Overview of forest law enforcement, governance and trade," *Forest Trends* (for FLEGT Asia Regional Programme), http://www.forest-trends.org/documents/files/doc_3159.pdf.

PART II

Local Society and Organizational Forms

5. Organizational responses of local societies in regional diversity: case study of a microfinance project in rural Indonesia

Motoko Shimagami

INTRODUCTION

Indonesia is the world's largest archipelagic country, comprising more than 17 000 islands and 237 million people. Across the archipelago, Indonesia consists of hundreds of ethnic and linguistic groups. This distinct cultural diversity is illustrated explicitly by a rich variety of folk terms used to express "village": *desa* in Java, Madura, and Bali; *nagari* in Minangkabau; *dusun* in South Sumatra; *gampong* in Aceh; *marga* or *merga* in Batak; *wanua* in Minahasa; *matowa* in the Bugis region; and *nagory* or *dati* in Maluku (Kartohadikoesoemo 1984, pp. 15–16).

A rural development project, even if implemented according to the same framework, takes different forms, demonstrating Indonesia's diversity of local societies. Performance of the IDT (Inpres Desa Tertinggal) project presents one such case. IDT is a microfinance project for poverty alleviation that was implemented throughout the nation by the Indonesian government for three years from 1994. The government grant was provided directly to groups of people in the form of a revolving fund.

According to Mubyarto (1996), project performance differs from place to place, even though the framework is the same. For example, the repayment rate differs distinctly by region: 99 percent in Java and Bali, 27 percent in Sumatra, and only 11 percent in Kalimantan. Additionally, the average loan size differs; loans for residents of Java and Bali are small and equally circulated to the members on an equitable basis, while larger loans for residents of other regions are granted to only a few individuals. Based on these data, Mubyarto argues that high group performance can be expected when the group emphasizes equity over efficiency.

Mubyarto's hypothesis is quite interesting, but it does not explain the distinct differences that have emerged between regions. When it is recognized that there are clear regional differences in group performance, a closer look should be taken at various local conditions that could cause such differences, such as economic opportunities, institutional settings, and resource endowments. It is conceivable that the high repayment rate was realized in Java and Bali because the project framework (for example, group size, unit, actors, and rules) was suited to the local conditions in those regions. To identify the local elements and their effects on the performance of development organizations, it is necessary to determine how local people organize themselves and manage their group activities.

To fulfill the stated research requirement, the discussion of this chapter proceeds as follows. First, it shows that the organizational responses of the people to the same development project differ according to the local or regional context in Indonesia. Second, it examines how the social system in each locality causes differences. Thus, it focuses on the salient features of locality groups, such as local administrative organizations and social organizations, and the relationships and interactions between these groups in the local society.

For the purposes of this study, this chapter provides an analysis of the performance of PNPM (known by Indonesians as the *Program National Pemberdayaan Masyarakat*, or National Program for Community Empowerment), which was launched in 2007 with the aid of the World Bank; it was designed to provide local people with funding to alleviate poverty and support community empowerment. This program requires that local people organize themselves to manage the fund, and it has been implemented nationwide under the same project framework. Therefore, it is feasible to compare differences in organizational activities according to a variety of local contexts. For the case studies, four villages from four provinces in Java and Sulawesi were selected and the performances of development organizations associated with PNPM in each village were compared.

This chapter is organized as follows. The next section reviews the characteristics of local organizations in rural Indonesia, with a particular focus on the relationships between social organizations and local administrative organizations. Development organizations that have been introduced mainly by the government are also presented. In the third section, PNPM is outlined. The fourth section shows the contrasts in the organizational responses of the four selected villages toward PNPM's unpaid loan problems. The fifth section includes a discussion regarding the reasons behind the differences in organizational responses. The concluding section summarizes the findings from the case studies.

LOCAL ORGANIZATIONS IN INDONESIA

As mentioned in Chapter 1 in this volume, there are two types of local organizations according to function, that is, development organizations and locality groups. Development organizations are formed to achieve specified targets, such as microfinance, joint marketing, or common-pool resource management. Locality groups coordinate and regulate members' behaviors; they include social organizations and local administrative organizations. This section provides an overview of both types of local organizations in rural Indonesia.

Village and Village Administration in Indonesia

Due to the distinct cultural diversity mentioned earlier, types of social organizations in Indonesia vary from place to place. Some are formed based on territorial bonds, while others are formed because of strong kinship relations. In some areas, caste-like organizations have been observed. Consequently, an important national agenda item for the Indonesian government has been defining and establishing administrative villages (local administrative organizations) by taking the diversity of social organizations into account.

Regional administration in Indonesia operates according to a four-tier system: (1) province (*propinsi*); (2) district (*kabupaten*) or municipality (*kota*); (3) sub-district (*kecamatan*); and (4) village (*desa*) or town (*kelurahan*). According to the current Act No. 32 of 2004 on Regional Administration (Act No. 32/2004, hereafter), provinces and districts/municipalities are designated as regional autonomous bodies, while sub-districts and towns are sub-organizations of districts/municipalities. Provincial governors and heads of districts/municipalities are elected by residents; in turn, these elected officials appoint the heads of sub-districts and towns from their district/municipal staffs.

Among these local administrative units, the village has a unique character. It is the lowest administrative unit in the rural area, equivalent to a town in the urban area. Unlike a town, however, a village is not a sub-organization of a district/municipality, nor is it a regional autonomous body. Act No. 32/2004 defines "village autonomy" as different from "regional autonomy," which is given to provinces and districts/municipalities. According to the Act, a village is "a unity of constitutional community which has borders and the authority to govern and manage the interest of the local people based on the history and custom of the local community." That is to say, village autonomy derives its authority from the indigeneity of a local community, while regional autonomy receives its authority as delegated by the central government.

This unique definition and position of a village is based on the stipulation of the 1945 Constitution that requires the state to recognize and respect the indigenous rights of village communities (*volksgemeenschap*), such as *desa* in Java and Bali, *nagari* in Minangkabau, *dusun* or *marga* in Palembang, and so on. In that sense, a "social organization" (an indigenously formed village) and a "local administrative organization" (administrative village) are supposed to be identical according to the Indonesian legal definition.

In reality, though, villages in Indonesia have endured substantial administrative reorganization and transformation. During the Suharto era (1966–1998), especially, the nationwide standardization of administrative villages was implemented based on Act No. 5 of 1979 on Village Administration (Act No. 5/1979, hereafter).

Act No. 5/1979 stipulated the standardization of the size and structure of administrative villages to mobilize people for participation in development, and to operate village administration more extensively and efficiently. The term "administrative village," for example, was standardized as *desa*, and the structure of village administration was made uniform. Further, the size of the village was regulated to be larger than 2500 people or 500 households, apparently using the Javanese *desa* as a basic model.

With the enactment of Act No. 5/1979, large-scale village reorganization has taken place, especially outside Java. As Table 5.1 shows, regions outside Java experienced more significant changes in the number of administrative villages. In most of the provinces outside Java, the minimum population requirement mentioned above seems to have been applied arbitrarily, and new *desa* were created by breaking up existing villages. In some cases, these enforced divisions tore apart the basic social organizations within the area.

Kato (1989) describes one such case by examining the experience of Koto Dalam village, Kuantan area, Riau Province, Sumatra Island.

Table 5.1   Number of administrative villages by region

Region	1974	1986	1998	2002	2008
Sumatra	9582	22263	21591	20839	23544
Java	21443	24540	24858	24948	25159
Kalimantan	7894	9285	6055	5892	6650
Sulawesi	3971	4481	7274	7474	9286
Other regions (except East Timor)	7241	5627	7705	8957	11027
Whole Indonesia	50101	67949	67925	68110	75666

Sources: Prepared by the author from the following literature and statistics: 1974, 1986, Kato (1989); 1998, Badan Pusat Statistik (1999); 2002, Badan Pusat Statistik (2003); 2008, Badan Pusat Statistik (2009).

According to Kato, an indigenous village unit in this area is called a *negeri*, which consists of a *koto* (a sort of capital of *negeri*) and several surrounding *banjar* (settlements). Due to the village reorganization, Koto Dalam village (*negeri*), which used to consist of a *koto* and four surrounding *banjar*, with a total population of 2511 people, was divided into seven *desa* (Kato 1989, p. 104). Consequently, various collective activities that used to be organized by the villagers of the entire *negeri*, such as maintenance of the school and the bridge, cleaning of the river, and coordination of the rice-planting calendar, were no longer taking place.

Kato argued that, in Koto Dalam, drastic village reorganization has torn apart the basic social organization and thereby brought about a negative impact on the collective activities of the people. This case leads to a hypothesis that the radical village reorganization that took place mainly in the provinces outside Java might relate to the poor development performance often observed outside Java, as in the case of the IDT project cited in the Introduction.

The same hypothesis has been used to criticize the "standardization" of administrative villages and advocate the revitalization of indigenous village units and structures, especially after the resignation of Suharto. The government changed its policy direction dramatically with the passage of the Act on Regional Administration (Act No. 22/1999, which was replaced by Act No. 32/2004). The legislation stipulates that the indigenous rights and cultural diversity of village communities must be acknowledged and respected, and it gives more regulatory authority to district/municipal governments (Table 5.2).

Responding to implementation of the Act, several regional governments took the initiative in establishing regional regulations to revitalize indigenous village units, replacing *desa* with *nagari* in West Sumatra, *gampong* in Aceh, *lembang* in Tana Toraja, and so on. However, a majority of the regional governments continue to use the *desa* as the village unit, and they utilize a structural framework similar to that of the *desa* (Figure 5.1). Moreover, as Table 5.1 shows, the number of villages continued to increase between 2002 and 2008.

The decision to reorganize a village in Indonesia raises several questions. To what extent is it relevant to revive indigenous village units, considering the drastic socio-economic changes that have occurred in Indonesia over the past several decades? If revitalization is still relevant, how can a certain village be identified as indigenous (or not indigenous)? In spite of the dramatic change in policy direction, why do most of the regional governments continue to use *desa* as the village unit? Does it mean that the exogenously introduced *desa* organization has been "indigenized" outside of Java? If so, how did this happen?

*Table 5.2   Major characteristics of village administration: comparison of
the two Acts*

	Act No. 5/1979	Act No. 32/2004
Term for village	Standardized nationwide as "*desa*"	Respect regional diversity Determined by the district/municipality regulation
Population criteria to set up new village	At least 2500 persons or 500 households	Diversified by region At least 1500 persons or 300 households (Java and Bali) At least 1000 persons or 200 households (Sumatera and Sulawesi) At least 750 persons or 75 households (Kalimantan and others)
Village head	Direct election Terms of office: 8 years (re-eligible for one time)	Direct election Terms of office: 6 years (re-eligible once)
Village officials	The village secretary, section heads, and sub-village heads Regulated in detail by the regulations of the Ministry of Home affairs	The village secretary, section heads, and sub-village heads. (Village secretary is appointed as district civil servant) Regulated in detail by the district/municipality regulation
"Village Assembly"	Village Deliberation Council (*Lembaga Musyawarah Desa*) Village head serves as chairman, and sub-village heads serves as members	Village Deliberation Board (*Badan Permusyawaratan Desa*, or other names) Village head and village officials cannot concurrently serve as members

Use of the organizational process approach may answer these questions. Here, importance was placed on understanding social organizations (indigenous villages) as critical elements of local social systems, not perceiving them in a static or idealistic manner. Rather, the purpose was to identify the organizing mechanisms of local social systems in which social organizations and local administrative organizations relate to and interact with each other by analyzing the performance of development organizations.

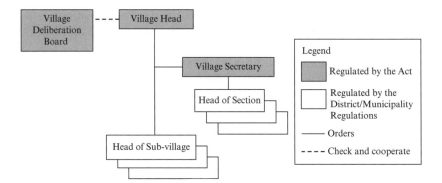

Source: Prepared by the author based on the Act No. 32/2004.

Figure 5.1   Structure of village administration in Indonesia

Development Organizations in a Village

Various development organizations have been established in Indonesian villages under the country's rural development policy, especially since the 1970s. Most development programs and projects have their own groups or organizations within villages to mobilize villagers' participation. The major ones include Women's Associations (PKK), the Village Development Committee (LKMD), the Youth Organization (*Karang Taruna*), Maternal and Child Health Groups (*Posyandu*), and Farmers' Groups. Besides development organizations established by the government or outside agents, various groups have been organized by villagers on their own initiatives to achieve specified targets, such as *arisan* (Indonesian traditional ROSCAs: rotating savings and credit associations), Islamic prayer groups, traditional art groups, and so on. To picture how these development organizations were organized, let us look at the case of KR village in Java, where I conducted intensive fieldwork in 1994 and 1995 (Shimagami 2001).

KR village is located in the Yogyakarta Province. At the time of my fieldwork in 1994–1995, the population was around 2500, or 900 households. Administratively, the village (*desa*) consisted of seven sub-villages (*dusun*), 16 RW (*Rukun Warga*, or bloc associations, consisting of several RT), and 37 RT (*Rukun Tetangga*, or neighborhood associations). Unlike Koto Dalam village, KR village had not experienced any village reorganization since the 1920s. Yet, KR village is not an indigenously formed village; it was formed as a result of administrative reorganization under the Dutch colonial government. As previous studies show, important social relationships in Javanese villages are dyadic, although they function in the context of residential proximity (Jay 1969, pp.188–190; Sekimoto 1978). No clear traditional unit, such as the *negeri*, has been observed in these villages. Yet, KR village in 1994 and 1995 appeared well organized in contrast to the Javanese village of the 1950s, which was characterized as "formless," "loose," and unable "to cooperate or to organize anything effectively" (Geertz 1959, p. 35).

Development organizations that were observed in 1994–1995 are listed in Table 5.3. Of 149 groups and organizations, around 120 were organized by government initiatives. Fourteen groups were organized at the village level (meaning that members are scattered around the whole village), 74 groups at the sub-village level (members are limited to the same sub-village), 38 groups at the RW level, and 23 groups at the RT level. Many groups, irrespective of their targeted activities, conduct *arisan* (ROSCAs) and savings and loan activities for the members on their own initiative.

Table 5.3 highlights several features of the organizational activities observed in KR village. First, the most common group size is around 30 members. Second, administrative units, such as the *dusun*, RW, and RT, usually represent boundaries of group members. Third, the majority of groups have been organized at the *dusun* level. Fourth, even in the development organizations formed under the government leadership, members independently organize their own activities, such as *arisan*.

From these features, it can be assumed that the most important locality group that functions as the host organization for collective action is the sub-village, and the optimal size of such a group is around 30 members living in proximity to one another. According to the 1994–1995 study, similar features were observed in other Javanese villages near KR village.

The case of KR village shows that it is possible to identify some characteristics of local social systems in the area by examining the features and performance levels of development organizations that were formed exogenously. The next section will look into PNPM, implemented nationwide under the same project framework. By examining the characteristics of local responses to the same development project implemented in different parts of Indonesia, it will explore how local society matters and try to identify the major characteristics of the mechanisms used by local people for organizing themselves.

DEVELOPMENT ORGANIZATIONS AND LOCAL SETTINGS OF SURVEYED VILLAGES

A Development Project (PNPM) as an Entry Point

PNPM is a national program aimed at alleviating poverty and empowering communities in rural areas. PNPM was launched in 2007 with funding

Table 5.3   Development organizations in KR village in 1995

Group name	Initiated by	Number of the groups	Members per group	*Arisan**
Groups organized at the village level (14 groups)				
Village Deliberation Council	Gov.	1	14	
Village Development Committee	Gov.	1	35	
Women's Association	Gov.	1	50	A
Women's Association: board members' meeting	Gov.	1	30	A
Youth Organization	Gov.	1	100	
Youth Red Cross	Red Cross	1	30	
Credit for literacy program participants	Gov.	1	250	
Credit for *desa* residents	Gov.	1	300	
Credit for rural economic activities	Gov.	1	50	
Credit for village women	Gov.	1	50	
Civil guards	Gov.	1	35	
Temple producers' group	Cooperative	1	10	A
Soccer team	Villagers	1	50	
Arisan among village officials' family	Villagers	1	30	A
Groups organized at the sub-village level (74 groups)				
Working Group of Village Development Committee	Gov.	7	10	A
Women's Association at sub-village level	Gov.	7	30–60	A
Maternal and Child Health Group	Gov.	7	30–60	A
Sub-unit of Youth Organization	Gov.	3	30–50	
Credit for sub-village residents	Gov.	7	50–60	
Credit for family planning participants	Gov.	1	50	
Rice bank credit	Gov.	1	20	
Farmers' group	Gov.	10	30–50	A
Water-using farmers organization	Gov.	1	20	A
Livestock raising group	Gov.	5	10	A
TV-watchers', radio-listeners' and newspaper readers' group	Gov.	7	30–50	A
Arisan among sub-village leaders	Villagers	1	20	A

Table 5.3   (continued)

Group name	Initiated by	Number of the groups	Members per group	*Arisan*
Groups organized at the sub-village level (74 groups)				
Arisan among the ex-soccer team	Villagers	1	40	A
Youth group for ceremony services	Villagers	1	25	
Traditional art groups	Villagers	12	20–30	
Sports groups	Villagers	3	30	
Groups organized at the RW level (38 groups)				
IDT groups	Gov.	16	30	A
Co-operative group	Cooperative	1	50	A
RW's monthly meetings	Gov.	7	30–40	A
Arisan among children	Villagers	2	20–30	A
Religious learning group	Gov.	10	30–40	
Islamic prayers group	Villagers	2	30–40	
Groups organized at the RT level (23 groups)				
Neighborhood Women's group	Gov.	9	10	A
Night watch system	Gov.	na	na	
RT's monthly meetings	Gov.	14	20–30	A

Note: * "A" indicates group that holds *arisan*.

Source: Rearranged from Shimagami (2001, pp. 524–525).

from the World Bank, based on the experience of the preceding (and similar) poverty alleviation program called PPK (a sub-district development program) that had been carried out in Indonesia since 1998.

The basic scheme of PNPM is as follows. Every year, a block grant in the range of Rp. 1–3 billion is allocated to each sub-district based on its population. Villages in the sub-district can propose their plans for: (1) small-scale infrastructure development; and/or (2) savings and loan organizations to support the income-generating activities of poor families. Plans are proposed, discussed, and selected by the villagers based upon a consensus reached through the participatory planning process, first at the sub-village level and then at the village level. Plans proposed by each village are discussed at the Sub-district Development Forum, where delegates from each village gather. Through Forum consensus, the block grant is allocated to fund prioritized plans. Since funding is limited, not all plans are funded every year.

Similar to the IDT project, savings and loan activities are implemented by organizing a group of poor families (especially women) who have demonstrated the potential for income-generating activities, such as cattle rearing, small-scale business, or craft making. A revolving fund is provided to each group, and group members can borrow money from the group and pay it back at a low interest rate. The group leader collects the repayment money and deposits it to the UPK (*Unit Pengelola Keuangan*, or Financial Management Unit) established at the sub-district level for managing the PNPM grant provided to the sub-district. The repayment money deposited at UPK will be provided to the same (or another) group in the same village as a revolving fund.

If a member cannot pay the money back in a specified period, the group members shall bear joint liability to pay it back. If the group cannot repay the money to the UPK in the designated period, the village that the group belongs to will lose its right to receive PNPM grant funds in subsequent years until the group repays its debt.

According to the basic scheme and rules mentioned above, PNPM has been implemented nationwide, becoming a very important development fund for Indonesian villages, which have limited development budgets. The following sections will examine the performance of PNPM in four villages in and outside of Java and explore how the villagers are organizing to respond to the development needs associated with the implementation of PNPM.

Brief Description of the Four Villages

The four villages selected for this case study include KR village (Yogyakarta Province) and BD village (Banten Province) on Java Island; and SA village (South Sulawesi Province) and LB village (Central Sulawesi Province) on Sulawesi Island. Basic information about these villages is summarized in Table 5.4, and the settlement patterns of each village are shown in Figure 5.2.

KR village is located in the Gunung Kidul District, Yogyakarta Province; it was mentioned in the previous section in the discussion of development organizations examined in 1994–1995. Almost all residents in this village are Javanese, and the population increased from 900 households in 1995 to 1600 households in 2011; quite a few newcomers have moved here from the nearby district capital. Houses are spaced closely and continuously, even between sub-villages. Because the village is located on a limestone plateau, villagers have been dependent upon dry-field farming, unlike the wet rice cultivation that is performed in many other Javanese villages.

Table 5.4 Basic information on four surveyed villages

Village region	Number of households	Total area (ha)	Village reorganization	No. of sub-villages	Population	Major livelihoods
KR Village, Gunung Kidul District, Yogyakarta	1600	514	No change since the 1920s	7	Javanese Newcomers are increasing	Dry-field farming, cattle rearing, public servants, small merchants, etc.
BD Village, Lebak District, Banten	812	1200	Limited reorganization	4	Bantenese and Sundanese A few newcomers	Wet-rice farming, collecting forest products, public servants, small merchants, etc.
SA Village, Tana Toraja District, South Sulawesi	490	1878	Frequent reorganization	4	Torajanese Some newcomers	Wet-rice farming, cacao and coffee, cattle rearing, public servants, merchants, etc.
LB Village, Donggala District, Central Sulawesi	490	696	No substantial reorganization	4	Kaili and others Some newcomers	Wet-rice farming, coconut palm cultivation, teachers, public servants, merchants, etc.

Source: Observation and interview at village office in 2011.

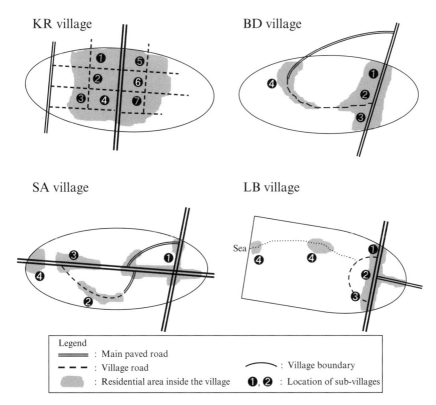

Figure 5.2 Settlement patterns of four villages and location of sub-villages

Though it is located on Java Island, BD village, Lebak District, Banten Province, has a different cultural and historical feature from the rest of the island. Formerly a part of West Java Province, Banten became a separate province in 2000 because of its unique origin under the influence of the Islamic Kingdom of Banten. Most villagers are Bantenese or Sundanese, and fewer newcomers have relocated here compared with KR village. Administratively, there are four sub-villages, with three sub-villages located along the main road; the other one is separated somewhat from the rest.

The two other villages are located on Sulawesi Island. SA village is in the Tana Toraja District, South Sulawesi Province. Tana Toraja literally means "Land of Toraja." As the name suggests, district residents are mostly Torajanese, and known for a magnificent death ritual during which they sacrifice large numbers of water buffalo and pigs. The Torajanese are known also for the ancestral house (*tongkonan*) constructed by the commonly acknowledged founder of the family branch. *Tongkonan* also refers to a group of family branch members that construct and maintain the ancestral house; it is the basic social organization for the Torajanese. As Torajanese kinship is bilateral, the scope of a *tongkonan*-based kinship group is quite broad. Administratively, Tana Toraja District experienced the most frequent and extensive village reorganizations among the surveyed areas (Table 5.5). The administrative village was first established in 1967. The number of villages, including towns (*kelurahan*), increased gradually from 65 in 1967 to 290 in 2001. In 2002, the number decreased to 141 due to the district's decision to revitalize the Torajanese traditional village unit (*lembang*). Since then, however, the number of villages has increased again, to 269 in 2004. SA village also experienced frequent reorganizations. Currently, it consists of four sub-villages (*kampung*).

LB village in the Donggala District, Central Sulawesi Province, is located along the seashore. Yet, the concentration of houses is 3–4 km inland alongside a paved road, except for approximately 20 fishery households near the seashore. Most residents are ethnic Kaili, although some residents come from different ethnic backgrounds, such as the Toraja and Bugis. Since 1902, LB village has not experienced substantial reorganization, except for one sub-village that was separated to become an independent village based primarily on population increase.

Performance of PNPM at the Four Villages

The basic information concerning PNPM implementation for each village is summarized in Table 5.6. In examining organizational responses to the implementation, attention was paid to the organizing process and development of savings and loan groups.

At KR village, information on PNPM's saving and loan program was distributed through the existing groups, namely PKK Dusun (the Women's Associations organized at the sub-village level). Each group recruited ten members, based on the project guideline recommendations. Since the Women's Association at the sub-village level functioned as the host organization, members of each PNPM's savings and loan group were composed automatically of residents from the same sub-village.

At the other three villages, the PNPM savings and loan groups were newly organized. The PNPM "village facilitator" appointed by the villagers approached candidates who engaged in potentially productive activities, on the premise that they would be able to repay loans. Ultimately, the facilitator organized these individuals into groups. At BD village, members of a group were from the same sub-village, but members were not limited to residents of only one sub-village for SA and LB villages.

As Figure 5.2 shows, houses and settlements are more scattered and

Table 5.5   Administrative reorganization in Tana Toraja

Year	Major administrative reorganization	Number of sub-districts (District*/ kecamatan)	Number of administrative villages/towns (desa/kelurahan)	Number of sub-villages (kampung/dusun/ lingkungan **)
1925	District system under the Dutch colonial government	32		410
1961	Reorganization of districts	15		133
1967	Establishment of kecamatan, desa gaya baru system	9	65	180
Around 1980	Introduction of desa system	9	65	n.a.
2000	Reorganization of kecamatan	15	290	n.a.
2001	Change of term from desa to lembang	15	290	n.a.
2002	Amalgamation of lembang	15	141	More than 485***
2004	Reorganization of kecamatan	19	145	n.a.
2004	Multiplication of lembang	19	269	More than 899***
2004	Reorganization of kecamatan and lembang/ kelurahan	29	269	n.a.

Notes:
*   "District" in this table is a unit introduced by the Dutch administration, different from the present district (*kabupaten*).
**   *Lingkungan* is a sub-organization under *kelurahan* (town).
*** In several *kelurahans*, number of *lingkungans* were not available.

Sources:
Prepared by the author from the following literature and statistics:
1925, 1961, 1967, 1980: Kabupaten Tana Toradja (n.d.).
2000, 2001, 2002, 2004: from appendix of the District Regulations of Tana Toraja regulating village reorganization of the respective years.

distant from each other in SA and LB villages than in KR village, yet for some reason the groups in SA and LB villages consist of residents from different sub-villages and settlements. Differences in the composition of group members create several questions that should be explored further. Are differences occurring because there are not enough potential candidates in one sub-village in SA and LB villages? Or does this mean that, unlike the case of KR village, the sub-village unit does not function as an important locality group that hosts collective action in SA and

Table 5.6 Implementation of PNPM in four villages, 2009–2011

| Village | Infrastructure project | | | Savings and loan groups | | |
	Year 2009	Year 2010	Year 2011	Number of groups	Group size	Composition of the members
KR	None	Drainage, nursery school facility	Drainage	10	10 members/ group	Members are from one sub-village
BD	None	Construction of elementary school	Road development	14	5–10 members/ group	Members are from one sub-village
SA	Road development	None	Road development	5	Around 10 members/group	Members are from different sub-villages and settlements
LB	Construction of elementary school	Road development, drinking water	Road development, public toilet	10	10–20 members/ group	Members are from different sub-villages and settlements

Source: Interview at the village office in 2011.

LB villages? If so, what is the important locality group for SA and LB villagers?

In all four villages, PNPM's repayment rates were better than rates of other government credit programs that had been implemented, because the project conditions included the requirement that a village could not receive a PNPM grant if one member failed to repay the money by the due date. However, each of the four villages had experienced situations in which a member failed to repay the money. Consequently, each village was trying to cover the unpaid loans on behalf of the problem borrower in its own unique way. The following section will examine how each village has responded to the unpaid loan problem by mobilizing its resources and organizational capacity.

RESOURCE MOBILIZATION MECHANISMS IN THE SURVEYED VILLAGES

Table 5.7 summarizes the responses to the unpaid loan problem that was identified in each village. Each village showed a very different response, thus illustrating characteristics of the varied organizing mechanisms within local societies.

KR Village

As noted in the previous section, quite a few development organizations were established in KR village during the Suharto era. Several character-istics became evident. First, the basic organizational unit was territorially based and consisted of approximately 30 members, mostly within the sub-village boundary. Second, the demarcation between endogenously formed activities such as *arisan*, and exogenously formed ones, as well as between social organizations and local administrative organizations, was not so clear. These characteristics continue to be relevant until today.

Although most of the development projects are well managed and gov-erned locally in KR village, a few members have failed to repay PNPM loans. According to the village head, the following measures were taken. First, the village head convened village leaders to discuss how to deal with the problem. At the meeting, the village head proposed to cover the unpaid loans from the assets of the village's credit institution (UED or *Usaha Ekonomi Desa*), managed by the village government, so that the village could continue to be eligible for PNPM grants. This proposal was agreed upon, and the problem borrowers were obliged to sign a written oath to pay the money back to the village government.

Table 5.7   Responses to the unpaid loan problems in four villages

Village	Response to the unpaid loan problems			Characteristic of resource mobilization mechanism
	Who took the initiative?	Asset mobilized to cover the unpaid loans	Original source of the asset	
KR	Village head	Asset of the village credit institution managed by the village government	Government grant once provided to the village groups	Close link between local administrative organizations and territorial based organizations
BD	Village head	Personal asset of the village head	Informal side income as a village head	Patrimonial (one-man) leadership of a village head
SA	Village head	Asset of the community development fund managed by the community	A part of animal sacrifice at rituals donated for community development	Resource mobilization through kinship groups at the time of rituals
LB	Head of the group	Savings collected by the group members	Members' savings	Resource mobilization through membership association

Source: Interviews and observation in 2011.

UED began as a government credit program at the end of the 1980s, but a village consensus has resulted in some reorganization of the program. In 2008, KR village decided to consolidate all assets of the existing government-subsidized credit organizations, including UED, Credit for Family Income Generation (UPPK), and IDT, into one asset to be managed by the restructured UED. Currently, UED functions as a sort of village bank in which all rules and regulations are determined by village consensus (no longer by credit organizations that follow government guidelines). In other words, UED began as a government program, but it has been "indigenized" and is now managed and governed by the villagers based on their initiative and consensus.

In KR village, the introduction of various kinds of development projects and programs seems to have strengthened the link between social organizations and local administrative organizations; in fact, they almost overlap each other. Later the development of this link will be examined.

BD Village

In contrast to KR village, BD village has few public and communal facilities, assets, or organizational activities, except for mosques and some Islamic prayer groups. A Women's Association was organized, but no substantial activities were identified. Further, there is no village office or village meeting hall. As a result, the private house of the village head functions as the "village office." A similar situation was observed in the nearby villages in the same sub-districts.

In BD village, PNPM's unpaid loans have been covered by the private earnings of the village head so that the village can continue to receive the PNPM grant. According to the village head, it is his responsibility to bear this risk for the village. On the other hand, the village head receives perks in the form of profits earned through implementation of development projects introduced to the village. For example, he recently received earnings for providing construction materials for village road development. From these earnings, he bought a car and renovated his house. He rationalized his purchase of a car by explaining that he is called upon at times to transport a sick villager to and from the hospital. He said the villagers acknowledge and approve this fact. If he pockets too much profit just for himself, he will lose votes in the next election. In striking contrast to KR village, BD village presents another type of resource mobilization mechanism, in which the resources for public and collective benefits are mobilized by the patrimonial leadership of the village head.

SA Village

Not as ample as those in KR village, public facilities in SA village include a village office and a village meeting hall. In the villages of Tana Toraja, communal assets related to the customs of the Torajan ancestral house (*tongkonan*) are conspicuous when compared to simple public facilities. A kinship group consisting of family members, including those who live outside the village, constructs and maintains the ancestral house. This kinship group plays a pivotal role in raising large numbers of animals and large amounts of money and labor for the death ritual. When SA villagers faced PNPM's unpaid loan problems, they took advantage of this kinship-based resource mobilization mechanism for rituals by utilizing the community development fund (*dana pembangunan kampung*).

At a death ritual, a huge number of animals are sacrificed in Tana

Toraja. The distribution of the meat of sacrificed animals is significant for the Torajanese. The amount and cuts of meat a person receives signify their socio-political status in society. Strict and detailed customs and rules apply to meat distribution. In the 1970s, people of SA village, a sub-village or *kampung* at that time, decided to establish a "community development fund" through which meat from sacrificed animals should be tendered and allocated. The fund is used for small-scale infrastructure development in the community, as well as for buying necessary equipment for rituals, such as tents, tableware, cooking units, mattresses, and so on. Community members can rent them at no cost.

When SA village initially faced PNPM's unpaid loan problem, the village head discussed the problem with village leaders, including customary leaders; ultimately, they decided to cover unpaid loans with money from the community development fund. However, borrowers are responsible for paying back to the fund through the village head. In a sense, the village head took the initiative to cover unpaid loans with "collective" assets of the villagers, in a similar fashion to the scheme in KR village. In the case of SA village, however, the community development fund provides a mechanism for the villagers to mobilize resources of kinship groups that usually extend beyond the geographical boundaries of the community. Later such mechanisms will be examined further.

LB Village

Similar to SA village, LB village has a simple village office and a meeting hall. There are several development organizations in the village, such as Women's Associations and Maternal and Child Health Groups, but they are not as active as groups in KR village.

One of the unique groups among them is an *arisan* that was organized on the initiative of a woman villager (a teacher) in 1963; it has continued to hold weekly meetings since then. As of 2011, approximately 50 women have joined. Most of the members live in the sub-villages along the paved road, yet some live in a distant sub-village or neighboring village. According to the group leader's explanation, members join this *arisan* not because of a territorial bond nor because of a particular kinship; rather, they choose to join based on their personal interests.

In the rotating savings and credit association (*arisan*), members basically do not keep any money or common assets in the group. At each meeting, members bring a predetermined amount of money to be used in a lottery. The member(s) who wins the lottery gets all the money that was collected at the meeting. Consequently, the group does not assume a great deal of financial management responsibility. Yet, the women in the *arisan* in LB village also manage a tableware rental activity for which the group collects a small amount of money from each member at every meeting to purchase tableware that can be rented to members for ceremonies at a low rate. In this sense, the women in this group maintain and manage a common asset.

In LB village, PNPM's unpaid loan problems were simply settled inside the group, which covered unpaid loans from the savings collected every month from members (in anticipation of an unpaid loan problem). The problem borrowers must pay the money back to the group.

As observed, responses to the unpaid loan problem by the four villages illustrate interesting features of resource mobilization mechanisms. Cases from the four villages indicate that contrasting types of organizing mechanisms are utilized by local societies. The first type provides a model for local administrative organizations and territorially based social organizations that are linked closely for mobilization of resources and mutual support as they respond to development needs. Second is a type in which the benefits and risks of village development reside in the hands of the village head who limits collective assets and activities. And third, another model encourages mobilization of resources through kinship groups, especially for the performance of rituals. Finally, individuals who are related loosely in territorial bonds and kinship relations are associated with activities based on their own interests and responsibilities.

LOCAL SOCIAL SYSTEMS IN THE JAVANESE AND TORAJANESE VILLAGES

I have noted that each of the four surveyed villages showed a different response to the problems that development organizations, namely PNPM's savings and loan groups, caused. One may assume that these differences are associated with differences in the various organizing mechanisms in the local societies. To explore further how the mechanisms work and to identify the connection between local social systems and such differences, let us examine the cases of KR village and SA village.

KR Village

As noted earlier, KR village consists of seven sub-villages that have not been reorganized since the 1920s. It is difficult to trace the history further, but it is assumed that this village and the sub-village units were not formed indigenously or naturally. Instead, they appear to have formed because of a particular administrative reorganization. RT and RW are administrative units that were introduced by the government according to the *tonarigumi* organization introduced during the Japanese occupation (1942–1945).

In spite of its exogenously established character, various development projects and numerous development organizations have transformed KR village into a unit with self-organizing and self-governing capacities. Each unit (that is, village, sub-village, and RT) plays a specific role.

The role of the village is to deal with outside agencies, direct village development, and to manage and govern the entire village. Important decisions, such as renovating a village hall, establishing a village corporation, or participating in the government's village development contest, are made at the village meeting, where the village head discusses plans with village leaders, including sub-village heads.

Yet, important plans that necessitate villagers' participation require their consensus at the sub-village level. In KR village, it has been the custom to hold a meeting at every sub-village, for which the sub-village head invites members of all local households to hear an explanation by the village head regarding proposed plans; villagers are requested to offer a consensus on the proposed plans. To implement a plan, the village head must engage the sub-village residents in the decision-making process.

The RT, consisting of 20–40 neighboring households, functions at the implementation level. Activities to mobilize villagers' participation, such as organizing voluntary labor to improve village infrastructure, collecting donations for village development, and night guarding at each RT, are performed at this level. In Javanese society, where territorially based social relationships are valued, the RT has become a good mobilizer for participation of villagers.

In summary, the village unit functions as an intermediary unit between the villager and the outside agent and makes important decisions regarding policies and development of the entire village. The sub-village is the unit that seeks a consensus among all residents through their direct participation in the consensus-building process. Finally, the RT is the institutional unit for mobilizing residents when implementing collective projects. Organizationally, these three levels of units are linked to each other. In most cases, the tasks of the village are reviewed at sub-village meetings, and the RT is mobilized for the collective projects planned at the upper levels.

SA Village

For the Torajanese, including those living outside Tana Toraja, the *tongkonan* is the very basic social organization and is regarded as a core of their identity. To ask "Who are you?" to a Torajanese is almost equivalent to asking "What is your *tongkonan*?" or "What is your genealogical position in the *tongkonan*?" According to the position and function of the founder, each *tongkonan* is ranked, such as the *tongkonan* of a royal family, that of ordinary people, that of slavery, and so on. Because Torajanese kinship is bilateral, a person may belong to several *tongkonan*, and the scope of the kinship group that a *tongkonan* covers is not fixed or certain. It is at the time of ritual when this *tongkonan*-based kinship group becomes tangible.

At a time of ritual, family members try to prepare as many animals as possible, because how many they can sacrifice directly relates to the socio-political status of a family as well as an individual who donates the animal. For example, at the death ritual of Mr T executed in SA village in 2012, 24 water buffalo and almost 100 pigs were gathered for sacrifice. Mr T used to be a high official of Tana Toraja District, and usually lived in Makale, the capital of Tana Toraja, yet his ritual was implemented at SA village where his *tongkonan* is located. The biggest donor of the animals was Mr T's brother, who lives and works in Jakarta. Animals are donated also from those who once received donations from Mr T's family, based on reciprocity. In other words, resources for organizing a ritual are mobilized through kinship relations, irrespective of geographical boundary.

What becomes tangible as well in the implementation of rituals is what Yamashita calls "ritual community," for which local terms differ in each region, such as *penanian, bua*, or *saroan* (Yamashita 1988, p. 109). Each ritual community follows different customary rules for implementing a ritual. According to an SA village leader, in the ritual community of Lampio, which covers the same area as SA village at present, a family which belongs to a high-ranked *tongkonan* should sacrifice at least 24 water buffalo at the death ritual. The ritual should continue for seven nights, including the coffin procession. Yet, in the neighboring ritual community of Bebo, even in the case of a high-ranked family, the ritual should end in five nights, without a coffin procession.

In every ritual community, there are several *tongkonan*, for example, 13 *tongkonan* in the case of Lampio, each of which has its own role and function, such as agricultural affairs, ritual affairs, military affairs, and so on, although most of them have lost substance in recent years. Meat from the sacrificed animals should be distributed to each *tongkonan* according to its customary role and function. Strict customary rules are still followed today concerning the distribution of the meat. According to Yamashita, who conducted field research in 1975–1976 in Tana Toraja, there are three types of meat distribution: (1) distribution according to the *tongkonan* system in the ritual community; (2) distribution according to the social hierarchy of each individual in the society, including a village head, a sub-district head, and officials of military, police, schools, and churches; and (3) distribution to all the households in the ritual community (Yamashita 1988, p. 206).

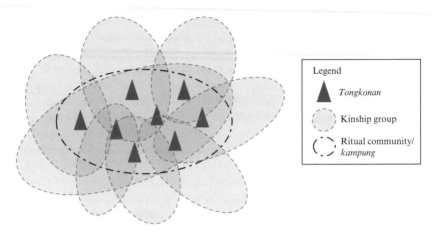

Figure 5.3   Local social system in SA village

The establishment of a community development fund can be categorized as one of the variants of type 3. In the 1970s, the geographical sphere
of the ritual community of Lampio was the same as that of a sub-village
(*kampung*) of an administrative village (*desa*) at that time. By establishing
a community development fund, the people in Lampio created a system to
utilize the resource mobilization capacity of the *tongkonan*-based kinship
group whose members exist irrespective of the geographical boundaries
for developing a territorial community (Figure 5.3). In other words,
the community development fund has become an effective development
organization because it created a link between social organization (ritual
community) and local administrative organization (*kampung*). In spite of
the frequent village reorganization, this system has been able to function
in SA village until today, as the unit of ritual community has become
an administrative unit, whether it is a sub-village (*kampung*), or a block
organization (RK), or a village (*desa* or *lembang*).

CONCLUSION

Certain development projects implemented in local societies are carried
out differently from one location to another. By examining the differences,
we may understand the characteristics of organizing mechanisms in local
societies. From this standpoint, this chapter presents an examination of
the performance of PNPM, a national program for community empowerment that was launched nationwide by the Indonesian government in
2007. The focus was on the responses of four surveyed villages to questions

about unpaid loan problems that each village faced in the process of implementing savings and loan activities of the program.

The responses showed clear contrasts. KR village in Yogyakarta managed to cover the unpaid loans by utilizing village assets that had been accumulated through microcredit activities organized in the village. In BD village of Banten, the village head covered the dues from his private earnings in return for the receipt of private benefits from various development projects that were currently under way or which had been implemented in the past. SA village, the Torajanese village in South Sulawesi, covered unpaid loans by using assets from the community development fund collected by kinship groups during certain rituals. In BL village of Central Sulawesi, the unpaid loan problem is settled by the group using members' savings. These differences associated with the same development project suggest that unique factors of local societies affect the way that local people organize themselves.

Therefore, the causes of the stated contrasts were identified and a closer look was taken at the locality groups in KR and SA villages, which responded to the default problem through collective asset management. As for KR village in Java, three layers of local administrative units were found, with different functions, that are linked with each other for collective actions organized in the village. The sub-village exists as a territorially based locality group that hosts most of the collective actions and builds consensus among the villagers. The existence of territorial social and administrative organizations worked as the basis for collective actions, including PNPM.

In SA village in Tana Toraja, South Sulawesi, irrespective of the frequent village reorganization, the unit of ritual community, has functioned as a local administrative unit, whether it is a sub-village, or a block organization (RW), or a village. Thus, synergy between the social organization and the local administrative organization has been created. The ritual community is recognized as a territorial social organization, and the sense of unity and resources among community members can be mobilized for the local administrative organization. In this case, the local society has a territorial basis for collective actions.

On the contrary, similar territorially based locality groups could not be found in BD and LB villages. In BD village, collective assets and activities are relatively limited, and a village head plays a dominant role in resource mobilization and distribution. In LB village, an organizational association functions with some efficiency. In both villages, the dyadic interaction among villagers and/or between the leaders and followers seems to work as the dominant social system.

REFERENCES

Geertz, Clifford (1959), "The Javanese village," in G. William Skinner (ed.), *Local, Ethnic, and National Loyalties in Village Indonesia: Symposium*, Yale University Cultural Report Series Southeast Asian Studies, Detroit, MI: Cellar Book Shop, pp. 34–41.

Jay, Robert R. (1969), *Javanese Villagers: Social Relations in Rural Modjokuto*, Cambridge, MA, USA and London, UK: MIT Press.

Kabupaten Tana Toradja (n.d.), *Sedjarah Ringkas Kabupaten Tana Toradja* (*Brief History of Tana Toradja District*), Tana Toradja: Kabupaten Tana Toradja.

Kartohadikoesoemo, Soetardjo (1984), *Desa* (*Village*), Jakarta: Balai Pustaka.

Kato, Tsuyoshi (1989), "Different fields, similar locusts: Adat communities and the Village Law of 1979 in Indonesia," *Indonesia*, **47**, 89–14.

Mubyarto (1996), "Efisiensi dan Keadilan dalam Program IDT: Kebhinekaan Ekonomi Rakyat" ("Efficiency and fairness in the Program IDT: Diversity of People Economy"), in Mubyarto, *Ekonomi Rakyat dan Program IDT* (*People Economy and Program IDT*), Yogyakarta: Aditya Media, pp. 47–51.

Sekimoto, Teruo (1978), "Nougyou wo meguru Hito no Kategori to Sougokankei: Cyuubu Jawa no Ichijirei" ("Human categories and interpersonal relations in agriculture: A case from rural Central Java"), *Bulletin of National Museum of Ethnology*, **3**(3), 345–415.

Shimagami, Motoko (2001), "Jawa Nouson niokeru Jumin Soshiki no Involution: Suharuto Seikenka no 'Sonraku Kaihatu' no Ichi Sokumen" ("Organizational involution in rural Java: A characteristic of 'village development' under the new order"), *Southeast Asian Studies*, **38**(4), 512–551.

Yamashita, Shinji (1988), *Girei no Seijigaku: Indonesia, Toraja no Doutaiteki Minzokushi* (*Politics of Rituals: Dynamic Ethnography of Toraja, Indonesia*), Tokyo: Konbun dou.

6. Forms of collective actions in a dyadically woven local society: the case of rural Philippines

Atsuko Hayama

INTRODUCTION

This study aims to clarify the organizational capabilities of rural Philippine society and its relationship with the performance of development organizations and programs and projects. In order to understand the failings of many community-based or participatory development programs and projects in the Philippines, it is important to identify the local mechanisms underlying how rural people organize themselves. Community-Based Forest Management (CBFM), the Philippine national program for sustainable state forestland management as well as for rural development, is one such failing development program. Like other community-based development programs and projects, the "community" facet of CBFM refers to a development organization formed by outside agencies with specific purposes. Although nearly 20 years have passed since the implementation of the CBFM policy, its goals have yet to be realized. Why so? Although many studies have discussed the causes of CBFM's poor performance, none of them have focused on the "community" itself or specifically on the mechanism that organizes people living in a rural society.

This study hypothesizes that CBFM's malfunction is attributable to the discrepancy between the organizational capability of rural Philippine society and what is expected of a development organization (that is, communities formed by outside agencies for CBFM purposes). The study consists of two parts. The first part (the second to the fourth sections) focuses on self-organizing processes and local social mores in rural Philippine society. The second part (the fifth and the sixth sections) further examines the characteristics of long-lasting local organizations, both endogenously and exogenously formed, in rural Philippine society.

Since this study was prompted by the failings of CBFM, the second section starts with an overview of CBFM in the Philippines and previous studies describing CBFM ineffectiveness. The third section remarks on endogenous functional organizations to identify the local social system for organizing people and the characteristics of the organizational capability of rural Philippine society. The fourth section, based on the characteristics of organizational capability extracted in the third section, discusses the fundamental cause of CBFM's failings. The fifth section scrutinizes the characteristics of organizational capability of long-lasting local organizations in rural Philippine society. Finally, the sixth section deliberates organizational capability in rural Philippine society and the relationships with the performance of development organizations.

OVERVIEW OF CBFM IN THE PHILIPPINES: WHAT IS LACKING IN PREVIOUS STUDIES

The apparent failure to attain sustainable forest management in the vast state forestlands, both directly by the government and through logging companies as concessionaires, in many developing countries has led to a forest policy reform that put state forestland management into the hands of local people. It has been perceived that local people living inside or adjacent to the forestlands, with their concerns and knowledge on their surroundings, can be better resources managers than the central government. "Community forestry," "community-based natural resource management," and "community-based forest management" thus became popular terms in forest policy in the developing world as well as in the development arena of donors.

The Philippines is one such country where local communities in the state forestlands, once considered as the culprits of forest destruction, are institutionally involved in state forestland management in place of logging companies. Executive Order No. 263, "Adopting Community-Based Forest Management as the National Strategy to Ensure the Sustainable Development of the Country's Forestlands Resources Providing Mechanisms for Its Implementation," signed by President Ramos, was issued in 1995. In the forest policy of CBFM, local communities are expected to rehabilitate degraded forestlands and conserve remaining forests (Lasco and Pulhin 2006). This forest policy reform has widely been espoused as realizing participatory forest management (Utting 2000), democratizing local people's access to forest resources, and thus contributing to poverty alleviation (Guiang et al. 2001), as well as crafting space for local forest management (Contreras 2003). At the same time, entrusting state forestland management to local communities is intended to eliminate de facto open access lands in the state forestlands and, thus, to lessen government administrative costs (Dalmacio et al. 2000).

The involvement of local people in state forestland management in the Philippines, albeit very limited in scale, emerged in the early 1970s. Three forestry programs in the 1970s – the Family Approach to Reforestation, the Forest Occupancy Management Program, and the Communal Tree Farming Program – aimed at reforestation by local people. The term "community" appeared there, but did not receive as much attention as it does today. These three forestry programs were consolidated into the Integrated Social Forestry Program in 1982 (Presidential Letter of Instruction No. 1260), in which a long-term state forestland usufruct right (25 years, and renewable another 25 years) was awarded to individuals in migrant communities and to communities as a whole in indigenous communities. It is estimated that some 25 million people (more than 30 percent of the total population) resided in state forestlands in 2000, of which some 6.3 million were indigenous people while 18.7 million were migrants (Guiang 2001, p. 106). "Indigenous people" here means those who have long resided in the forestlands, even before they were nationalized, or in their so-called ancestral domains, while "migrants" are those who have settled in the logged-over forestlands after World War II. The Integrated Social Forestry Program emphasized the security of long-term land tenure to local people so that they would invest in sustainable forestlands use through planting perennial crops, reforestation, and erosion control.

The fall of President Marcos in 1986 brought about a new development in local people's involvement in state forestland management. The reorganization of the forestry agency and forest policy reform, shifting from logging company-centered state forestland management to local people-centered management, attracted many international and foreign donors to financially, institutionally, and technically assist with the involvement of local people in sustainable resources management (Korten 1994, p. 973). Donor assisted-forestry projects have surged since the late 1980s (DENR n.d.). Pulhin et al. (2007, pp. 870–871) describe that in the Philippine forestry sector, 1988 to 1994 was a period of "experimentation and heavy infusion of external assistance," with each donor attempting its own "people-oriented" forestry programs and projects with different schemes and strategies. The term "community" became noticeable in the forestry sector when many donor-assisted people-oriented forestry programs and projects in the late 1980s and 1990s included "community" in their titles, such as the Asian Development Bank (ADB)-assisted Low Income Upland Communities Project and the German Agency for Technical Cooperation (GTZ)-assisted Community Forestry Program. To unify and integrate all such people-oriented forest programs and projects under one umbrella, the policy of CBFM was proclaimed in 1995. In 1996, the Department of Environment and Natural Resources (DENR, the government office with jurisdiction over the state forestlands) issued the Department Administrative Order (DAO) No. 96–29 (which was revised in 2004 to reduce some requirements) "Rules and Regulations for the Implementation of Executive Order 263."

The DENR's Revised Master Plan for Forestry Development in 2003 stated that out of 15.9 million hectares of total state forestlands (53 percent of the total land area), 5.7 million hectares were under CBFM (including all people-oriented forestry programs and projects with various forms of tenure instruments) in 2000, and envisioned that in total, 9 million hectares would be under CBFM by 2010 (FAO et al. 2003, p. 158). To enhance CBFM, another Executive Order (No. 318, "Promoting Sustainable Forest Management in the Philippines"), signed by President Arroyo and restating CBFM as a primary strategy in state forestland management, was issued in 2004.

Section 4 of the DAO No. 96–29 defines "community" as: "A group of people who may or may not share common interests, needs, visions, goals and beliefs, occupying a particular territory which extends from the eco-system geographical, political/administrative and cultural boundaries and any resources that go with it." Although not articulated in the DAO, it is postulated in the policy that "A group of people who may share common . . ." are indigenous people; while "A group of people who may not share common . . ." are migrants. In CBFM, local people are required to form an organization, that is, a People's Organization (PO), which is defined in the DAO as: "A group of people, which may be an association, cooperative, federation, or other legal entity, established by the community to undertake collective action to address community concerns and need and mutually share the benefits from the endeavor." One CBFM area covers one *barangay*, the smallest administrative village in the Philippines, or several *barangays*. When the natural forest extends to, for example, three *barangays*, these three *barangays* may form one community for CBFM. Several neighboring *barangays* where a donor-assisted reforestation project was established may also form one community. One community has one PO, which is a receiving organization of the CBFM Agreement (a sort of contract for legal resources use in the state forestlands) with the DENR and external resources.

As stipulated in the DAO, for a group of people to be legally recognized as a PO, they have to register as a legal entity with the government agency in charge. This is because, according to the DENR, it is the only way to guarantee the credibility of a group of people which the government can contact and grant the long-term land tenure. The majority of them are registered as cooperatives at the Cooperative Development Authority. Registration as a cooperative requires several qualifications specified by the Republic Act No. 6938, "An Act to Ordain A Cooperative Code of the Philippines," such as organizing with at least 15 members, preparing by-laws and collecting capital shares from members (minimum 1000 pesos). Once it is registered as a cooperative, the PO (now a cooperative) has to apply for a CBFM Agreement with the DENR by submitting several documents. These application documents are reviewed and checked at each level of the administrative organization of the DENR from local to central, that is, Community Office, Provincial Office, Regional Office, and Central Office. Documents with deficiencies are returned to the PO. A CBFM Agreement is awarded to a PO only when the DENR Secretary approves it. This procedure alone takes a long time.

The latest Philippine Forestry Statistics show that 1790 POs covering aggregately 1.634 million hectares have been awarded with CBFM Agreements (Table 6.1). The majority of CBFM Agreement-awarded POs are foreign-funded projects. The tenured area under the CBFM Agreement in 2011 is much smaller than the above-mentioned 5.7 million hectares under CBFM in 2004. Most CBFM areas have not yet been awarded such a privilege, primarily due to a lack of financial and technical assistance needed to forge the agreement with the DENR. Without a CBFM Agreement, POs are not legally permitted to use forest resources, particularly timber. Upon receiving a CBFM Agreement, POs have to prepare plans for the use of state forestland resources (the Community Resource Management Framework, which is "a strategic plan of the community on how to manage and benefit from the forest resources on a sustainable basis,") and a Five-Year Working Plan (DAO, No.2004–29, Section 18), with the assistance of the DENR Community Office, Municipality Office, and non-governmental organizations (NGOs), and submit them to the DENR Community Office. Without the DENR's consent, POs cannot embark on their resources use activities. In this regard, CBFM is the strategy both to lessen DENR management costs for the state forestlands and to retain the DENR's control over them. POs are, thus, the DENR subcontractor.

Table 6.1 shows that one PO consists of 180 households, covering 913 hectares on average. Not all the households in a CBFM area are PO members. This is because becoming a PO member is optional, and if it is a cooperative the payment of a minimum capital share of 1000 pesos is quite heavy for many people.

It is rarely stated that CBFM has been effectively enforced as envisioned by the government. It is frequently observed that POs' activities malfunction after external assistance ends at the sites. The above-mentioned Revised Master Plan for Forestry Development in 2003 writes that: "Enhancement of CBFM implementation would put onto the right track many CBFM projects where POs became inactive due to various reasons" (FAO et al.

Table 6.1   The number of Community-Based Forest Management Agreements as of 2011 by region

Region	Tenured Area (ha)[1]	Number of POs[2]	Number of participating households[3]	Area/PO (ha)	Number of households/ PO	Area/ household (ha)
Philippines	1633891	1790	322248	913	180	5.1
CAR	56625	87	13762	651	158	4.1
Region 1	40272	127	15514	317	122	2.6
Region 2	259879	103	92391	2323	897	2.8
Region 3	79517	131	12502	607	95	6.4
Region 4-A	18401	47	3098	391	66	5.9
Region 4-B	92615	78	10229	1187	131	9.1
Region 5	47925	83	12328	577	149	3.9
Region 6	40715	105	17142	388	163	2.4
Region 7	57609	208	16056	277	77	3.6
Region 8	116739	132	14405	884	109	8.1
Region 9	79207	131	12886	604	98	6.1
Region 10	213770	298	34021	717	114	6.3
Region 11	207264	94	26114	2205	278	7.9
Region 12	95739	53	10607	1806	200	9.0
Region 13	217613	113	31193	1926	276	7.0

Notes:
CAR: Cordillera Administrative Region located in the Cordillera Mountains in Northern Luzon.
Region 1–Region 5: Luzon and surrounding islands, Region 6–Region 8: Visayas islands, Region 9–Region 13: Mindanao and surrounding islands.

Source: (1), (2), and (3) 2011 Philippine Forestry Statistics (DENR 2011 p. 31).

2003, p. vx). Many studies point out the various reasons for the ineffectiveness of CBFM. Pulhin et al. (2007, pp. 874, 876, 878) enumerate them as follows: (1) financial limitations for supporting CBFM due to a decrease in donors assistance since the early 2000s; (2) lack of adequate institutional support to provide benefits to local communities; (3) limited local governments' capability to provide support in extension, capacity building, and infrastructure to local communities; (4) insecurity in the right to resource use caused by frequent policy changes regarding timber production; (5) complex and tedious requirements and proceedings for local communities regarding timber production; (6) lack of income-generating activities and viable enterprises owing to the technically, managerially, and organizationally poor livelihood projects of POs; (7) local people's mentality regarding the CBFM program as a project that terminates after the withdrawal of external assistance; (8) weak managerial capabilities of PO members with regard to, for example, accounting and bookkeeping. Many studies have also criticized the government for retaining control over state forestlands by limiting the devolution of the right to use resources to local communities, which hampers the effective achievement of CBFM (Dalmacio et al. 2000; Gauld 2000; Pulhin et al. 2007, p. 876; Guiang 2008; Chokkalingam et al. 2006; Suh 2012).

It can be seen in many studies that, in spite of these problems, CBFM could be properly implemented if CBFM policy design is adequately reformed and local communities are given sufficient time, support, and incentives. Many studies thus conceive that the performance of CBFM (dependent variable) is the function of variables such as policy, project design, support, and incentives (independent variables). The assumption here is that CBFM functions well when these variables are fully satisfied. Little attention, however, has been paid to community itself, especially to migrant communities. For example, one chapter of *Community-Based Forest Management in the Philippines: A Preliminary Assessment* (Guiang et al. 2001, pp. 93–114) is titled "Community," describing indigenous community and migrant community. It claims that "community" among indigenous peoples refers to social groups of family, clan, or tribe, which share commonalities such as history, norms, and a sense of identity. Community members are bonded with traditionally and locally shared rules. They manage their own forests based on customarily developed social institutions such as monitoring, sanctions, and rewards for collective action. Community among migrants, on the contrary, is defined by PO membership (that is, participants of a development organization), geographic boundaries (that is, *barangay* or *sitio*, which is a subdivision of a *barangay*), or a combination of these two. The remarkable difference between indigenous communities and migrant ones, according to this study, is that the former are self-initiated while the latter are delineated by external agents. This study states that economic incentives and benefits are the major factors that bind migrant communities for collective action. If these are weak, CBFM activities begin to decline upon the termination of external assistance. It is stressed, thus, that community organizers in migrant communities need to attend to community cohesion as much as to organizational capability building (ibid. p. 111). In this study too, the premise for CBFM is that rural local society (indigenous communities as well as migrant communities) can mobilize people collectively and sustainably for forestland management when conditions are all satisfied.

No attempt has been made to explore the characteristics of organizational capability in rural society, especially in migrant communities. As Shigetomi (2011, p. 24) articulates, local societies have their own systems for helping to organize people, on which their organizational capabilities depend. Organizational capability is defined as "the capability for local societies for creating and managing development organizations" and, more specifically, "the ability to shoulder the problem-solving process, which consists of understanding a problem process, planning process and implementation process, for creating organizations" (ibid. pp. 24, 25). This study hypothesizes that the fundamental cause of CBFM malfunction is not that policy, project design, support, and incentives are insufficient, as many studies suggest, but that there is a discrepancy between the organizational capability in rural Philippine society and what is expected of a development organization for CBFM purposes.

CHARACTERISTICS OF ORGANIZATIONAL CAPABILITY IN RURAL PHILIPPINE SOCIETY: ENDOGENOUS FUNCTIONAL ORGANIZATIONS

Migrant Community in the State Forestlands

This section examines how local social systems contribute to the formation of rural organizations in the Philippines. My focus here is, thus, to understand the self-organizational process of rural people. The study site for this purpose is Barangay El Salvador in the Municipality of New Corella, Province of Davao del Norte, Mindanao, in the southern part of the Philippines. Barangay El Salvador is a typical migrant community in the state forestlands, which was formed after World War II with those who spontaneously migrated into the logged-over area of commercial logging operations.

The entire *barangay* area (some 1500 hectares) of El Salvador is within the state forestlands. Topographically, these forestlands are steep, rolling hills. Since settlements in the forestlands are formed in flat and gentle slope areas, they are some distance from each other. The size of the settlements in these forestlands is generally small. One *barangay* in the forestlands consists of several settlements. Barangay El Salvador comprises six *puroks* (subdivisions). Before the term *purok* was adopted in the Philippine administrative organization, *sitio*, the administrative term used during the Spanish colonial period, was used for a settlement or an enclave. The six *puroks* of El Salvador are synonymous with the previous six *sitios*, respectively. Migrants spontaneously formed settlements one by one, to a total of six, before the area became a *barangay*.

The total number of households in Barangay El Salvador as of March 2007 was 240, out of which 233 were interviewed. The total population of 233 households was 1052 (male 582, female 470). Table 6.2 summarizes each *purok*'s number of household and kinship groups and the

Table 6.2   Number of household and kinship groups in each purok *and distance from Purok 1*

Purok	Number of households	Number of kinship groups	Number of households belonging to the biggest kinship group/*purok* households	No. of Males	No. of Females	Population	Walking distance from Purok 1
Purok 1	62	8	54/62 (87.1%)	151	153	304	–
Purok 2	16	6	7/16 (43.8%)	38	26	64	1 hour
Purok 3	28	5	24/28 (85.7%)	82	57	139	1.5 hours
Purok 4	24	6	19/24 (79.2%)	49	32	81	2 hours
Purok 5	44	10	19/44 (43.2%)	121	100	221	0.5 hours
Purok 6	59	12	46/59 (78.0%)	141	102	243	0.5 hours
El Salvador	233	40	168/233 (72.1%)	582	470	1052	–

Source: Fieldwork in March 2007.

walking distance from Purok 1. Purok 1 is the administrative, religious, and commercial center of the *barangay*, where the meeting hall, health-care center (no medical workers assigned), elementary school, basketball court, chapel, two Protestant churches, and several *sari-sari* stores (small groceries) have been established. A chapel pastor who resides in the nearby town, Nabunturan (the provincial capital of the Province of Compostela Valley), comes for every Sunday service. A priest only comes to give Mass on special occasions. The biggest and smallest *puroks* are Purok 1 with 62 households and Purok 2 with 16 households, respectively.

The characteristics of migrant settlements in the logged-over forest-lands are based on blood relations. This is because the first migrants, most of whom were male, called upon their parents, siblings, and relatives to migrate. Many Barangay El Salvador residents are migrants from Bohol in the Visayas region (central part of the Philippines) and Davao del Sur in Mindanao. Most newly-wed couples reside in the husband's or wife's parents' settlement. The majority of settlement residents are, thus, blood-related or marriage-related to each other, belonging to one kinship group. There are 40 kinship groups in Barangay El Salvador. The biggest kinship group amounts to 168 households (72.1 percent) out of 233 households, and the second-biggest amounts to only 11 households. Table 6.2 shows that the majority of Purok 1 and Purok 3 residents belong to the same kinship group. The majority of *barangay* residents know each other. It should be noted, however, that local people do not identify a kinship group as an organization. As will be seen below, a kinship group for an individual includes only several blood- and marriage-related relatives.

Endogenous Functional Organizations

Shigetomi (2011 p. 26) classifies rural organization into four types based on two axes of function ("achieving a specified target" and "coordination and control of members") and origin ("endogenous" and "exogenous"). I focus here on endogenous organizations with the purpose of achieving a specified target to examine the social system. Three endogenous functional organizations can be identified in Barangay El Salvador: a mutual fund organization for funeral services, a mutual fund organization for wedding receptions, and a fund-raising organization for food expenses on special occasions.

Mutual fund organization for funeral services (*dayong*)

The mutual fund organization for funeral services is locally known as *dayong*, which literally means in Cebuano (the people's mother tongue) "carrying on the shoulders of two or more persons." *Dayong* is the oldest endogenous functional organization, operating in Barangay El Salvador since the early 1960s, when pioneer migrants from Bohol introduced it as their practice there. In urban areas and rural areas in the lowlands, it is common for local people to depend on a funeral business (undertakers) that has an office there. In the forestlands, on the contrary, local people can hardly depend on such a business.

A household as a unit joins *dayong*. When joining *dayong*, a member has to pay 100 pesos (the daily wage for agricultural labor in the *barangay* is 150 pesos). The treasurer stores all the money collected from the members. When a family member of a member household dies, the treasurer collects 100 pesos in kind (rice, canned goods, firewood, other food, and so on) from all the member households. All the money stored and these goods are then provided to the bereaved household. Moreover, all the member households are assigned roles such as to inform *barangay* members about the death, the purchase of food, cooking, cutting firewood, making a coffin, and digging a grave. Absence is fined. Immediately after the funeral, all the member households are called to the assembly to pay 100 pesos, which are again stored by the treasurer until the next funeral. Two consecutive absences in the assembly are fined or result in a removal of *dayong* membership. Joining, withdrawal, and rejoining are unrestricted. Joining is, however, allowed at the time of assembly held right after the funeral. A household who has a member at death's door is not allowed to join *dayong*. If a family member dies when the household had not yet paid 100 pesos, or has withdrawn from *dayong*, no service is provided to the household.

As of March 2008, there are four *dayongs* in Barangay El Salvador. The biggest *dayong* consists of Purok 1, 2 and 6 residents, amounting to 54 households. Other *dayongs* are 23 households in Purok 3, 25 households in Purok 4, and 17 households in Purok 5.

Mutual fund organization for wedding receptions (*gala*)

The mutual fund organization for wedding receptions, *gala*, was established when one resident who had single sons introduced it to Barangay El Salvador about ten years ago. *Gala* in Cebuano literally means "merry festival." In the Philippines, it is custom that a bridegroom shoulders all the expenses for a wedding reception. *Gala* thus comprises only those households with unmarried sons. While in *dayong* withdrawal and rejoining can happen at any time, in *gala* the members are fixed when it is formed. Once a household has joined *gala*, withdrawal is not allowed.

As of March 2008, there were two *galas* in Barangay El Salvador. One consists of 20 households including the resident who introduced it to the *barangay*, who are residents in all the *puroks* except Purok 3. The other *gala* consists of 15 households in Purok 3. Every time the marriage of a member's son is decided, 1000 pesos are collected from each member household. The 20 000 pesos and 16 000 pesos (since one member pays for two sons) collected from the respective *gala* are given to the member whose son marries. *Gala* lasts until all the sons marry. If a son dies unmarried, the member households can retrieve all the money it has contributed from other members, or use the money for another son. Even if a son and/or a member household leave Barangay El Salvador, they are still *gala* members.

Like *dayong*, all member households are assigned roles in a wedding reception, such as purchasing food, cutting firewood, and cooking. Absence is also fined.

Fund-raising organization for food expenses on special occasions (*socio*)

Socio is a fund-raising organization for food expenses on special occasions. *Socio* is a Tagalog word meaning, "joining and investing for a business." The practice of *socio* was introduced in the mid-1990s by a resident who had encountered it in other places in Mindanao. The purpose of fund-raising is to collect sufficient money to buy food for special occasions such as the fiesta (celebration of the patron saint of the *barangay*), Christmas and New Year's Day. It is the practice on such occasions to prepare a banquet and entertain relatives and visitors. Butchering a *carabao* (water buffalo) or a pig is considered the best banquet.

A *socio* is formed for an occasion in the following year and its duration is one year. For example, *socio* Christmas is formed in December for the next year's Christmas. *Socio* is formed to buy specific foods, for example, *socio bigas* (rice), *socio carabao*, and *socio baboy* (pig). A proposer recruits members and forms a *socio*. Every member contributes the same amount of money, for example 500 pesos. All the money collected is loaned to *socio* members with a monthly interest of 10 percent (simple interest) and to non-*socio* members with a monthly interest of 15 percent (ditto). All the money collected from the *socio* members is loaned out and no money remains with them. When loaning to a non-*socio* member, a *socio* member should provide a joint surety to pay back the loan if the non-*socio* member cannot settle the payment. After one year, 1000 pesos loaned to a non-*socio* member turns into 2800 pesos. With the augmented money, the members buy a planned item. The purchased item, such as a *carabao*, pig, or rice, is equally divided among the *socio* members. Since local people need loans, according to *socio* members, *socio* has no difficulty in finding borrowers. Once default happens, however, *socio* fails.

As of March 2008, there were 12 *socios* in Barangay El Salvador, participated in by 67 households (an aggregate of 150 persons). The biggest *socio* consisted of 42 persons, while the smallest one consisted of three persons (Table 6.3). The average was 11.7 persons. The big *socio* mainly comprised closely blood-related members (parent–child and/or siblings) and/or married couples. Many of the same *socio* members resided in the same *purok*. Among the 23 households of the biggest *socio*, 20 of them resided in Purok 4. Among the 12 households of the second-biggest *socio*, all resided in Purok 6.

Characteristics of Endogenous Functional Organizations

As observed, no endogenous functional organization exists to mobilize all the *barangay* members, in spite of the fact that the majority of them belong to one kinship group and they all know each other. No endogenous functional organization exists to mobilize all the *purok* members either.

Two common characteristics can be found in the three endogenous functional organizations. One is that all are small organizations, bound with close dyadic relationships. Three endogenous functional organizations are formed among *purok*-based or settlement-based people, that is, a small social group of blood-related people and people with common ties to a place.

Close dyadic relationships guarantee one's credibility. In *gala* and *socio*, a proposer permits persons whom they trust to join the organization. In this regard, these organizations are membership organizations founded on the close dyadic relationships of a proposer. The *gala* proposers invite one by one the people whom they can trust. In *socio*, when a member's aberrant

Table 6.3   Relation of socio *members (as of March 2008)*

Socio	Number of participants	Number of participating households	Number of blood related participants	Number of married couples
A	3	3	0	0
B	7	5	0	2 couples
C	5	5	0	0
D	4	4	0	0
E	20	10	Two pairs of 2 persons are blood related respectively	10 couples
F	4	3	0	1 couple
G	42	23	7 persons, 10 persons, and 4 persons are blood related respectively	19 couples
H	9	7	2 persons and 3 persons are blood related respectively	0
I	7	5	2 persons are blood related	2 couples
J	23	12	6 persons and two pairs of 2 persons are blood related respectively	11 couples
K	12	7	Two pairs of 2 persons are blood related respectively	5 couples
L	4	2	2 persons are blood related	0
Average	11.7	7.2	–	–

Source: Fieldwork in March 2008.

behavior, such as their default, or failure to observe their responsibility in providing joint surety when a non-*socio* member fails to pay back the loan, appears, the proposers never invite them to their *socio* again. Once they lose their credibility, no *socio* proposers would invite them into their *socio*, which is a heavy sanction to local people.

In circumstances where a settlement is small, located some distance from other settlements, and close contact between settlements is infrequent, the size of a functional group such as *dayong, gala,* and *socio* will be small. Shigetomi (2011, p. 31) also characterizes rural Philippine society with dyadically related people by citing Valsan (1970) and Hayami and Kikuchi (2000).

The other characteristic of the three endogenous functional organizations is that they are all short-term resource-pool organizations. In *dayong*, all the money collected by the members is pooled by the treasurer until the next funeral of a member household. At the time of a funeral, all the pooled money is given to the bereaved household and the fund, then, is at zero. After the funeral, money is again collected from all the members and pooled by the treasurer. The period of the money pool is, thus, only until the next funeral. In *gala*, money is collected from the members right before the marriage of a son of a member household is decided. Since all the money collected is immediately given to the bridegroom household, the period of the money pool is almost none. In *socio*, the period of the organization is exactly one year. Since all the money invested by the members is loaned, the money pooled by *socio* groups is always at zero.

The longer an organization pools money, the bigger the management cost becomes and the bigger the possibility of deviation or embezzlement by members. By making the period of pooling money short, the organization can curb the management costs as well as the possibility of deviation by members. By shortening the money pool period, rural local society enables endogenous functional organizations to function continuously.

To increase the profit from organizing collective action, rural local society tries to reduce the organizational costs such as the cost of credibility inquiry for would-be members, the cost of consensus making among members, and the cost of management of pooled resources. Close dyadic relationships centering on one individual reduce the credibility inquiry cost for would-be members and the consensus-making cost among members recruited by him or her. Moreover, making the period that resources are pooled short can lessen the management cost of pooling as well as curb deviation by members. In other words, it is also deduced that rural local society cannot control local people's behaviors over a longer period, which is the organizational capability of rural Philippine society.

MALFUNCTION OF THE CBFM DEVELOPMENT ORGANIZATION: DISCREPANCY WITH THE ORGANIZATIONAL CAPABILITIES OF RURAL SOCIETY

I have extracted the characteristics of endogenous functional organizations in rural Philippine society, that is, utilizing the social system of close dyadic relationships and forming short-term resources-pool organizations. It can be seen here that these characteristics do not correspond to what is expected of a development organization or the PO for CBFM.

The PO for CBFM in Barangay El Salvador was organized to sustainably manage the total land area of the *barangay*. A few years after the PO started timber production, the operation of the PO malfunctioned. The planned sustainable timber production under the PO had not been achieved.

In 1988, the ADB/JBIC (Japan Bank for International Cooperation; then the Overseas Economic Cooperation Fund, OECF)-funded contract reforestation project started in the country. Barangay El Salvador was one of the project sites. Most of the *barangay* residents took an active interest in the project, since the project was to pay contractors if they planted and maintained trees during the three-year contract period, and they would be able to harvest these trees to sell when they matured. The whole *barangay* area, in spite of being state forestland, is de facto owned by individuals. As the reforestation project contractors, they planted trees (all fast-growing species) in their claimed lands. Nearly half of the *barangay* area was planted with fast-growing trees.

After the concept of CBFM was introduced by the DENR Community Office to Barangay El Salvador, a PO was formed by a DENR-appointed NGO. In 1998, the PO was registered with the assistance of the NGO as the El Salvador Farmers and Tree Planters Industrial Cooperative (ELFATPICO) at the Cooperative Development Authority. Again, with the assistance of the NGO and the DENR Community Office, ELFATPICO was awarded the CBFM Agreement by the DENR to legally use forest resources. Despite the fact that the majority of households in the *barangay* had been engaged in contract reforestation and planted trees on their land, only 35 households, about 17 percent of the then total households, joined ELFATPICO. They were the ones which could afford to pay the capital share of 1200 pesos, which was fixed as the minimum amount in the ELFATPICO by-laws. Moreover, most of the *barangay* residents did not feel the necessity to join ELFATPICO, since anyone, even non-ELFATPICO members, could harvest their planted trees to sell.

With the help of the DENR Community Office and the NGO, ELFATPICO prepared the state forestlands resources use plans. Timber production started in 2003 when the Resource Use Permit, which is the timber production right issued by the DENR to CBFM Agreement-awarded POs, was issued to ELFATPICO. If timber production had operated in accordance with the plans, many of the reforested trees would still exist in the *barangay*. Instead, most of the reforested trees were harvested in a short period.

In March 2008, 58 households (about 25 percent of the total *barangay* households) in Barangay El Salvador were members of ELFATPICO. There were also 29 member households who resided outside the *barangay*, among which 16 households were previous residents and land claimants in the area, while 13 households had never resided in the *barangay* and had purchased the land for speculation purposes. Although CBFM is ostensibly an advocate for the welfare of state forestland residents, it is often observed in CBFM sites that non-resident members, particularly those with speculation interests, are included in POs. The board of directors (which is the executive body of elected members) meeting of ELFATPICO decided to include non-residents to increase the capital share.

The direct cause of the malfunction of ELFATPICO is that it could not control residents' behaviors, especially in timber harvesting. In CBFM, it is ELFATPICO that has the exclusive right to harvest trees in the *barangay* area and sell timber. In reality, however, many middlemen came to buy directly from the owners of trees. The majority of the owners of trees cannot afford to shoulder harvesting costs such as hiring laborers for logging and hauling. They asked either ELFATPICO or the middlemen to harvest for them. It did not matter to them who harvested and bought the trees, as long as they could sell them at a high price. ELFATPICO could not control the influx of middlemen. The resources use plans soon became void, only for most of the reforested trees to be harvested in a short period.

Later it was revealed that a large sum of money had been embezzled by the ELFATPICO chairman (who was elected by all the members at the assembly meeting). The treasurer and the bookkeeper (who were appointed by the chairman) had been aware of it, but kept silent for fear of being discharged by the chairman.

The malfunction of ELFATPICO is not an exceptional case in CBFM. Rather it is one of the typical PO malfunctions in CBFM. The fundamental cause of the malfunction of the PO is not a policy design problem, insufficient support, or frequent changes in forest policies, as many studies suggest, but the discrepancy between the organizational capabilities of rural local society and the expectations for a PO. It is expected that the PO will mobilize all the *barangay* residents for sustainable forest resource management, sustainable timber production in particular, and make use of the capital it produces and pool it for rural development. It is expected, thus, that the PO in the form of a cooperative will continue to manage and control local people and capital for a long period of time. The characteristics of endogenous functional organizations in rural society which I have described in the previous section do not correspond with the nature of the PO (that is, a small group based on close dyadic relationships versus a large group covering the entire *barangay*, or sometimes extending to several *barangays*; and short-term resources-pool organization versus long-term resources-pool organization).

It is quite natural, thus, that any development organizations which are inconsistent with the organizational capability, that is, using the social system of close dyadic relationship-based and short-term resources-pool-type organizations, do not survive in rural society.

ORGANIZATIONAL CAPABILITY OF LONG-LASTING LOCAL ORGANIZATIONS

As I have observed, organization of a small-sized group based on close dyadic relationships and pooling of resources for a short period of time can reduce organizational costs, resulting in increased profits. There are two ways in which such a strategy can make profits bigger: (1) when a small-sized organization shifts from short-term to long-term resource pooling; or (2) after enacting long-term resource pooling, the organization moves from small-sized to large-sized. However, the longer resources are pooled and the bigger the size of the organization, the harder it becomes to control people's behaviors, thus increasing organizational costs.

Unlike the PO for CBFM that failed, one can also point to functional development organizations in rural Philippine society. Exemplars of such organizations are Grameen-type microfinance organizations (MFOs) or savings and credit cooperatives. These organizations have utilized a long-term resources pooling strategy. The question arises how the organizations conquered hardships as they amassed the necessary resources. While a Grameen-type MFO is a small-sized operation, some savings and credit cooperatives in rural areas have large memberships. Another question is how these organizations solved the problem of expanding their base in a rural area where there is no other social system except close dyadic relationships. Let us examine these questions below.

Grameen-Type MFOs in Barangay El Salvador

Shigetomi (2011, p. 28) articulates that, in comparison with savings groups as the most popular MFOs in rural Thai society, Grameen-type MFOs are the most popular MFOs in rural Philippine society. Shigetomi (2011) did his study in the Central and Southern Luzon regions. In Barangay El Salvador too, the most popular MFO is the Grameen-type. The structure of the Grameen-type MFO is that a small group of people is formed by an outside agency and that an individual member can loan from the agency but the group is responsible for the payment of the individual loan. Grameen-type MFOs are based on close dyadic relationships in rural Philippine society.

The majority of the MFOs in Barangay El Salvador are Grameen-type and were formed by private financial institutions. In March 2008, six private financial institutions provided savings and loan services to women there. An aggregate of 119 women or 37 percent of the total households in the *barangay* were provided with such services. Five of the financial institutions required those who wanted to receive such services to organize themselves. The number of members in the five Grameen-type MFOs was 4, 11, 12, 29, and 33 respectively. The MFOs with 4, 11, and 12 members each formed one group, and the MFOs with 29 and 33 members each formed two groups. The biggest group among the seven groups consisted of 17 members.

As discussed by Shigetomi (2011), the *barangay* is bypassed in the process of organizing *barangay* members. Persons from the private financial institutions contacted the *barangay* captain (headman) to get *barangay* clearance, which is the document permitting outsiders to carry out activities in a *barangay*, and permission to hold meetings at each *purok*. The outside agencies, not the *barangay* captain, invited *barangay*'s women residents to the meetings. Representatives from the private financial institutions requested *barangay*'s women residents who showed an interest in the microfinance service to form a group. These *barangay* individuals then recruited others to their group. Staff from the private financial institutions then visited the houses of would-be members to check their assets in order to judge their eligibility. Many of the members of Grameen-type MFOs reside in the same *purok*. For example, among the members of the 33-membered MFO, 21 persons reside in Purok 1. Among the members of the 29-membered MFO, 13 and 11 persons reside in Purok 5 and Purok 1, respectively. Members are not necessarily blood-related, but they are settlement-related. When joining the MFOs, all the members were requested by the financial institutions to take an oath that the group had collective responsibility for the payment of individual loans.

What is clear from the Grameen-type MFOs is that their organization is based on close dyadic relationships, generally in the same settlement. The recruitment of group members by *barangay* individuals is a way to ensure credibility and so curb default problems by the group members.

Unlike the three endogenous functional organizations described in the previous section, in which funds or capital are provided or invested by members, funds in the Grameen-type MFOs are provided by outside institutions. To control members' behaviors to ensure repayment and to curb default problems, the outside institutions require all the group members to assemble at the institution offices in the nearby town, Nabunturan, for repayment every week or every two weeks. Members of Grameen-type MFOs are supervised among themselves and at the same time frequently administered by outside institutions. It is outside institutions, not development organizations, that pool funds; that is, the management cost for pooling funds is shouldered by outside institutions. Therefore, the reasons why the Grameen-type MFOs have been long established in rural Philippine society can be attributed to the utilization of the social system of dyadic relationships and the outside institutions' frequent supervision, as well as the outsider-shouldered management costs of pooling resources for a long period of time.

Thirteen-Member Savings and Credit Group

Another study site for this purpose is Barangay Cabuluan, the Municipality of Villaverde, Province of Nueva Vizcaya, Luzon, in the northern Philippines. Barangay Cabuluan is located in the lower part of the Cordillera Mountains. The *barangay* is situated in rolling hills. The distance from the center of Barangay Cabuluan to Solano, the biggest business and commercial center in the province, is about one and a half hours by motorcycle.

The 13-member savings and credit group has no organizational name and was endogenously formed in 2004, and had lasted eight years when the survey took place in 2012 (with originally 15 members, but two out-migrated). The members are all women, consisting of relatives and neighbors, in Barangay Cabuluan. Every Sunday afternoon from 1 pm to 3 pm, all the members gather in the house of one member. They have to deposit their meager savings of 10 pesos. Everyone has her own passbook, which was prepared by the leader. The leader records their savings in each passbook and keeps the books with her. All the money deposited is instantly loaned among the members and/or non-members at an interest rate (simple interest) of 2 percent and 3 percent, respectively, per month. The leader also has a record book for loans. The organization-pooled money is, thus, always zero. To keep the management cost for pooling the deposited money at zero, members are forced to borrow it. No serious default has occurred. In December, profits are equally divided among the members. The organization has not deposited money at any banks. This is because, according to the leader, banks are quite far from the *barangay*, requiring a large transportation cost. After eight years of operation as of 2012, the biggest saving among the members amounted to 8700 pesos.

This organization is a typical small-sized group using the social system of close dyadic relationships. To increase profits, the organization needs to last a long time. In order to overcome the problem of increased organizational costs and the possibility of resources being embezzled by managers, the 13-member savings and credit group practices a total loan-out of pooled deposits. No management costs are required. No risk of embezzlement is entailed.

VMPCO, Exogenous Savings and Credit Organization

Grameen-type MFOs and the 13-member savings credit group are all small-sized groups based on close dyadic relationships. Here, I examine the larger-sized organizations.

The study site is Barangay Nagbitin, the neighboring *barangay* of Barangay Cabuluan, the Municipality of Villaverde. Solano is only 30 minutes by motorcycle from the center of Barangay Nagbitin. Barangay Nagbitin (some 1110 hectares) consists of a flat area and rolling hills.

The household number of Barangay Nagbitin in August 2012 was 555 with a population of 2004 (male 1055 and female 949). Barangay Nagbitin is composed of seven *puroks*. Unlike Barangay El Salvador, where settlements are far from each other, settlements in Barangay Nagbitin are markedly formed only in Purok 1 and Purok 4. In other *puroks*, houses are built along the road, and there are no distinct boundaries between the neighboring *puroks*. Purok 1 and Purok 4 are old settlements and other *puroks* are created in accordance with population increases.

In Barangay Nagbitin, there are three long-lasting cooperatives. As of 2012, they were the nearly 25-year-old Villaverde Multi-Purpose Cooperative founded in 1988 (hereafter VMPCO), the Kapatirang Damayan Auto-Saving Group founded in 1989 (hereafter KADASA), and the more than 10-year-old Nagbitin Development Cooperative founded in 2001 (hereafter NADECO). They are all savings and credit organizations, having their offices in Purok 1. The number of their members as of August 2012 was 310, 146, and 385 respectively. I will start with VMPCO.

In 1984, to financially and technically assist indigent members in Barangay Nagbitin, Plan International (PI), an international NGO, organized them into small groups. These small groups were reorganized in 1988 by PI to establish the savings and credit organization. The organization started its business with an initial capital of 21 000 pesos invested by 48 members' capital share and 130 000 pesos from PI. The organization was registered as a multipurpose cooperative in 1990. After PI retreated from the *barangay* in 1991, VMPCO has been financially and technically assisted by several outside agencies. Since 1997, VMPCO has been linked with the Land Bank of the Philippines, the government-owned bank.

VMPCO has two types of membership: regular members who invest 1000 pesos (the daily wage for agricultural labor in the *barangay* is 170 pesos) as a minimum capital share and can borrow, and associate members who invest 500 pesos but cannot borrow. Regular members are required to invest 1000 pesos every year until they accumulate 15000 pesos. Regular members can borrow, for the first time, twice their capital share with an interest rate of 1 percent or 2 percent per month (simple interest), depending on the term of loan. If a regular member can pay back their loan without an extension of the term, from the second time onwards they can borrow a bigger amount depending on their collateral. A loan of more than 2000 pesos requires collateral. The collateral is a land title, an animal document (which is issued by an animal seller to the owners of a *carabao* or horse to guarantee their possession), a motorcycle, or any kind of vehicle. The maximum loanable amount is 50 percent of the value of the collateral.

As of August 2012, VMPCO had in total 310 members, with 173 regular members and 137 associate members, of which about 50 percent are Barangay Nagbitin residents. Among Barangay Nagbitin resident members, nearly half of them reside in Purok 1. The residences of the remaining 50 percent of the members extend to six *barangays* in the Municipality of Villaverde and the neighboring municipality of Solano. To understand how VMPCO deals with the problem of default, I focus on regular members and defaulting members (Table 6.4).

The manager, who is responsible for the management of VMPCO, decides whether a loan is approved to a person (regular member). The credibility check on a person is, thus, done based on close dyadic relationships centering on the manager. When the membership population extends to the entire municipality and eventually to neighboring municipalities, the number of those whom the manager does not know well, or at all, also increases. Of course, relying on close dyadic relationships is impractical for credibility checks. For the persons whom the manager does not know well or at all, the seven members of the board of directors are responsible for credibility checks in their assigned areas. The credibility check on a person is done through interviews by a loan investigation officer with their neighbors about their reputation on money matters, especially whether bill collectors from moneylenders often come to their house or not.

The default rate among the regular members of VMPCO as of August 2012 was 26 percent (45 defaulting members out of 173 total regular members), but it was higher before, especially among the members who joined the organization in the incipient year of the establishment. The reason for this, according to the manager, is that they had been accustomed to money doled out by outside agencies and thought that the loan was a gift. It took time, the manager said, to change their mindset by convincing them to pay their loan back.

Those who cannot pay their loan back within a given period have their payment rescheduled. The chance of rescheduling a repayment is given

Table 6.4 *VMPCO regular members and delinquent members by residence and joining year (totalizing every 5 years)*
(Delinquent members/All regular members)

| Joining year | Barangay Nagbitin[1] | | | | | | | Other barangays in the Municipality of Villaverde[2] | | | | | | SL[3] | Total |
	P1	P2	P3	P4	P5	P6	P7	BN	BS	CB	IB	SM	PZ		
1988–1992	15/34[4]	0/2	0/3	1/5	0/1	1/3	0/0	0/0	0/0	0/3	0/0	0/0	0/0	0/0	17/51
1993–1997	0/1	0/0	1/3	0/2	0/0	1/2	0/0	0/0	0/0	0/0	0/0	0/0	0/0	0/0	2/8
1998–2002	5/8	0/1	5/12	2/2	0/0	1/3	0/0	0/0	0/0	3/10	0/0	0/0	1/2	0/0	17/38
2003–2007	0/5	0/1	0/3	0/0	0/0	0/0	0/0	1/3	1/1	0/8	0/4	0/1	1/1	0/0	3/27
2008–2012	1/5	1/11	0/0	0/3	0/0	0/0	0/0	1/5	0/2	1/15	0/3	1/1	0/2	1/2	6/49
Total	21/53	1/15	6/21	3/12	0/1	3/8	0/0	2/8	1/3	4/36	0/7	1/2	2/5	1/2	45/173

Notes:
(1) P1, P2, . . . P7 are Purok 1, Purok 2, . . . Purok 7 in Barangay Nagbitin.
(2) BN: Barangay Bintawan Norte, BS: Barangay Bintawan Sur, CB: Barangay Cabuluan, IB: Barangay Ibung, SM: Barangay Sawmill, and PZ: Barangay Pieza are *barangays* in the Municipality of Villaverde, Nueva Vizcaya.
(3) SL: Municipality of Solano, the neighboring municipality Nueva Vizcaya.
(4) 15/34 means 15 delinquent members out of 34 regular members.

Source: Calculated by the author based on an interview with the VMPCO officer.

three times. Before the third (and last) chance, the defaulting person is taken to the *barangay* captain (headman) to make an oath of payment in front of the captain and to prepare a written oath. This shows that the organization makes use of the formal authority of the *barangay* captain; which is, however, not always effective in repayment. VMPCO can sell the collateral when the defaulting member who cannot pay the loan any more sends a voluntary surrender letter of the collateral to VMPCO. If there is no voluntary surrender letter of the collateral from the lingering default-ing member, VMPCO forecloses the collateral. For VMPCO to own the collateral to sell, it has to register in the registry of deeds, which requires a large cost for VMPCO.

To collect money from the defaulting members who seldom come to the office for repayment, VMPCO assigned one collection officer, from the Province of Iloilo, Visayas region, to pay frequent visits to their houses. The collection officer is not familiar with people in the area which means the officer can, then, make businesslike decisions. If they knew each other well, the officer might sympathize with the defaulting members' economic hardships, which makes the collection of repayment harder. It is also a VMPCO policy to allow the collection officer to stay for a short time only at the defaulting member's house. If the officer stays longer, she may be entertained with a drink and a snack by the defaulting member, which again makes the collection of repayment harder. Table 6.4 shows that VMPCO is able to control the default problem in newly joined regular members. To decrease the default rate, VMPCO plans to assign board of directors members to collect money in the areas where they are not famil-iar with residents.

We can observe here that the formation of the organization is based on the social system of close dyadic relationships. Since the size of the organization is increasing, covering a wider range of geographical settings, it is harder for all the members to be tied with close dyadic relationships. To make organizations larger and more profitable, VMPCO is now shift-ing from an informal to a formal model for managerial relationships. An informal relationship means the organization is based on a social system of close dyadic relationships, while a formal relationship means the organi-zation is not based on any social system, but on a formalized set of rules. Credibility investigations by a loan investigation officer, and collection from defaulting members by a collection officer who is not familiar with residents, contribute to the formalization process.

The social system of close dyadic relations often works adversely, espe-cially for money collection from defaulting members. As mentioned above, personal closeness between managerial personnel and members often hampers the collection of money. Because of the closeness between them, the former can easily take pity on members' economic hardships, resulting in a high default rate. To make VMPCO sustainably profitable in the business of savings and credit, it has had to conquer this problem.

Rural Philippine society does not have a social system that can mobilize a large number of people or widen their cooperative relationships, thus the only way to conquer this problem is to enact a formal set of rules for each organization.

NADECO, Exogenous Savings and Credit Organization

Barangay Nagbitin was one of *barangays* assisted by the European Union (EU)-funded project, the Caraballo and the Southern Cordillera Development Program. The idea of a savings and loan group (SLG) was introduced to the *barangay* by the project in 1999. One group consisted of 5 to 15 persons. Each deposited 10 pesos per week for loans to members. There were 13 SLGs formed in the Municipality of Villaverde (six in Barangay Nagbitin), among which only two survived. One of the surviving SLGs was in Barangay Nagbitin. The manager of NADECO was the leader of the surviving SLG. With the assistance of the EU, a savings and credit organization based on the SLG was formed in Barangay Nagbitin in 2001. The organization started its business with 30 members. It was registered as a multi-purpose cooperative in 2008.

As of August 2012, the number of members had reached a total of 385, out of which about 40 percent were residents in Barangay Nagbitin (about half of which resided in Purok 1) and 27 percent were residents of the neighboring *barangay* of Barangay Ibung. The members' places of residence also extended to the entire municipality. The 385 members consisted of 239 regular members who invested a minimum capital share of 1000 pesos and can borrow, and 146 associate members who invested 500 pesos but cannot borrow. Like VMPCO, when the organization was small, credibility checks for loans to regular members were not a problem. Once the organization grew to cover a larger geographical setting, a loan investigation officer conducted credibility inquiries for regular members, thus formalizing the relationship between the managerial body and members. NADECO's rules for loans are almost the same as VMPCO's.

The default rate as of August 2012 was 29 percent (70 defaulting members out of 239 regular members) (Table 6.5). The collection of money from the defaulting members who seldom come to the office for repayment is done in the same way as VMPCO, by assigning a collection officer who is not familiar with the place to pay frequent visits to them. It is thus observed that, like VMPCO, NADECO has also been in the process of formalizing the relationship, from an informal one based on the social

Table 6.5   NADECO regular members and delinquent members by residence and joining year (totalizing every 5 years)
(Delinquent members/All regular members)

Joining year	Barangay Nagbitin[1]							Other barangays in the Municipality of Villaverde[2]						SL/BY[3]	Total[4]
	P1	P2	P3	P4	P5	P6	P7	BN	BS	CB	IB	SM	PZ		
2001–2005	3/7[5]	2/5	2/2	0/1	1/2	0/1	0/0	2/5	0/0	0/4	5/16	0/0	0/0	1/2	17/46
2006–2010	5/20	2/7	1/8	3/11	0/1	5/13	0/2	8/24	3/12	1/4	15/42	0/4	4/4	0/0	47/152
2011–2012	0/1	0/1	1/5	0/4	0/0	1/2	0/1	1/7	1/4	0/4	2/10	0/2	0/0	0/0	6/41
Total	8/28	4/13	4/15	3/16	1/3	6/16	0/3	11/36	4/16	1/12	22/68	0/6	4/4	1/2	70/239

Notes:
(1)   P1, P2, . . . P7 are Purok 1, Purok 2, . . . Purok 7 in Barangay Nagbitin.
(2)   BN: Barangay Bintawan Norte, BS: Barangay Bintawan Sur, CB: Barangay Cabuluan, IB: Barangay Ibung, SM: Barangay Sawmill, and PZ: Barangay Pieza are *barangays* in the Municipality of Villaverde, Nueva Vizcaya.
(3)   SL/BY: Municipality of Solano and Municipality of Bayombong, Nueva Vizcaya.
(4)   One delinquent member's residence could not be identified.
(5)   3/7 means 3 delinquent members out of 7 regular members.

Source: Calculated by the author based on an interview with the NADECO officer.

Table 6.6   KADASA regular members and delinquent members by residence and joining year (totalizing every 5 years)
(Delinquent members/All regular members)

Joining year	Barangay Nagbitin[1]							Other barangays in the Municipality of Villaverde[2]						Outside[3]	Total
	P1	P2	P3	P4	P5	P6	P7	BN	BS	CB	IB	SM	PZ		
1998–2002	3/7[4]	0/0	0/0	0/0	3/6	0/0	0/0	0/0	0/0	0/0	0/0	0/0	0/0	1/1	7/14
2003–2007	2/2	0/0	0/0	0/0	0/2	0/0	0/0	0/0	0/0	0/0	2/2	0/0	0/0	0/0	4/6
2008–2012	9/13	0/0	1/2	2/3	1/2	0/0	1/1	1/2	2/3	9/32	8/16	0/0	1/1	13/13	48/88
Total	14/22	0/0	1/2	2/3	4/10	0/0	1/1	1/2	2/3	9/32	10/18	0/0	1/1	14/14	59/108

Notes:
(1) P1, P2, . . . P7 are Purok 1, Purok 2, . . . Purok 7 in Barangay Nagbitin.
(2) BN: Barangay Bintawan Norte, BS: Barangay Bintawan Sur, CB: Barangay Cabuluan, IB: Barangay Ibung, SM: Barangay Sawmill, and PZ: Barangay Pieza are barangays in the Municipality of Villaverde, Nueva Vizcaya.
(3) Outside: outside of the Municipality of Villaverde which the Municipality of Solano, the Municipality of Dupax del Norte of Province of Nueva Vizcaya, Province of Tarlac, and Province of Isabela.
(4) 3/7 means 3 delinquent members out of 7 regular members.

Source: Calculated by the author based on an interview with the KADASA officer.

154

system of close dyadic relationships, to one based on a formalized set of organizational rules.

KADASA, Endogenous Savings and Credit Organization

Unlike VMPCO and NADECO, which were formed by outside agencies, KADASA was an endogenous savings and credit organization. *Kapatiran* means brotherhood and *damayan* means helping each other. A person who used to work as an accounting assistant in VMPCO called his siblings and relatives to form a savings group in 1989 for emergency purposes. He is the manager of KADASA. The original membership was ten, all siblings and relatives. They deposited 10 pesos per month. When membership grew including non-relatives, KADASA started the business of savings and credit in 1998. KADASA had expanded its membership to 146 as of 2012. Members were mainly concentrated in Purok 1 and Purok 5 of Barangay Nagbitin. This is because the original members of siblings and relatives are residents there. Members were also concentrated in Barangay Cabuluan, the neighboring *barangay* to Barangay Nagbitin. This is because the manager, who is an elementary teacher, was once assigned there and he recruited the residents to KADASA. Because of his recruitment, 63 joined in 2010. The 146 members consisted of 108 regular members who contributed 1000 pesos as a minimum capital share and who can borrow, and 38 associate members who contributed 500 pesos but cannot borrow.

In August 2012, KADASA experienced a high default rate of 55 percent (59 defaulting members out of 108 total regular members) (Table 6.6). KADASA's by-laws state that the loanable amount is five times one's capital share. The manager clarified that with the same by-laws KADASA could control default problems when the membership was small. Because this rule was favorable to borrowers, those who joined KADASA in 2010 borrowed 5000 pesos each (with their capital share of 1000 pesos). KADASA could not collect the money from defaulting members in 2011 and ended the loan business in 2012.

This is one typical case in which savings and credit organizations malfunction. The social system of close dyadic relations functions well for the credibility check but finds difficulty in the collection of money from defaulting members. KADASA's survival depends on whether it can adopt schemes for formal relationships and businesslike transactions.

CONCLUSION: ORGANIZATIONAL CAPABILITY IN RURAL PHILIPPINE SOCIETY

This chapter has examined the organizational capability of rural Philippine society. The study was prompted by the research question of why CBFM malfunctions despite outside agencies' efforts to enhance it. Understanding the organizational capability of rural Philippine society is necessary to determine the fundamental cause for CBFM's malfunctioning.

As observed in this chapter, rural Philippine society has the capability to form organizations that are based on the social system of close dyadic relationships and that pool resources for a short period of time. This type of organization can reduce organizational costs by decreasing would-be members' credibility inquiry costs and consensus-making costs, to which the social system of close dyadic relations contributes, and resource management costs by pooling resources for only a short period of time, resulting in making the organization profitable. The social system of close dyadic relations naturally renders the size of such organizations small. I have not encountered any endogenous functional organizations that cover all *purok* residents or all *barangay* residents, even in the *barangay* where the majority of people belong to the same kin group and know each other. Development organizations formed by outside agencies can function only when they correspond to the above-mentioned organizational capability in rural society. The Grameen-type MFO is the typical successful development organization to match the organizational capability in rural Philippine society, but it is outside agencies, not organization members, that shoulder organizational costs to pool resources for longer periods.

Figure 6.1 focuses on two characteristics of organizations in rural Philippine society, that is, member relationships and pooling resources periods. The former includes informal relationships and formal relationships. Informal relationships use the social system of close dyadic relations, in which individual and personal relationships are crucial to making organizations function. Conversely, formal relationships do not use the social system. Instead, group relationships based on formal rules are crucial to making the organization function properly. This is because rural Philippine society has no social system, other than dyadic relationships, to mobilize people and control their behavior. Pooling resources periods can comprise short-term resources and long-term resources pools. There are three types of organizations observed in rural Philippine society, that is, "informal relationship and short-term resources pool" type (Type A organizations), "informal relationship and long-term resources pool" type (Type B organizations) and "formal relationship and long-term resources

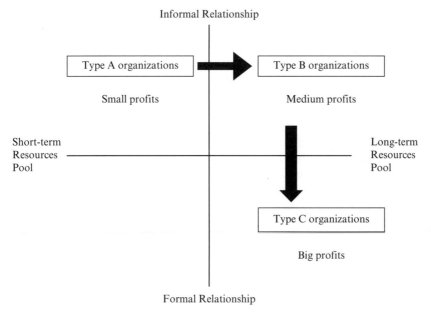

Source: Prepared by the author.

Figure 6.1   Two characteristics of organizations in rural Philippine society

pool" type (Type C organizations). As I have discussed, Type A organizations are predominant in rural Philippine society.

Type C produces the biggest profits among the three types, followed by Type B, and then Type A. To increase organizational profits, Type A has to shift to Type B and to Type C. The shift of the types is done from Type A to Type B and from Type B to Type C. The shift directly from Type A to Type C hardly ever happens because the hurdle for the shift is very high.

The typical Type A organizations I observed are mutual fund organizations for funeral services and for wedding receptions, and fund-raising organizations for food expenses on special occasions. They are small in size and pool resources for short periods of time. The typical Type B organizations I observed are Grameen-type MFOs and the 13-member savings and credit group. These are still small in size, but pool resources for longer periods of time. Type B organizations enjoy bigger profits than Type A organizations. However, the shift from Type A to Type B is not easy, because it takes time until organizational profits become noticeable to members. Until such a time, organizations need to last. However, as I have already discussed, the longer the organization lasts, the greater the organizational costs become and the greater the possibility of deviation or embezzlement by members. A scheme is indispensable for organizations to overcome these problems. In Grameen-type MFOs, member behaviors are policed internally as well as by outside agencies that shoulder the organizational costs necessary to pool resources for a longer period of time. The 13-member savings and credit group adopts the scheme of loaning all the deposited money out, so that the organization incurs no costs for pooling money. Most Type A organizations, however, do not overcome the hurdle to shift to Type B organizations in rural Philippine society.

Type C organizations enjoy much bigger profits than Type B organizations. If Type B organizations want to make bigger organizational profits, organizational size should grow in terms of membership. To shift from Type B organizations, which already have experience in pooling resources for longer periods, to Type C organizations, the membership size should be greater. Informal relationships between managers and members of the social system of close dyadic relationships do not serve to control a large number of members' behaviors. Because of the non-existence of social systems in rural local society that can lengthen cooperative relationships, the formalization of the relationship, into one which is based not on social systems but on a formalized set of organizational rules, is required to keep organizations functional. The formalization of the relationship has been under way in the two cooperatives of VMPCO and NADECO. Type C organizations, thus, do not use the social system to bind members. Instead, formal organizational rules bind members, like those in enterprises and government offices. Once Type C organization members are aware that obedience to formal rules produces bigger organizational profits, the organizations can be firmly established. The shift from Type B organizations to Type C organizations – that is, the formalization of the relationship – is, however, not easy. The two cooperatives I observed were struggling with the shift.

Table 6.7 indicates the difficulty of the shift from Type B organizations to Type C organizations. I classify 19 517 operating cooperatives in the country as rural, urban, or semi-urban cooperatives. Rural cooperatives are located in rural *barangay* like Barangay Nagbitin, and their members are mainly rural residents. Urban cooperatives are located in urban *barangay* and their members are mainly urban residents who have permanent jobs. Semi-urban cooperatives are located in rural *barangay* but their service area extends to a whole province. The average number of members per rural cooperative is 76, much smaller than the 354 of urban cooperatives. As observed in the two cooperatives in Barangay Nagbitin, the average number of regular members, who can borrow, is much smaller (about 60 percent of total cooperative members). If we apply this ratio to a rural

Table 6.7 The number of cooperatives and average members/cooperative in rural and urban areas by region (as of August 2012)

Region	Rural Cooperative[1]		Urban Cooperative[2]		Semi-urban Cooperative[3]		Unidentified[4]
	Number of cooperatives	Average members/ cooperative	Number of cooperatives	Average members/ cooperative	Number of cooperatives	Average members/ cooperative	Number of cooperatives
National	9265	76	9561	354	136	6835	555
CAR[5]	365	102	366	317	17	5806	12
Region 1	704	93	570	457	11	7826	25
Region 2	459	86	357	686	7	13308	0
Region 3	762	56	1275	444	4	2653	64
Region 4	817	97	1438	276	20	2032	54
Region 5	315	72	449	304	5	14493	75
Region 6	606	89	688	194	18	11578	65
Region 7	627	88	902	391	15	4561	41
Region 8	361	93	278	524	10	8963	44
Region 9	395	93	342	734	6	1958	24
Region 10	758	64	715	369	8	10256	33
Region 11	811	83	886	293	3	7195	31
Region 12	514	71	518	275	6	1539	31
Region 13	667	71	385	237	6	6136	25
ARMM	1104	31	392	74	0	0	31

Table 6.7 (continued)

Notes:
(1) Rural cooperative is located in rural *barangay*.
(2) Urban cooperative is located in urban *barangay*.
(3) Semi-urban cooperative is located in rural *barangay* but its service area is the entire province.
(4) Unidentified cooperatives are those that cannot be identified as any of the three types. Identification of cooperatives is done one by one to check the *barangay* name in their address, which was provided by the Cooperative Development Authority with the National Statistics Office Website, which provides information on some but not all urban and rural *barangays* in the country. Cooperatives without a *barangay* name in their address could not be identified.
(5) CAR: Cordillera Administrative Region located in the Cordillera Mountains in Northern Luzon, Region 1–Region 5: Luzon and surrounding islands, Region 6–Region 8: Visayas islands, Region 9–Region 13: Mindanao and surrounding islands, ARMM: Autonomous Region in Muslim Mindanao.

Source: Calculated by the author based on the data gathered by the Cooperative Development Authority.

160

cooperative, the average number of regular members is about 45. This fact shows that most rural cooperatives still remain in Type B organizations and cannot shift to Type C organizations.

Moreover, it is reported that in February 2008 there were 70 154 registered cooperatives in the Philippines, including 21 068 operating cooperatives (30 percent), 21 473 non-operating cooperatives (31 percent), 15 427 cooperatives that had been dissolved (22 percent), and 12 286 cooperatives that had had their registration cancelled (18 percent) (CODE-NGO 2009, p. 3). Only one-third of all the cooperatives registered (including rural, urban, and semi-urban types) can survive. This fact too shows the difficulty for organizations to pool resources for a long period of time. Many cannot stay even in Type B organizations.

POs or development organizations formed by outside agencies for CBFM to cover a *barangay* or bigger area require significant mobilization. The sustainable management of state forestlands, including profiting from timber production for rural development, requires long-lasting organizations that pool resources over a significant period of time. POs, thus, should be Type B or Type C organizations. As observed, it is obvious that rural Philippine society barely has the organizational capability to form Type B and Type C organizations. The majority of organizations in rural society remain Type A of a small size, using the social system of close dyadic relationships, as well as short-term resources pool organizations. It is apparent that development organizations that do not match the organizational capability of rural Philippine society will not last.

REFERENCES

Caucus of Development NGO Networks (CODE-NGO) (2009), *Assessing the Philippine NGO Environment: Regulation, Risks and Renewal*, Quezon City: Caucus of Development NGO Networks.

Chokkalingam, Unna, Antonio P. Carandang, Juan M. Pulhin, Rodel D. Lasco, Rosa Jane J. Peras, and Takeshi Toma (2006), *One Century of Forest Rehabilitation in the Philippines: Approaches, Outcomes and Lessons*, Bogor: Center for International Forestry Research.

Contreras, Antonio P. (ed.) (2003), *Creating Space for Local Forest Management in the Philippines*, Manila: La Salle Institute of Governance.

Dalmacio, Marcelino, Ernesto S. Guiang, Bruce Harker, and William F. Hyde (2000), "Secure forest tenure, community management, and deforestation: A Philippine policy application," in William F. Hyde, Gregory S. Amacher, et al. (eds), *Economics of Forestry and Rural Development: An Empirical Introduction from Asia*, Ann Arbor, MI: University of Michigan Press, pp. 151–180.

Department of Environment and Natural Resources (DENR) (2011), *2011 Philippine Forestry Statistics*, Quezon City: Government of the Philippines.

Department of Environment and Natural Resources (DENR) (n.d.), *Completed DENR-Foreign Assisted Project Profile*, Quezon City: Government of the Philippines.

Food and Agriculture Organization of the United Nations (FAO), Forest Management Bureau (FMB), and Department of Environment and Natural Resources (DENR) (2003), *The Revised Master Plan for Forestry Development*, Quezon City: Government of the Philippines.

Gauld, Richard (2000), "Maintaining centralized control in community-based forestry: Policy construction in the Philippines," *Development and Change*, **31**, 229–254.

Guiang, Ernesto S. (2001), "Impacts and effectiveness of logging bans in natural forests: Philippines," in Patrick B. Durst, Thomas R. Waggener, Thomas Enters, and Tan Lay Cheng (eds), *Forests Out of Bounds: Impacts and Effectiveness of Logging Bans in Natural Forests in Asia-Pacific*, Bangkok: Food and Agriculture Organization of the United Nations Regional Office for Asia and the Pacific, pp.103–135.

Guiang, Ernesto S. (2008), "Resource use rights and other challenges to the sustainability of community-managed forests and forest lands in the Philippines," in Karin L. Collin and James L. Kho (eds), *After the Romance: Communities and Environmental Governance in the Philippines*, Quezon City: Ateneo de Manila University Press, pp.49–91.

Guiang, Ernesto S., Salve B. Borlagdan, and Juan M. Pulhin (2001), *Community-Based Forest Management in the Philippines: A Preliminary Assessment*, Quezon City: Institute of Philippine Culture, Ateneo de Manila University.

Hayami, Yujiro and Masao Kikuchi (2000), *A Rice Village Saga: Three Decades of Green Revolution in the Philippines*, London: Macmillan Press.

Korten, Frances F. (1994), "Questioning the call for environmental loans: A critical examination of forestry lending in the Philippines," *World Development*, **22**(7), 971–981.

Lasco, Rodel D. and Juan M. Pulhin (2006), "Environmental impacts of community-based forest management in the Philippines," *International Journal of Environment and Sustainable Development*, **5**(1), 46–56.

Pulhin, J.M., M. Inoue, and T. Enters (2007), "Three decades of community-based forest management in the Philippines: Emerging lessons for sustainable and equitable forest management," *International Forestry Review*, **9**(4), 865–883.

Shigetomi, Shinichi (2011), "Organizational capability of local societies in rural development," *Social Development Issues*, **33**(1), 24–34.

Suh, Jungho (2012), "The past and future of community-based forest management in the Philippines," *Philippine Studies Historical and Ethnographic Viewpoint*, **60**(4), 489–511.

Utting, Peter (ed.) (2000), *Forest Policy and Politics in the Philippines: The Dynamics of Participatory Conservation*, Quezon City: Ateneo de Manila University Press.

Valsan, E.H. (1970), *Community Development Programs and Rural Local Development: Comparative Case Studies of India and the Philippines*, New York: Praeger.

7. Common fund procurement through rent collection: a form of collective action for public works and public services in Indian villages

Akina Venkateswarlu and Shinichi Shigetomi

INTRODUCTION

In post-World War II India, many new economic theories on how best to promote development arose. One such theory, advocating the modernization of production and restructuring of traditional production factors, required two economic policy measures at the local level: (1) the regional resource development approach; and (2) the allocation of production factors (Yogo 1986). The former measure was meant to enhance production through improvement of the production infrastructure. However, even after the improvement had been implemented, this measure faced a problem in that the modern production factors were not sufficiently procured through market mechanisms. As a result, the productivity of small producers did not increase. To cope with this "deficiency of market" problem, the latter measure was implemented to allocate production factors through local administrative organizations. However, such an allocation through governmental hierarchy faced another problem, namely "the limitation of administration." It was often the case that cohesion between the local administration and the rural elites was built into the allocation system of the production factors, resulting in the apparent intensification of disparities among the traditional rural classes.

Observing these issues, the government of India recognized – well before other developing countries – the endogenous development capability of local communities as an important aspect of regional planning (Holdcroft 1978). Small producers could perhaps correct market deficiencies through collective access to the market. They could access the administratively allocated resources through their organizations. Community involvement with popular participation was regarded as necessary to support local people to organize themselves for these collective actions.

Broad-based community participation is premised on the assumption that people in a given community can cooperate to address their collective needs and problems together. Homogeneity of members tends to be regarded as a positive factor in a community's ability to take collective action (Agrawal and Gibson 1999). In the villages of India, however, residents are divided into caste groups, and social segregation among castes is still practiced. Vishwambhar Nath, formerly of the Planning Commission of the Indian government during the period of implementing the Community Development Programme, observed the difficulty of forming organizations based on egalitarian principles (such as co-operatives) among people who are governed by traditional hierarchical organizations (that is, castes) (Nath 2010, p. 172). Political struggle among political parties is rife even in the village-level administration. Wade (1988, p. 57) commented through his detailed study of a village in Andhra Pradesh that there was little sense of the village as an entity over time. Hence, the following question arises: how could the populations in Indian villages unite to participate collaboratively in rural development projects?

There are, in fact, many reports of cases in which Indian villagers organize themselves for the purpose of improving their social and economic conditions. In this chapter, we study three villages in Andhra Pradesh State as cases where collective actions of local people are documented in action. We show that the mechanisms used for collective action at this local level are especially successful in procuring (financial) resources from individuals both within and outside their villages, pooling such resources as a common fund, and using them for public works and services in their villages. This chapter examines the organization of collective actions in these villages and attempts to clarify the local conditions that enable them.

This chapter consists of five subsequent sections, to examine the central research questions. The next section provides preliminary information about local administration and social organizations in rural India. In the third section, we describe the process of resource procurement and utilization in a case village, Pindiprolu, in detail. In the fourth section, we examine the experience of two other villages in the context of our findings in the Pindiprolu case study. In our conclusion, we summarize the salient features of collective actions observed in the three village case studies, and discuss the local social systems at work behind the scenes in each case. We will also offer some concluding comments on current rural development policies in India.

SOCIAL AND LOCAL ADMINISTRATIVE INSTITUTIONS IN RURAL INDIA

Local Units at the Grassroots Level

In India, the word "village" is used in different senses depending on the context.[1] A village may refer to: (1) a habitation or hamlet; (2) a "revenue village"; or (3) a *panchayat* village. A habitation is an aggregate of several households sharing the same locality for residence. It is identical to a natural village with borders, either defined or undefined. All villages with separate and independent names can be called habitations. When a habitation has some dependence on a neighboring habitation, for either economic activities or administrative purposes, the dependent habitation is called a hamlet, and the other is called the main village or main habitation.

In the current local administration system, a *panchayat* village is the statutory body for local self-government administration while a revenue village is the local unit for managing revenue collection by state government. Both are usually clusters of habitations, though sometimes each can consist of a single habitation, depending on its size and degree of dependency. As of April 1, 2012, at the national level, the average number of habitations per *panchayat* is 6.76 and the average number of habitations per revenue village is 2.80. Different states have different demarcations. For example, in West Bengal in East India, a *panchayat* village includes about 10–12 habitations with a total of about 10 000 residents (Ghatak and Ghatak 2002). In each revenue village, there may be one or more village *panchayats* while two revenue villages may exist under a single *panchayat* village. Often, a revenue village and a *panchayat* village cover the same territory.

Village Communities and their Administration

India's village communities from the pre-British period have long been portrayed as self-sufficient village economies, called "village republics." On the one hand, this term connotes the simplicity of organization for production in these self-sufficient communities based on the communal ownership of land; on the other, it suggests the economic interdependence between farmers (agricultural activities) and non-farmers through the caste system (non-agricultural handicrafts and services).

Even on the eve of British entry into India, there were indications of the disintegration of village communities caused by internal changes (Singh 1981). Many social changes occurred under British colonial domination. The introduction of centralized governmental administration, the revenue system, the institutions of the police and courts of law, and the extension of modern means of communication and transportation, ended the total isolation of many villages. Thus came the end of the self-sufficient village community. During India's post-Independence period, the village community experienced further changes because of the constitutional ban on untouchability. As the ascription of occupation by the caste system disappeared, so did the interdependency among villagers caused by division of labor (Nath 2010, p. 183).

By the late 1950s, rural India no longer enjoyed the reputation of a quiet, idyllic, rural haven (Marriot 1955). The fact that the village community did not adopt egalitarianism was illustrated quite clearly in scholarly works, such as M.N. Srinivas's study in the early 1960s (Srinivas 1989 [1962]). Rural–urban migration became a demographic trend because of the quick demise of village handicrafts during the 1960s and 1970s due to the Indian government's adoption of industrialization policies, development of the public sector, and encouragement of the private sector after 1956.

Even in ancient times, the village community had an institution for self-administration via the *panchayat* or village council (Matthai 1915, p. 18). The word *"panchayat"* here refers to an organization for village administration.[2] It was formed by the leaders of various castes and *sanghs* (associations) for discussing village affairs (Srinivas 2002). The village *panchayat* looked after various village matters such as village defense, dispute arbitration, village public works, and tax collection on behalf of the government (Madan 1990, pp. 4–7). It had survived during the pre-British period (including Muslim rule) and endured through the British period with modifications. Thus, this type of *panchayat* system can be considered self-administration, which is dependent on the voluntary system.

Thus, the *panchayat* of ancient times formed the basis of the modern local self-governing *panchayat* (Ramesh 2011). When the state governments of India adopted a statutory local self-government system for local administration in the late 1950s, the word *"panchayat"* no longer referred to the institution of the village community. In acknowledgment of the historical heritage of the village *panchayat* system, the government of India (Indian constitution) named the entire statutory local self-government system the Panchayati Raj System at the district, block/*mandal* and village levels; and its institutions are called Panchayati Raj Institutions (PRIs). We can differentiate the new system of local self-government, dependent on elections and statutory laws, from the old *panchayat* system of self-administration.

Though the old *panchayat* system for self-administration has diminished, when people have the initiative to develop the habitation or village, self-administration in the form of the village council still remains (Wade 1988; Krishna 2002, pp. 135–137; Mallik 1929, p. 41). This institution plays a crucial role in the collective actions we observe later in the case studies.

As a part of self-administration, Indian villagers have long made efforts to secure common funds for public needs. The village common fund has historical roots in both the pre-British and British periods. Madan (1990, p. 17) wrote that there were certain common needs of the villagers, such as the construction and repair of the village temple, the village hall, the wells and tanks, the streets and defense walls, the embankments and canals, and the roads.

Even in the British period when the government took over many activities from the village *panchayat* and discouraged village councils (ibid., pp. 7–8), it was observed in South India that villagers either contributed voluntarily or paid fees or rent to use the village commons. Singh (1981, pp. 96–97) also wrote that village funds were derived from the proceeds of communal lands or from the annual sale of fishing rights to the pond, and from trees that were jointly owned by the community. The funds helped small communities to possess a common temple, a village hall, a village watch, a company of artisans, pasture grounds, cattle yards, threshing floors, water tanks, and irrigation channels.

Panchayat Villages and Local Administration

The autonomy of the *panchayats* declined considerably during the rule of the British East India Company (1757–1858). The creation of the roles of the *patwari* (who became the official record keeper for a number of villages) and the magistrate (who carried out policing functions) completely disempowered the village community. When the British government directly took over the reins of the Indian government in 1858, it tried to restore the *panchayat* by giving it powers to try minor offenses and resolve village disputes, but these measures were not enough to restore the lost powers of the village community.

When India gained independence in 1947, the ruling class wanted to realize Mahatma Gandhi's vision of establishing "self-governing village republics" in rural India. In 1957, a state committee recommended decentralizing power to levels below the state in the form of a three-tier system of rural local government, with the village *panchayat* at the grassroots level.[3] These local administrative systems, referred to as PRIs, came into existence in 1959 in many states. This was the beginning of the present *panchayat* villages. However, until the 1990s, the decentralization of administrative authorities was limited. It was the 73rd Constitutional Amendment of 1992 that accorded the PRIs sweeping powers and the authority to conduct local development works.

The village *panchayat* is expected to be the agent promoting the development of agriculture, education, and drinking water supplies (Sharma

2009, p.111). It is represented by the president, who also administers the *panchayat* village, along with ward members, all of whom are elected by public vote. Political parties compete in the election of the president and ward members, which sometimes produces political conflict and division among villagers. There is also an assembly of voters in the village called the *gramsabha*. The village *panchayat* has to conduct the *gramsabha* every six months and submit proposals and accounts to the *gramsabha* for approval. The agenda and minimum attendance rate in the *gramsabha* are also regulated by law.

Regarding the fiscal aspect, the *panchayat* village has long faced a shortage of revenue. A typical *panchayat* village had four sources of development funds: (1) its own independent income; (2) a share of assigned revenue; (3) government grants; and (4) deposits and donations. In many villages, independent income, accruing for the most part from local taxes, was quite meager. Assigned revenue was also a negligible amount. Grants from state and central governments, which had flowed in annually since 1989–1990, were to be spent for specified purposes only. Deposits and donations were conspicuously absent. Any further taxing of villagers (thus incurring their resentment) was not an advisable option for any political party in power. Overall, the total revenue received by the *panchayat* was not enough to carry out the general development functions assigned to it.

Revenue Villages and Revenue Administration

When the British East India Company began to occupy India in 1757, it first adopted the system of permanent settlement in Bengal in 1793, conferring the authority to collect land revenues to new landlords (*zamindars*). This *zamindari* system further entrusted the collection of land revenues to many intermediaries between the state and the *zamindars*. This system caused many problems for the actual farmers, so when the British conquered Western and Southern India, they decided to settle the land revenues with the actual cultivators and maintain land records and collect revenues directly through an official agency in each village. This came to be called the Ryotwari Settlement (Dandekar and Rath 1971).

Under both systems, land revenues were assessed by the British government at the village level. This village unit was called a "revenue village." When India became independent in 1947, throughout the next two decades, the Indian government implemented land reforms including the abolition of the aforementioned intermediaries. The revenue village remained the unit of land revenue assessment, so the revenue village is to this day the basic unit of land revenue administration throughout India.

Under India's current system of revenue administration, the rural areas are divided into revenue divisions, which are divided into *tahsils* or *mandals*, which are further divided into revenue villages. When a cluster of habitations is treated as a revenue village, the main habitation becomes the headquarters for revenue administration, and it bears the name of the revenue village.

Caste Institutions

In Hindu society, each member belongs to a particular caste by birth, depending on the caste of his or her father. In ancient India's Hindu society, the menial or impure occupations were assigned to *chandalas*, the excommunicated, and thus they became (were branded) "untouchables." Hindu tradition has created a highly inequitable social structure in socio-economic terms, simultaneously inflicting humiliation on the untouchable caste (Guru 2009). Kroeber (1930, p. 254) defined caste as "an endoga-mous and hereditary subdivision of an ethnic unit occupying a position of superior or inferior rank or social esteem in comparison with other such subdivisions."

At the village level, the caste institution is not merely a social stratum but also has some organizational aspects. The ascribed occupation for each caste used to be incorporated into the division of labor under the commu-nal administration. Within each caste group, there is an institution called a caste council that acts as an intracaste dispute-settlement mechanism as well as a representative for intercaste affairs with authority to enforce penalties and punishments.

With improved transportation and communication facilities and higher educational levels over the years, the caste stigma for untouchables has continued to decline in urban areas nationwide. In rural areas, it has slowly declined as well but has not been completely eradicated. Intercaste dining has become more common, but intercaste marriage is still stigmatized. Occupations are no longer ascribed, which means that the division of labor among castes at the village level has also disappeared. The role of the caste council has diminished, but the council does still exist in some villages – including those surveyed as part of this study – settling small disputes and overseeing associational activities such as festivals and worship activities.

COMMON FUND FORMATION AND ITS USE IN VILLAGE PINDIPROLU

Consisting of 950 households as of 2006, Pindiprolu is the main habitation of Panchayat Pindiprolu, which also includes two smaller habitations with

110 and 120 households, respectively. We conducted a detailed field survey here in 1993 and collected additional data on this location in 2006 and 2012. In addition, a detailed report on Pindiprolu has been previously published by one of the authors of this chapter (Venkateswarlu 2011). There is an annual village festival called Muthyalamma, organized by the elder villagers and celebrated by the entire Hindu population of Habitation Pindiprolu. As for the other two habitations, one has a temple and its own village festival, while the other had plans for a temple of its own at the time we visited in 2012. Each habitation has its own primary school as well. In this way, each habitation has its own set of assets or resources that resembles those of the other habitations.

Pindiprolu's Early History: Armed Political Struggle of the Communists

As inhabitants of a part of the Telangana Region of Andhra Pradesh, in 1946, the people of Pindiprolu initiated an armed struggle against feudalism and oppressive landlords, under the banner of the Communist Party of India (CPI). The struggle was spearheaded primarily against the tyrannical practice of bonded labor (*vetti*) and excessive grain levy, and in favor of better agricultural wages (Thirumali 1992; Dhanagare 1981, p. 495). Long before this, the people of Pindiprolu had waged a legal battle against the landlord (*dora*), under the leadership of Rayala Venkatanarayana (RVN), in favor of the tenants, who emerged as the victors. This victory served to motivate the youth throughout the region to forge the Library Movement, and their rising consciousness eventually led them to form the CPI Village Committee in Pindiprolu in 1946. At that point, Pindiprolu became a center of communist activities and the CPI became the largest political party in the habitation.

From 1946 to 1951, the cadre of the Pindiprolu CPI participated in the armed struggle that made a tremendous impact on every walk of life in Pindiprolu. After the Police Action of the Indian government in 1948, the communists continued their struggle. In that process, out of the 16 activists in the CPI, five were killed by the military, and one was murdered by *goondas*. The other party cadres and sympathizers were forced to go underground; some were compelled to go into the forests, while others were arrested. After the Police Action, a police camp was installed in Pindiprolu, and the villagers were subjected to mental and physical torture by the police.

After the return of the CPI cadres from the jails and underground, when the Panchayati Raj System was introduced in 1959, the CPI obtained a clear majority in Pindiprolu Village Panchayat in the *panchayat* elections of 1959, 1962, and 1965. After the 1962 *panchayat* elections, a village education committee was formed to raise additional funds for more school buildings, and eventually a high school was established in the village.

However, in the 1960s, there occurred division within the communist group, and its dominant faction boycotted the 1970 *panchayat* elections. The Congress Party got a chance to win a majority of seats. Under a *panchayat* that was then dominated by the Congress Party, there was neither an election held (until 1981), nor any major developmental activities undertaken. After the mid-1970s, the student activists who were studying in Khammam (the District Headquarters) returned to the village and became active communist leaders. They formed a youth group, most of the members of which were associated with the revolutionary politics of the Communist Party of India (Marxist Leninist – New Democracy) or CPI (ML-ND). By that time, the other political parties existing in Pindiprolu were the Communist Party of India (Marxist) (CPI (M)) and the Congress Party.[4] This youth group sold tickets to plays and cultural events held in the village, and deposited the proceeds at the Block Office to obtain subsidies from the government to build a primary school building. In this way, the young communist leaders regained the trust of Pindiprolu villagers. CPI (ML-ND) member Sri Rayala Nageswara Rao, who took the initiative for village development in later years, was one of the leaders of this youth group.

Formation of the Village Development Council

The 1981 elections of the village *panchayat* were the first in a decade; the CPI (ML-ND) won eight of the 11 ward seats. CPI (ML-ND) member Rayala Nageswara Rao was elected as the president of the village *panchayat* in 1981.[5] Soon after taking the helm, Rayala Nageswara Rao proposed the formation of an unofficial body to take the initiative in development projects in the village instead of relying on the official self-governing institution (the *panchayat*). This unofficial organization was named the Village Development Council (VDC).

Rayala Nageswara Rao invited political leaders to participate on the VDC, not only from the communist parties but also from the Congress Party, as well as the leaders of social organizations, such as caste group leaders and senior villagers. In the beginning, the VDC had 43 members, 37 of whom were residents of Habitation Pindiprolu. The other six habitations at that time sent one representative each to the VDC. Although the other habitations were represented, the VDC was actually administered by the 37 members from Habitation Pindiprolu, consisting of the representatives of political parties, the major caste groups, social groups such as the youth group, and other villagers, who were expected to serve as advisors.

According to the village leaders, the reasons for forming the VDC instead of using the *panchayat* for village activities were threefold. First, they wanted to avoid the formal rules imposed by the government on any collective activities at the village level. Even before the 1981 election, the village elders had the practice of collecting a concession fee from liquor distributors, which they would then pass to Rayala Nageswara Rao for the common purposes of the village. They feared that the management of this fund would be taken over, or bound by government regulations, if it were transferred to the control of the *panchayat*. Second, the village *panchayat* lacked the funds for development projects, and could not expect to receive enough resources from the government. Third, the VDC was far more representative of the entire village population than the *panchayat*, which had been a forum characterized more by political competition than consensus building for the common good of the village. Moreover, the *panchayat* did not include informal leaders, especially caste leaders. In Pindiprolu, caste councils still played an important consultative and arbitrating role among caste members. Indeed, the representatives from caste groups reported on VDC meetings to their caste members.

Revenue Procurement through Concessions

Even with this new unofficial institution for village development projects, the village faced a shortage of resources to implement development projects. Panchayat Pindiprolu was not exceptional among the villages of India in this regard. Since its establishment in 1959, it had faced a perennial shortfall in funding from the government and was limited in its ability to levy or raise taxes from the villagers.

The first and most effective effort at fundraising by the village began in 1982, when the VDC tried to impose a concession fee upon liquor distributors who wanted to do business in their village. As noted earlier, liquor was sold under an agreement with the village until 1981, with the village receiving a fee from the distributor or contactor. However, the government changed the system in 1982, allowing a bidding system, through which the winning bidder at the district level could then monopolize the sale of liquor throughout the district. The distributor would then raise the retail price of liquor, thereby gaining a significant profit. The leadership of Village Pindiprolu took note of this, and acted to claim a part of the economic rent gained by the distributor. The VDC demanded that: (1) the price of the liquor could only be raised in consultation with the VDC; and (2) the liquor distributor must contribute to the village development fund. The distributor did not abide by these demands, so the villagers began a boycott of liquor that lasted for 79 days in 1982. The distributor tried to open shops in the village with the help of police and its own private hood-lums, but was not successful. Eventually, the liquor seller accepted the two conditions of the VDC.

Since then, a new distributor had come almost every year to sell liquor, causing the Pindiprolu people to continue their relentless protest against undue price increases. In 1991, such a disagreement went on for three months, and again, the distributor acquiesced to the demands of the village. This mechanism for revenue procurement from the liquor distribu-tor continued until 1993, when the state government prohibited the sale of liquor in Andhra Pradesh. Subsequently, the VDC lost its source of revenue from liquor sales.

In order for this arrangement to have been effective and successful as a means of obtaining revenue to apply to village development projects, the leaders of the VDC of Pindiprolu had to hold some power or influence over not only the outsiders (the liquor distributors) but also the villagers; otherwise, the boycott would not have been effective. It was necessary for the VDC to mobilize the villagers for collective action, and convince them not to buy liquor for a few months in 1982 and 1991. The VDC could rely on the CPI (ML-ND), which had been prepared to use force for their own struggle in the past, to resort to the use of pressure on any villagers who did not adhere to the boycott. Indeed, the villagers felt that corporal punishment would possibly be applied against non-adherents. Although this did not actually happen, one villager received a threat from the village leadership when he prepared to sell liquor in his shop.

Once the liquor fees were no longer a source of revenue, the village administration found new sources of income, such as rent collected from merchants who used the market place and shop buildings within the village domain. However, since the market place was a public domain and the shop building was built by government subsidy to the village *panchayat*, the rent related to their use by merchants was incorporated into the village *panchayat*'s budget, after 1993.

Village Development through Public Works

Since 1981, several development activities have been initiated in Pindiprolu. These activities have been implemented generally through a strategy of co-production, with partnership between the VDC and the village *panchayat* or with the support of the government at higher levels. The co-production strategy was mostly related to the purchase of sites for proposed buildings and structures related to important public facilities such as building space for the *panchayat*, the Primary Agricultural Credit Society (PACS), and women's organizations, schools, a junior college, a health sub-center, and a veterinary hospital. Once sites were purchased through local efforts, the *panchayat* and the VDC sought finances from the government at higher levels for the buildings and structures, through "matching funds." In the case of the junior college, for instance, not only was the land purchased but also the required buildings constructed entirely through VDC funds. The VDC also met expenditures for the maintenance of the teaching staff for the first four years. Table 7.1 shows the variety of infrastructures formed in the village and their funding sources. The VDC contributed nearly 40 percent of total expenditure while the village *panchayat* provided less than 2 percent during the period 1981–1993.

After 1994, even though the VDC reduced its role in providing funding, it still worked in tandem with the village *panchayat* for bringing government funds in for development activities. For example, for the development of a water system, the VDC paid 250000 INR (Indian rupees), and the *panchayat* requested a government subsidy of around 2.5 million INR.

Other Collective Actions of Pindiprolu Villagers

Compared with its prominent role in asset formation and fundraising, the VDC played a limited role in organizing villagers. Since the 1980s, Pindiprolu villagers have been persuaded by the government to form women's Self-Help Groups (SHGs), and since the late 1990s, the project has been financially assisted by the World Bank as part of a microfinance scheme. Each group, consisting of 10 to 15 women, collects savings from its members, to lend back to them to establish new self-owned businesses. As many as 42 SHGs had been formed by 2012 in the village, with satisfactory results. However, it was the state-level village development agent, rather than the VDC or the other village organizations, who organized these groups. This field worker contacted village women who might be potential leaders and let them organize trusted women as the members. The village *panchayat* and the VDC did not play any active roles in this process.

Another economic organization that was once active was the credit cooperative known as the Primary Agricultural Credit Society (PACS). Although the PACS has been in existence since 1957, CPI (ML-ND) leaders were elected to the PACS leadership in 1987, resulting in a rapid increase in membership since then. Total membership increased from 503 members in 1987 to 1247 members in 1993, while the number of members from Pindiprolu increased from 350 to 574. The PACS membership expanded beyond the sphere of Pindiprolu and included inhabitants from eight habitations in 1993 (Venkateswarlu 2011, p. 94). This co-operative was not based on any village organizations of Pindiprolu. It finally

Table 7.1 Expenditure on different community assets and VDC share in village panchayat of Pindiprolu, 1981–93 (unit: Indian Rupees (INR))

Serial No.	Item	Total	Government	Panchayat	Village Development Council
1	Junior College site and Buildings	1 240 000	250 000	0	990 000
2	School Buildings and Amenities	383 000	305 000	0	78 000
3	Internal Roads	545 841	165 841	67 000	313 000
4	*Panchayat* Building and Furnishings	359 712	96 212	0	263 500
5	Drainage Canals	297 736	287 736	0	10 000
6	New Electric Transformers and Street Lighting[1]	118 000	0	0	118 000
7	Drinking Water Schemes	844 000	830 000	0	14 000
8	Irrigation Schemes for Scheduled Castes	720 000	720 000	0	0
9	Health Sub-Centre Site and Building	172 000	140 000	0	32 000
10	PACS Godown Site and Buildings	193 000	135 000	0	58 000
11	Veterinary Hospital Site and Building	78 520	78 520	0	0
12	Village Deity Expenditure	5 000	0	0	5 000
13	Village Bullock and Male-Buffaloes Maintenance	20 000	0	0	20 000
14	Cattle Pound Site	22 400	0	0	22 400
15	Women's Association Building Deposit	10 000	0	0	10 000
16	Community Latrines	45 724	45 724	0	0
17	Mini Shopping Complex	55 088	55 088	0	0
18	Bus Shelter	80 000	80 000	0	0
19	Scheduled Tribe (ST) Housing Colony Deposit	20 000	0	0	20 000
	Total Expenditure	5 210 021	3 189 121	67 000	1 953 900
	Share of Each Source (%)	100.0	61.2	1.3	37.5

Note: (1) Some materials were provided by the government.

Source: Venkateswarlu (2011, pp. 73–85).

stopped lending money after 1993 to the members who were at default, when repayment defaults became serious.

There were also other women's organizations and youth organizations in the village that were active at one time or another. However, these were organized along political party lines, and their activities were guided or directed by the party policies. In addition, villagers sometimes gathered informally to voice their concerns to the government, but such gatherings were usually initiated by communist leaders, rather than the VDC.

OTHER CASE STUDIES OF VILLAGE COMMON FUND AND VILLAGE ADMINISTRATION

The case of Pindiprolu is not exceptional in South India. Another village institution very similar to the VDC of Pindiprolu as a resource procurement mechanism for public interest was also observed in the other villages we surveyed in 2012.

The Case of Village Karimaddela (Kottapalle)

Karimaddela in Andhra Pradesh is the village that Robert Wade studied in the early 1980s, which he reported as the case of Kottapalle (Wade 1988). In 2012, this village functions as a habitation, and at the same time, a single-village *panchayat*. It has a long history of an active village council, discussed by Wade in his book. The village council is an unofficial institution functioning as the body for self-governance along with the village *panchayat*. The local name for the village council is *grama peddala mandali* or *grama peddalu* (*grama* means village, *peddalu* means elderly people, and *mandali* means council). From its local name, it can be deduced that the village council might have originally been a council of elders. However, these days, the members of the council are not necessarily senior villagers, as five out of the eight members were below 50 years old in 2012. As for the caste composition, six of the eight belong to Reddy caste, an upper caste, while two are from a backward caste (BC). The upper caste representatives take the majority in the council, even though the household numbers of upper caste and backward caste are about 200 and 500, respectively, among the 1120 total households of this village. The candidates for council members are recommended by senior villagers and approved in the entire village meeting. Since the village council manages the village fund for various activities, it has a bank account. However, the account is in the name of an individual villager since the council is not a legal body. Although the village council is formed by the landed class in the village, the council works most of the time for the benefit of overall village development, using the surpluses of the village fund.

Even though the village council is an unofficial institution, its activities for the common benefit of the villagers are remarkable. The council actively increases the fund by tapping into some of the profit from the villagers' economic activities. Wade reported in detail about the example of the concession given to shepherds who came to the village and left their sheep in the fields after harvest. The village council opened a bidding system among the shepherds for the right to do this, and took the winning bid amount for the village fund. The shepherds would be repaid their money from the farmers who would pay them to have the sheep in their fields.[6]

Another source of village funding reported by Wade is the fee paid by the landowners for water allocation to their paddy fields in the form of rice, 10 kg per acre. To manage the irrigation water supply, the village council hired 17 common irrigators and one supervisor, paying them wages in the form of rice for their work of allocating water to each paddy plot in the territory of Karimaddela. Whatever surplus exists after the payment of wages goes to the village fund. To pre-empt the issue of possible temptation to draw more water than allowed, the landowners themselves are not allowed to visit the place of water allocation. The villagers do not rely on mutual control and collaboration with regard to irrigation, so that they take the strategy to hire workers for this task.

The third source of funding, which was introduced after Wade's village survey, is the practice of collecting fees on the sale of agricultural produce. Each year, the council holds an auction and chooses the highest bidder, who pays the quoted price to the village council and weighs farm products with his own weighing machines when village farmers sell their products to merchants at a rate determined by the council. This practice was introduced in the last 30 years, when the village needed new sources of income for infrastructure development such as road maintenance.

While these were the main sources of village funds in 2012, Wade also reported that the liquor franchise was another important funding source in the years that he surveyed. From his description (ibid., pp. 104–105), we learn that Village Karimaddela used the same tactic as that of Village Pindiprolu, collecting fees from the liquor distributor, although later on, this revenue source might be discontinued, as it was in the case of Pindiprolu. In this way, Village Karimaddela found a source of village funding according to changing opportunities in the village.

The villagers said they were obliged to follow the rules that were agreed to in the village council and supported by the majority of villagers, even if they were not satisfied with the agreement. Wade wrote that there was little sense of the village as an entity, and villagers had only a weak sense of morally motivated obedience to the village organization. At the same time, however, he found that, "The council's superordinate position is seen in the fact that it both makes policies and enforces them, wielding substantial and specific sanctions in support of its decisions once arrived at" (ibid., p. 133). Wade's observation suggests that this South Indian village is effectively equipped with institutions for enforcing collective agreement.

Generally, the village fund is used for both public services and public works. In addition to managing irrigation workers, the village council also hired four field guards for nine months, paying wages in cash. These field guards have various tasks: preventing stray cows from entering fields, keeping watch on farmers to prevent them from moving animal dung from the others' fields to their own, and preventing crop thefts. Another type of guardsman, the "total field guard," was hired to be responsible for preventing theft in any part of the village territory. The management of irrigation is another public service provided by the village council, which we have already described.

The village council also looks into the requirements of the village public works and the formation of important community assets. In the last few years, the council took care of repairs of the village's internal roads whenever urgent repairs were required, using mud on the roads. It also used funds for the repairs of the *gramasavidi*, the village council office. Other important construction activities included reconstruction of the temple and the purchase of a site for the high school. In the case of the temple building's reconstruction, the council collected donations and used them to draw matching funding from a religious funding agency. For the school, the council purchased 3 acres of land and received a matching grant from the government for the construction of the school building. According to the village leaders, the village *panchayat* is short of funds for public works, so the village council took the initiative. The *panchayat* building collapsed several years ago, but work to reconstruct it has not yet started, and the reconstruction site remains vacant, symbolic of the low regard the villagers hold for the *panchayat*, the official local self-government body. As Wade describes it, the *panchayat* is the institution only for government works, while the village council, invisible to the state, is concerned with village betterment (ibid., pp.106–107).

The Case of Village Gangadevipalli

Gangadevipalli is another Andhra Pradesh village that has a Village Development Council (VDC) acting as the headquarters of village development activities. Gangadevipalli was once a habitation in the Panchayat

Village of Matchapur, and became an independent *panchayat* village in 1994 (Gangadevipally Village 2010, p. 15). In 2012, this village included about 280 houses and 370 families, of which three are from forward castes, ten from a scheduled caste, and the rest from backward castes and a Muslim family. There is no village temple, but there are some village-level festivals.

From 1952 to 1972, there was a conflict with the main village of Panchayat Matchapur about the land allocation, which was the main reason the Gangadevipalli people wished to separate their habitation from Panchayat Matchapur. After the dispute was settled, there remained internal problems about the method of dispute arbitration. There was no village council in this village to serve this purpose; the customary means of resolving disputes was that caste leaders accepted a deposit from those who voiced a grievance, and then made a judgment. However, these caste leaders tended to spend the deposited money for their own purposes, and did not award it to the damaged party, who should have received the money as compensation.

Koosam Rajamouli, a youth group leader, formed a new committee for their habitation, Gangadevipalli, for arbitration and invited a respected villager to serve as the chairman. This new committee took its task of conflict arbitration seriously, and did not use the deposited money for its own benefit. Understandably, the villagers preferred to rely on the new committee, rather than the old one, and put their trust in Rajamouli. This committee could keep some of the deposited money as a fund for some public works, such as purchasing electric bulbs for street lights, repairing roads, and digging wells in the village.

From 1982 to 1985, there was a Communist Party campaign in Andhra Pradesh against drinking liquor; Rajamouli convinced his fellow villagers to join in the campaign. Although the villagers did not prohibit the drinking of liquor, they did not permit its sale within the village and its vicinity. The village showed some sort of unified action against the offender. Reportedly, a villager who prepared to make liquor sales during this time was forced to walk around the village with a liquor distillation pot on his head, as severe social punishment.

After the success of the anti-liquor campaign, Rajamouli proposed that the villagers establish a VDC in 1985. Consensus was reached in a village meeting, and 11 members were elected in the meeting, including Rajamouli as the VDC chairman. Since Gangadevipalli was a habitation, there was no formal or governmental institution for its self-administration. Village affairs had been discussed by caste leaders up to this point. With the establishment of its VDC, the village had a formal, albeit unofficial, institution for collective decision making for village development.

In Gangadevipalli, there were many problems concerning drinking water. The VDC first addressed this in 1993; Rajamouli identified a non-governmental organization (NGO) that was willing to subsidize the building of a tank for drinking water. He sought the help of the NGO for the implementation of this project in his village. The NGO imposed a condition that 15 percent of the total project funds should come from the villagers. To mobilize these funds, Rajamouli held several meetings and personally convinced several people through individual meetings. A water committee was formed under the leadership of Rajamouli. Eventually, it was decided that 1000 INR could be collected from each household that wanted a tap connection, and also that each household would be required to contribute some labor in the construction and management of the overhead tank. In the end, 65 villagers participated in the project, and the village received the subsidy from the NGO. In the same manner, the village constructed another water tank in 1998. The water committee collected fees from the water users. There was a tacit agreement that the surplus revenue of the water committee could be used for the benefit of the entire village. Indeed, the funds generated from drinking water projects have been used for village development activities since 2004, such as the purchase of land for a temple, the construction of an office for the water committee, and the purchase of land for a veterinary hospital, as well as for providing other services in the village. The total expenditure amounted to about 123 500 INR with a surplus of 350 000 INR by July 2010.

After the water committee was formed, the villagers created other new committees to meet specific needs, such as public health, microfinance, entertainment, and environmental conservation. In 2004, the village established a coordination committee, which took over the role of the VDC in coordinating various activities in the village. In 2009, the village formed the internal audit committee to check the accounting of every committee in the village, since some of them, such as the water committee, dealt with funds. There were 20 committees in the village as of 2012.

As mentioned before, Gangadevipalli became a *panchayat* village, the official administrative body, in 1994. As a result, it now has formal local administrative bodies such as the *gramsabha*, or the village assembly, for collective decision-making by direct participation of villagers. By law, the *gramsabha* must be held a certain number of times a year, during the daytime, and most of its agenda items are predetermined by the government. This does not provide a convenient or direct manner for the villagers to discuss their local needs or issues. Therefore, the village organized another assembly called the *sadharana gramasabha* (general village assembly), which is held in the evening, for the convenience of villagers. The agenda is determined by the needs of the villagers. For example, in one meeting, the villagers discussed a silt-dredging project proposed by the government. Since the cost of dredging could not be covered by the government budget, the villagers discussed whether it was appropriate to require the owners of the land where the silt was disposed of to pay a fee, since the silt would make their land more fertile.

The various committees, which are a unique village development strategy, have never been under the village *panchayat* administration. Rajamouli first became *panchayat* president in 2006, so he chaired only the coordination committee and water committee.[7] If the committees were to be put under the authority of the village *panchayat*, the *panchayat* president would be required to represent every committee, according to government regulation. Rajamouli's opinion is that such a regulation does not promote independent and creative activities on the part of these committees.

CONCLUSION

We summarize the salient features of the collective activities observed in the three Southern Indian villages studied as follows. First, in all three cases, the villagers secured financial resources at the village level and pooled them into a common village fund. Second, the resources were obtained by tapping the profits gained from economic transactions between villagers and outsiders (in the cases of Pindiprolu and Karimaddela), or by charging fees to the villagers who received services from the village (in the case of Gangadevipalli). In other words, the village claimed a portion of the economic rent that individuals gained, under the condition that the village monopolized certain economic transactions. Third, the procured resources are managed and utilized by the decision of the village leaders for the benefit of the entire village, that is, for public works and public services. In our three case examples, it appears that the village shows its talent in the securing of collective resources rather than in mobilizing its people into collective action. For example, in Village Karimaddela, the village raised a fund and hired workers for the task of water allocation and field watch, rather than calling the villagers to perform those tasks for the common good.

These collective actions are based on the local social systems, which have the following characteristics. First, the natural village or habitation is the locality group that functioned as the host organization of the collective actions. Wade (1988, p. 57) asserted that the sense of loyalty to the village or the sense of assuming the village as an entity could not be observed in his survey village (Karimaddela) and the other Indian villages. Indeed, the villagers are socially divided into castes. There were political conflicts between political parties and groups, as seen in Pindiprolu. The field guards and common irrigators in Village Karimaddela were necessary, because the villagers did not trust each other. The assertion of Wade may be true, but at the same time, there appears to be the common idea among local people that the habitation, rather than the *panchayat* village, is the unit for organizing collective actions.

However, note that the habitation does not have an institution for self-administration. Even in the case where the *panchayat* village overlaps a single habitation, such as in Karimaddela and Gangadevipalli, the institutions of *panchayat* do not effectively facilitate the collective actions of villagers for their own needs. We found that the *panchayat* president of Gangadevipalli institutionalized an unofficial village assembly to perform public works and services, while the *panchayat* building had been left abandoned and in disrepair in Village Karimaddella. In this setting, where local people lack the institutions for self-administration, the villagers formed an unofficial local group, a VDC, or utilized the existing village council as the platform for development activities. This is the second important feature of local social systems, which we found in the three case villages.

Third, there appears to be some kind of social mechanism that encourages villagers to comply with a village-level agreement. As we have seen in the case studies, the villagers of Pindiprolu knew that corporal punishment was a possibility if they did not abide by the liquor boycott, and they saw a villager receive a threat from the village leadership. In Village Gangadevipalli, an offender against the village agreement regarding liquor sale prohibition was forced to walk around the village with a liquor distillation pot on his head. If there had been no social mechanism for enforcement, the liquor boycott in Pindiprolu and Gangadevipalli would not have succeeded. Fee collection from farmers in Karimaddela would not have been possible unless the village had some form of authority to enforce compliance among the farmers. Indeed, the villagers of Karimaddela expressed the feeling that they were obliged to follow the consensus of the village council. Wade's observation of this village in the 1980s supports this claim as well. Although there seems to be little sense of community in the villages of India, as Wade stated, this social pressure appears to be successful in discouraging disobedience to the collective will.

Regarding this point, the hierarchical social structure of villages may be evaluated now in a different light than the conventional understanding seen in community development literature. In Indian villages, the informal authority given to the leaders may be key to the extent of their power to control villagers in resource procurement activities.

Given these observations and conclusions, some comments on rural development policies and practices in India are possible. Proposing asset formation type projects, or public works projects that require the securing of financial resources, through the habitation rather than through the village *panchayat* may receive a more positive response from the residents.[8] With regard to this point, the matching grant system, which has been widely practiced in India, is to be appreciated. However, since the habitation is not officially empowered to administer resource procurement, there remains a need for establishing a more formal institution to be the platform of collective actions for village development.

ACKNOWLEDGEMENT

We express deep gratitude to the late Dr G.K. Chadha, the former President of South Asian University in New Delhi, for his advice on our rural studies in India.

NOTES

1. In India, a rural area is defined in terms of what is not an urban area. Then, the problem arises as to what is an urban area. The approximate definition of an urban unit since the 1971 Census has been as follows: (a) all places with a municipality, corporation, cantonment board, or notified town area committee, and so on; (b) all other places that satisfied the following criteria: (i) a minimum population of 5000; (ii) at least 75 percent of the male working population engaged in non-agricultural pursuits; and (iii) a population density of at least 400 per sq. km. Thus, in India, an area that fails to satisfy one of the above criteria is to be treated as rural area. The rural area is composed of villages.
2. The *panchayat* was also called *gram sabha*.
3. This committee was the Balwant Rai Mehta Committee appointed by the government of India in January 1957. It submitted its report in November 1957, suggesting the decentralization of local rural self-government into three tiers via the village *panchayat*, block *panchayat*, and district *panchayat*, based on elections. Implementation began in 1959. However, by 1985 the block was divided into a few *mandals* in Andhra Pradesh. So now the village *panchayat*, mandal *panchayat*, and district *panchayat* comprise the three tiers.
4. A new party gained a presence in the village in 1982, the Telugu Desam Party (TDP).
5. Rayala Nageswara Rao of CPI (ML-ND) assumed presidentship of the Panchayat of Pindiprolu successively in the 1981 and 1988 elections. After reservation for presidentship became mandatory, in the 1995, 2001 and 2006 *panchayat* elections, Rayala Nageswara Rao had to yield to backward class male, scheduled caste male, and backward caste female candidates, respectively, all of whom were members of the CPI (ML-ND). Rayala Nageswara Rao has nevertheless been active as village headman, and is also the chairman of the VDC.
6. From the date of allowing sheep folding, 60 days will be the total period of folding. For example if four shepherds are chosen and if each shepherd can fold sheep in a field for four days, then each shepherd can fold sheep in the fields of 15 farmers. Thus, all four shepherds can fold sheep in 60 farmers' fields in a year. The shepherds get back their money from the farmers, who want to have the sheep folded in their fields. But there will be competition among the farmers for the sheep folding. So every four days, there will be

bidding for the sheep folding among the farmers of the village. On every bidding day, four farmers will be selected, based on the highest bidding. Thus, the shepherds get back what they pay to the village council, sometimes more than what they paid to the village council.

7.   When the first *panchayat* was elected in 1995 (after the separate *panchayat* of Gangadevipalli was formed in 1994), it was unanimously resolved by the villagers that all *panchayat* members would be elected from among women only, as if the *panchayat* is reserved completely for women, though this practice is not mandatory. In the 1995 and 2001 *panchayat* elections, the wife of Rajamouli was elected as president of village *panchayat* of Gangadevipalli for two successive terms. Thus, Rajamouli could assume presidentship in the 2006 *panchayat* elections.

8.   Recently, the government of India has begun to consider habitation level as important for certain development activities. In the Fifteenth Meeting of the National Advisory Council of India held on July 28, 2011 in New Delhi, it was suggested that the works or projects to be undertaken at the local level should be planned in the context of "natural village or hamlet" basis rather than using the existing pattern of undertaking works on the basis of revenue villages (*Indian Express* 2011). In 2000, the Prime Minister's Rural Roads Programme under the Ministry of Rural Development decided that the unit for the program of building rural roads in India is a habitation, and not a revenue village or *panchayat* (http://www.worldbank.org/sartransport).

REFERENCES

Agrawal, Arun and Clark C. Gibson (1999), "Enchantment and disenchantment: The role of community in natural resource conservation," *World Development*, 27(4), pp. 629–649.

Dandekar, V.M. and Nilakanth Rath (1971), "Poverty in India," *Economic and Political Weekly*, 6(2), pp. 106–146.

Dhanagare, D.N. (1981), "Social origins of the peasant insurrection in Telangana (1946–51)," in A.R. Desai (ed.), *Peasant Struggles in India*, Delhi: Oxford University Press, pp. 486–516.

Gangadevipally Village (2010), "A case study on Gangadevipally: A model village," paper submitted for National Seminar on Building of Model Villages through Panchayat Raj Institutions, July.

Ghatak, Maitreesh and Maitreya Ghatak (2002), "Recent reforms in the panchayat system in West Bengal: Toward greater participatory governance?," *Economic and Political Weekly*, 37(1), pp. 45–58.

Guru, Gopal (2009), "Caste and contemporary India – Closing Plenary Session," Caste and Contemporary India conference, October 17, Columbia University, video available at http://www.academicroom.com/video/caste-and-contemporary-india-conference-day-2-closing-plenary-session.

Holdcroft, Lane E. (1978), "The rise and fall of community development in developing countries, 1950–65: A critical analysis and an annotated bibliography," MSU Rural Development Paper No.2, East Lansing, MI: Michigan State University.

Indian Express (2011), "Plan NREGS works at hamlet level: NAC," July 29.

Krishna, Anirudh (2002), *Active Social Capital: Tracing the Roots of Development and Democracy*, New York: Columbia University Press.

Kroeber, A.L. (1930), "Caste," *Encyclopedia of the Social Sciences, Volume 3*, New York: Macmillan, pp. 254–257.

Madan, G.R. (1990), *India's Developing Villages*, Bombay: Allied Publishers.

Mallik, S.N. (1929), "Local self-government in India", *Annals of the American Academy of Political and Social Science*, 145, Part 2: India (September), pp. 36–44.

Marriot, McKim (1955), *Village India: Studies in the Little Community*, Chicago, IL: Chicago University Press.

Matthai, John (1915), *Village Government in British India*, London: T. Fisher Unwin.

Nath, Vishwambhar (2010), *Rural Development and Planning in India*, New Delhi: Concept Publishing.

Ramesh, Chauhan (2011), "The structure of Gram Panchayat in ancient India," *Shodh, Samiksha and Mulyankan*, 13(33), pp. 12–13.

Sharma, Rashmi (2009), *Local Government in India: Policy and Practice, With Special Reference to a Field Study of Decentralizatiton in Kerala*, New Delhi: Manohar.

Singh, V.B. (1981), "Village community", in V.B. Singh (ed.), *Economic History of India: 1857–1956*, New Delhi: Allied Publishers, pp. 88–103.

Srinivas, M.N. (1989 [1962]), *Caste in Modern India*, Bombay: Media Promoters & Publishers.

Srinivas, M.N. (2002), "The Indian village: Myth and reality," in Vandana Madan (ed.), *The Village in India*, New Delhi: Oxford University Press, pp. 51–70.

Thirumali, Inukonda (1992), "Dora and Gadi: Manifestation of landlord domination in Telangana," *Economic and Political Weekly*, 27(9), pp. 471–482.

Venkateswarlu, Akina (2011), *The Role of Village Panchayats and Village Development Councils in Rural Development*, Delhi: Abhijeet Publications.

Wade, Robert (1988), *Village Republics: Economic Conditions for Collective Action in South India*, Cambridge: Cambridge University Press.

Yogo, Toshihiro (1986), "Research proposal on self-organization capability of local communities," mimeo, Nagoya: United Nations Centre for Regional Development.

8. Communal resource-driven rural development: the salient feature of organizational activities in Chinese villages

Nanae Yamada

INTRODUCTION

It has long been said that it is hard to find any unity or cohesion except for kinship and bilateral networks in Chinese society. Sun Yat-sen indicated insightfully in his *Three Principles of the People* in the early 1900s that Chinese people were separated like grains of sand, with no source of cohesion except for family and kinship (Sun 1989). Famous sociologist Shaotong Fei indicated that Chinese rural society was a collection of elastic, bilateral relations called *guanxi*. A series of rural investigations mainly conducted in the North China Plain by the Japanese South Manchuria Railway Research Department before World War II did not reveal any strongly tied territorial communities like those seen in German and Japanese villages (Hatada 1973). Collective actions observed in rural China are not an expression of the unity of the village community but merely an aggregation of market-oriented, rational people who are tied by common necessity or interests (Suga 2009). Chinese society is the web of personal network that consists of individual, bilateral relations and groups of individuals that appear fluidly and flexibly from time to time (Tahara 2006).

In the people's commune era in the 1950s to 1970s, members of people's communes were compelled to be organized by order and enforcement. After the dismantling of the people's commune system in the early 1980s, it seems that the rural society returned to what it used to be, in which there was no integration and unity among local residents, but only bilateral networks and market transactions (He 2002; Ako 2010). Since then, it has crucially been required to establish new popular organizations at the village level to supply administrative and public services for local residents, though a series of such efforts have not been successful. The establishment of village committees at the administrative village level in the 1980s was one of the first institutional experiments for such purposes. Three decades after the introduction of village autonomy, some scholars make the criticism that the ability of village committees to provide public services is too limited, while others say that trust in leaders has declined because of nepotism and corruption (Takida 2009). In fact, as the capabilities of village committees were limited, the central government has strongly encouraged the establishment of some "participatory" development organizations for rural development since the mid-1980s, including financial organizations, agricultural co-operatives called Farmers' Professional Associations (FPAs for short), and water users' associations, some of which were initiated by international organizations (Plummer and Taylor 2004). Yet, most such existing organizations were initiated under strong pressure from local government, and the abilities of these private organizations are still too weak for them to operate independently of government involvement. Some are exclusively on-paper organizations, only appearing on the registration list of the government.[1] To understand the causes of such failure to organize people it is helpful to examine the nature of Chinese rural society as background.

The objective of this chapter is to clarify the functions of Chinese rural society by extracting some patterns of collective action or popular participation observed in the management of communal resources owned by rural collectives – administrative villages, and village groups – therein through case studies. As addressed above, in Chinese villages there is scarce "popular participation" in terms of its usual meaning, which is generally associated with equal commitment by a group of organized, homogenous people in decision-making and cost-sharing processes for the common purpose; but this does not mean there are no collective actions in China at all. In post-Maoist China, the rural collectives have legal ownership over rural resources such as land, forests, and irrigation facilities, and such communal resources need collective decision-making for their management.[2] There are some remarkable discussions on the origin of such collective assets. At the beginning of the collective farming era, private assets including land, agricultural tools, and livestock were compulsorily accumulated at the village level and such collections of assets were called "collectives," which generated clear boundaries among villages (Sasaki and Karasawa 2003, p. 336), although before 1949 the boundaries of villages were not clear in China (Hatada 1973). That means that Chinese villages are created by such collected assets; assets of collectives are not created by villages (Takida 2005).

By detailed observation, I found that local villagers participate in the decision-making of who manages the communal resources and how, and this style of participation reflects the nature of the local society. It is generally believed that "cooperation" or "collective action" is generated among a group of homogenous people on a voluntary basis, but in present-day China popular participation is more likely to occur under the strong initiative of a trustworthy leader who encourages people to take part (Tahara 2009). This hypothesis seems to be reliable due to the fact that powerful leaders often have sole discretion over resources of a certain size in China. For instance, FPAs are led by leaders of local administrative organizations, local elites, or merchants, while local residents have limited commitment to them (Fock and Zachernuk 2006). Some scholars also point out that there is a strong relationship between the size of the common property and the strength of the social network among the members of the collective (Kato 1995; Tahara 2006).[3]

This chapter will analyze two case areas: one from the North China Plain and another from the Yangtze River Delta in southern China. The reason for choosing these two areas is that the socio-economic and natural conditions and village structures are completely different between the northern and southern banks of the Yangtze River; therefore, it is likely that these two cases may provide a clear contrast of the collective actions in the different local contexts. I do not intend to generalize upon the characteristics of Chinese rural society, nor to extract all types of it, but this chapter will try to understand the capability of local society better by focusing on the style of communal resource management.

The contents of this chapter are as follows. The following section introduces the basic structure of Chinese rural administrative organizations and related institutions in the post-Maoist era. It gives an overview of the change in the local administrative hierarchy, distribution of rural resources, and grassroots-level institutions in the post-Maoist era. The chapter then describes the case studies performed in two areas. I focus on how collective members participate in the communal resource management; in effect, who performs the management, which methods are used, and how the profit is distributed among the concerned parties. I present two principal types of resource management: land shareholding co-operatives in the North China Plain, and bilateral contracts in the Yangtze River Delta. Administrative villages and village groups play crucial roles in resource management and coordination, but in different styles according to the regions.[4]

THE STRUCTURE OF RURAL ADMINISTRATIVE ORGANIZATIONS AND INSTITUTIONS IN THE POST-MAOIST ERA

Organizational Structure and Resource Distribution

Figure 8.1 shows the structures of administrative and autonomous organizations after the early 1980s. China has a five-tiered administrative hierarchy with central government at the top, followed by the provincial, district, prefecture, and township levels, in that order. The organizations below the township level are sometimes termed "rural grassroots" organizations.

In 1982, the revised National Constitution formally regulated that newly founded township governments, village committees, and village groups would replace the former people's communes, production brigades, and production teams, respectively, as grassroots autonomous organizations (Yan 1995: p. 216). Each administrative village has a village committee and a branch of the Chinese Communist Party. In the Maoist era, the production team was both the basic labor unit and the owner of the farmland. In the post-Maoist era, the individual household became the basic unit of production, and the village group (the former production team) became a sub-organization of the administrative village. In the northern region, the production team was reorganized into the village group, but with different membership and boundaries, and land rights were concentrated in the administrative village; while in the southern region, property rights were directly transferred to the new village group. In general, one administrative village includes several tens to several hundreds of households, while a village group includes several tens of households.

The scale, scope, and geographic relation between natural village and village group vary from region to region according to population: some village groups correspond to natural villages, while others include multiple natural villages, and vice versa. A natural village in northern China usually includes multiple families and is larger in size than those in southern China, so most administrative villages there include one or two natural villages. Population fluidity has traditionally been greater in northern China than in the south. Many areas in the North China Plain, including the present-day Beijing, Hebei, and Shandong Provinces, originated with migrants from other areas after the Ming Dynasty, whereby several migrant families formed one natural village; this made the size of natural villages larger in those areas.[5]

In contrast, in southern China, a natural village has a smaller population, in many cases consisting of single kinship; in most such cases, one administrative village includes multiple natural villages. In the Yangtze

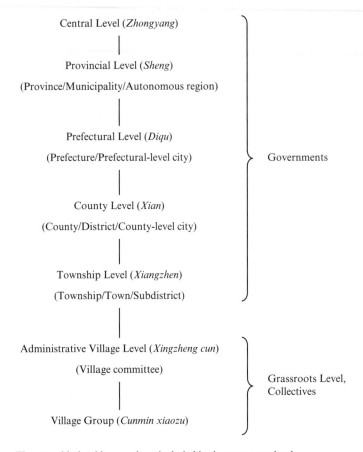

Note: The township level is sometimes included in the grassroots level.

Figure 8.1   Hierarchy of the administrative divisions of the PRC in the post-Maoist era (since the 1980s)

River Delta, the boundaries of the natural villages and their farmland were fixed as early as the Land Revolution of the early 1950s, and they have remained almost the same until today. Even in the Maoist era, production teams in this area were organized in terms of membership in natural villages, and this unit was the direct successor to the current village group.

Economic and Financial Institutions

In China, where the formal budget redistribution function is not sufficient, the budget for grassroots activities has basically been kept outside of the formal finance scheme; this means that collectives have to derive profit from some business activities for the provision of public services by considering their endowments of natural resources and other socio-economic conditions, just as an enterprise would.[6] According to Takida (2005), the evaluations of such commercialization of administrative villages by researchers are divided into two types: one is affirmative evaluation based on the observation of successful super-villages which can afford to provide villagers with sufficient public services (Qian and Weingast 1997; Zhe and Chen 2000); other works imply that it often induces nepotism (Liu 2005; Ruf 1998). Rozelle and Li (1998) examined the efficiency of resource management by villages and concluded that the management methods have varied widely from village to village and administrative village leaders tend to behave in such a way as to maximize their private interests and to minimize the administrative cost.

At the end of 1978, the regime shift to the Household Production Responsibility System led to change in the financial system at the grass-roots level. In the post-Maoist era, the major sources of revenue for township governments and administrative villages were taxes and levies from farmers and Township and Village Enterprises (TVEs) (Oi 1992). Besides these taxes and levies, construction of public infrastructure was accomplished through enforced labor by local residents. TVEs were privatized in the late 1990s, and all agricultural taxes and levies on them were finally abolished by 2005 after being phased out in a step-by-step manner.

Especially since the tax reform of the late 1990s, village incomes mostly depend on the management capacity of village leaders. After that reform, administrative villages' main revenue sources have been government subsidies and use fees from common resources. It was decided that administrative village leaders' salaries, and part of a fund for infrastructure construction, would be financed by subsidies; but upper-level government places limits on each type of spending. Therefore, the ability to make profits under such a decentralized financial system depends on factors like resource endowment, geographical conditions, transportation, and the management capacity of administrative village leaders. The income gap among regions – and even among administrative villages within the same region – has expanded in the last three decades. More and more administrative villages have increased their financial dependency on revenue from land leased to enterprises or government, especially in less developed areas.[7] The conversion of farmland to other use has become a more significant source of revenue for local government since the introduction of the tax-sharing system in the mid-1990s. Many local government and administrative village leaders expropriate farmland illegally without the agreement of local residents, and sell the land use rights to real estate developers or industries at high prices.

Land Management System

After the introduction of the Household Production Responsibility System, every household was granted land use rights for individual farming on a contract basis from the collective to which it belonged. Although farmers' land use rights have been strengthened since then, land property rights are still maintained by the collectives (that is, administrative villages or village groups).[8] At the outset of implementation of the Household Production Responsibility System, the central government decided that the land use contract would expire 15 years after 1984. After the expiration of the first contract, many administrative villages have adjusted or redistributed land use rights among households every few years in consideration of the shift in population. The central government was worried that farming productivity might decrease because of land fragmentation via frequent adjustment of land use rights. Thus, the Land Contract Law of 2003 formally strengthened farmers' land use rights through extensions of contract terms and relaxing of the conditions for transactions involving land use rights, such as transfer, borrowing, lending, and inheritance; that notwithstanding, there are still no property rights for farmers. Though farmers' land use rights have been strengthened, the collective still has power over land use. Many disputes involving illegal transfer of farmland among local governments, administrative village leaders, and villagers have been reported.

Decision-Making System

The Organic Law of the Village Committee, which was adopted and announced in 1986 and became effective in 1998, decided the responsibilities and election and conference structures of village committees.[9] The main contents of this law are as follows: first, a village committee consists of three to seven remunerated leading members, including a chairman, a vice chairman, a treasurer, and so on. Second, the leaders should be elected from villagers by direct election every three years; re-election is possible. Appointment and dismissal of the leaders should be done only by election; no organization or individual has the right to appoint, dismiss, or recall leaders. The election should be monitored by the Election Management Committee under principles of transparency, fairness, and justice. Third, the village committee is responsible for conducting a Villagers Representative Conference as the body for decision-making. Important issues like the annual budget, fee collection from villagers, and public projects should be discussed at the Conference.

RESOURCE ENDOWMENT AND MANAGEMENT IN TWO CASE AREAS

Profile of Research Areas

This section will analyze the methods of rural resource management at administrative village level in two regions to understand the mechanisms of popular participation there. The location and a brief profile of research area are shown in Figure 8.2 and in Table 8.1. The first research area is located in Daxing and Chanping Districts in the suburb of Beijing Municipality, less than two hours' drive from Beijing City (site no. 1). The second one is located in Yixing Prefecture, Wuxi City in Jiangsu Province, less than 2 hours' drive from Nanjing and 3½ hours' drive from Shanghai City (site no. 2). Site no. 1 is located in the North China Plain region, whereas site no. 2 is located in the Yangtze River Delta, which is known as one of the most industrialized regions in China; its development model was dubbed the "Sunan model," in which local, collectively owned TVEs played a key role. In these two sites, farmers' per capita income is more than 10 000 RMB, a comparatively high level for China. The survey was implemented by myself in one-to-one interviews with administrative village leaders and villagers.[10]

As for farming in these sites, the climate in site no. 1 is dry and cold; it traditionally thrives via double cropping of wheat and corn using dry-field farming. Farming of greenhouse vegetables targeted for Beijing City, and green tourism in watermelon and peach orchards too, have developed of late. In contrast, because of the temperate and humid climate in site no. 2, farmers mainly engage in paddy agriculture for self-consumption. As most of the farmland in this area is located on a swampy plain with numerous small canals that stretch in meshed patterns, and ponds called *dang* along the coast of nearby Taihu Lake, many farmers have access to inland water fisheries that utilize the rich water resources. In both sites, the majority of the younger generation have gone to large cities for education or work, but the older generation stay in the rural areas and engage in part-time jobs at factories in nearby industrial parks. The influx of migrant labors is large in these areas.

Table 8.2 contains a brief profile of the researched administrative villages in these two sites: three administrative villages from ZZY Township in Daxing District and one administrative village from BS Township in Chanping District in site no. 1; and five administrative villages from three townships – QT, FQ, and HQ – in site no. 2.[11] The populations of the administrative villages in site no. 2 are larger, because the former administrative villages were recently synoecized several times into a larger

Source: Okamoto (2008, p. iii), revised by the author.

Figure 8.2   Location of research area

administrative village. The present QT, SY, and YS were established in the mid-2000s by combining four, two, and three former administrative villages, respectively. In site no. 1, except for ZZ (which was formed by synoecism of five nearby administrative villages in the 1970s), no other administrative villages had experienced annexation.

I now discuss the administrative and autonomous organizations at the grassroots level. Figure 8.3 contains a conceptual map of typical villages in the North China Plain and the Yangtze River Delta. In the targeted villages in site no. 1, the territory and members of natural villages mostly correspond with administrative villages; in contrast, in site no. 2, each

Table 8.1   Basic information on the research areas

Region	Site no. 1 (Beijing Municipality)		Site no. 2 (Jiangsu/Wuxi)
City	Daxing district, Beijing	Chanping district, Beijing	Yixing county, Wuxi city, Jiangsu prov.
Distance from nearest city (by car)	2 hours' drive from Beijing	2 hours' drive from Beijing	2 hours' drive from Nanjing, 3.5 hours from Shanghai
Language	Mandarin	Mandarin	Wu dialect/Mandarin
Living population (× 10 000)	136.5 (2011)	166.5 (2011)	123 (2010)
Rural population (× 10 000)	32.2 (2011)	26.3 (2011)	–
Per capita income	10 103 RMB (2008)	10 102 RMB (2008)	10 267 RMB (2010)
Type of agriculture	Grain production for self-consumption	Grain production for self-consumption	Grain production for self-consumption
Main agricultural products	Wheat, corn, vegetable	Wheat, corn, vegetable	Rice
Fishery, animal husbandry	–	–	Inland water fishery
Population fluidity	High	High	High

administrative village contains multiple natural villages. As stated earlier, the relations between the realms of natural village, administrative village, village group, and the former production team are different between northern and southern China.

The significance of the village group also differs between these two sites. In site no. 1, some villages have never established village groups, and even in those with village groups, several neighboring households are automatically bundled into a village group to facilitate communication. Such village groups have no continuity with former production teams or the farmland owned by the former production team. This means that in site no. 1, the village group is only an artificial unit.

On the other hand, in site no. 2, the membership and scope of farmland managed by the production team has remained the same in the village group. In most cases, one village group consists of one or a

Table 8.2 Profiles of target village

Province/Pref.	Site no. 1 (Beijing Municipality)				Site no. 2 (Jiangsu/Wuxi)				
County/Township	Daxing/ZZY			Changping/BS	Yixing/QT			Yixing/FQ	Yixing/HQ
Administrative Village	ZZ	LB	NF	SZY	QT	SY	BZ	YS	TL
Population	1300	963	1720	–	3126	1150	–	2240	3652
No. of hamlets included	5	1	1	1	25(4)	N.A.(8)	22(4)	N.A.(9)	31(4)
No. of VG	0	0	4	28	38	14	55	25	46
No. of VG Chief	0	0	4	28	38	14	55	25	46
Continuity with PT	No	No	Yes	No	Yes	Yes	Yes	Yes	Yes
No. of PT	–	3	4	–	38	14	55	25	46
Area (mu)	4200	4500	–	–	4347	1800	8000	3669	4710
Farmland area (mu)	2200	1800	4200	2700	2600	1400	4000	3440	3500
Land area expropriated (mu)	0	0	0	0	300	200	–	–	700

Notes:
1. Mu is a Chinese unit of land area. One mu equals one-fifteenth hectare.
2. VG and PT are short names for village group and production team, respectively.
The numbers in the brackets in "No. of hamlets included" express the number of original administrative villages before annexation in the 2000s

Source: Prepared by the author.

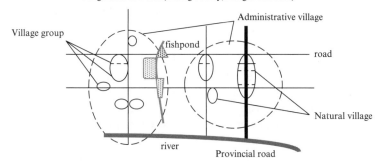

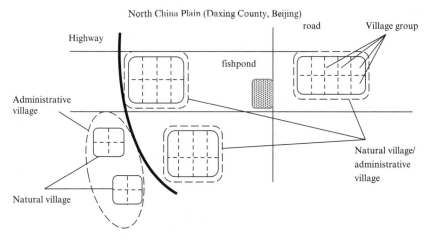

Note: Farmland that belongs to each administrative village or village group is not shown on the map, because for historical reasons, the boundaries of some villages are very complicated and sometimes remote from residences (Kojima 1996; Tahara 1997).

Figure 8.3   Conceptual map of the typical villages in research areas

few group(s) of relatives by which the farmland has been owned since the Land Reform of the 1950s. This means that in this area, the unit of the village group has not experienced dismantling or reorganization since then. In other words, this has always been the most basic social unit in site no. 2, with tight networks of relatives owning resources of land or water facilities, though the unit has changed its name from time to time.

THE RELATIONSHIP BETWEEN THE ADMINISTRATIVE VILLAGE AND THE VILLAGE GROUP IN SOUTHERN CHINA

The relationship between administrative village and the village group in southern China is different from that in northern China. This will be detailed via the example case of the allocation of governmental land compensation in QT (administrative village) in site no. 2.

In site no. 2, the village group plays a key role for decision-making and arbitration of disputes among beneficiaries only in special cases that relate to the interests of its members, although originally, village groups only functioned as mediators for simple administrative tasks.[12] As already mentioned above, in this area there are many opportunities for expropriation of rural land by local government for the purpose of diversion to industrial use. The distribution of compensation from such expropriation is one of the villagers' most significant interests, and the village groups play an important part in making decisions and mediating among interested parties.

The interviews with leaders of the QT Village committee indicated that some village groups in QT had experienced conflicts among members over the sharing of compensation for government land expropriation. Though the expropriated land included plots for which the use rights had been held by members of a village group, the rest of the members were not satisfied with the idea of distributing benefits only among the owners of those land use rights. Through discussions, they agreed that half of the compensation would be distributed according to title to the area of land concerned, while the other half would be distributed equally among all members of the village group. The administrative village did not interfere with the decision-making of village groups if no illegal behavior was found in the process. The administrative village allocated part of the compensation to public construction in the administrative village.

In this case, the village group directly represented its members' interests, while the administrative village played an income-leveling role among village groups through redistribution of pooled funds. In QT Village, there exist economic disparities among village groups because of population mobility, redistribution of estates by marriage, and most significantly, governmental compensation by land expropriation. When a wealthier village group needs to maintain common resources like irrigation facilities, it may collect fees from its beneficiaries. An administrative village may provide subsidies for poorer village groups in such cases, or if support from the administrative village is not sufficient, the village group can apply for a subsidy from upper government.

The Stagnation of Collective Actions Observed in Research Areas

For research areas, I chose four kinds of activities in which collective actions were observed or used to be observed – agricultural production, social mutual aid, security maintenance, and cultural activities – to confirm by field survey whether or not voluntary collective actions currently exist in China, and whether there were any changes in their content and involved parties. Table 8.3 indicates the present situations of these activities or organizations in the researched areas. In fact it shows the scarcity of collective actions in present-day Chinese villages, but it confirms the existence, even if scarce, of villagers' voluntary participation for the common purpose such as FPAs, which will be detailed below.

Agricultural production

The only type of organization observed with regard to farming was FPAs, which were seen in some administrative villages in both sites. The FPAs established in site no. 1 were both land shareholding co-operatives (systems in which participant villagers invest their use rights to land plots as stock). The FPA manages the recollected land just like a shareholding enterprise would. The farmer (that is, stockholder) can be granted dividends from annual profits according to land area invested. In contrast, there are also two FPAs in site no. 2, but they are nominal in nature and do not organize any co-operative activities, even though they are formally registered with the Ministry of Civil Affairs. The cases of FPAs will be elaborated later.

The practice of labor exchange among a few neighboring villagers was generally observed in the North China Plain in the 1930s–1940s (Uchiyama 2003: 111), but in the researched areas, labor exchange among villagers seems to have already disappeared. Fukutake (1946) indicated that this practice did not sustain larger organizations: membership was not stable. He also says that collective actions in farming practice were rare and that employment was more common, even at that time. It is likely that the decline in labor exchange was caused by the spread of agricultural machines. In site no. 1, most farmland is cultivated by FPAs equipped with large-scale agricultural machinery; while in site no. 2, villagers often employ a neighboring farmer equipped with agricultural machinery as such equipment can be found in one farm out of several tens in this area; or they can employ professional contractors from outside for cultivation, harvesting, and other farming practices.[13] Such utilization of machinery by employment or contract is currently widely accepted in China.

Table 8.3 *Present situations of private organizations in researched villages*

Province/Pref.	Site no. 1 (Beijing Municipality)						Site no. 2 (Jiangsu/Wuxi)		
County/Township	Daxing/ZZY			Chanping/BS	Yixing/QT			Yixing/FQ	Yixing/HQ
Administrative village	ZZ	LB	NF	SZY	QT	SY	BZ	YS	TL
Agricultural production									
Farmers cooperatives	No	No	Yes	Yes	No	No	Yes, but nominal	No	Yes, but nominal
Labor exchange	No	No	No	No	No	No	No	No	No
Social mutual aid									
Funeral group	No	Yes	No	No	Yes	Yes	No	N.A.	N.A.
Construction team	No	Yes	No	Yes	Yes	No	N.A.	N.A.	N.A.
Security maintenance	Yes	Yes	Yes	Yes	Yes	Yes	Yes	Yes	Yes
Cultural activities	Yes	Yes	Yes	Yes	Yes	Yes	No	Yes	Yes

Source: Prepared by the author.

Social mutual aid

Among ceremonial functions, only funerals have specific organizations dedicated toward them. Wedding ceremonies are held at hotels or restaurants, with the assistance of private companies. The fees are generally paid by the bridal couple's families. In both sites, there are voluntary groups consisting of members of the older generation that manage everything necessary to the funeral ceremony. Before the 1980s, almost every natural village had a funeral group, and even now, some of the researched administrative villages have funeral groups with several to more than a dozen members.[14] The function of these groups is limited to arranging the ceremony and contacting the people concerned. Funeral groups do not pool any funds for the activity in either research site; all expenditures are usually paid by the bereaved family (or by the administrative village if the bereaved family is too poor to afford the expenditure). The bereaved family often gives special treatment to funeral group members or (in some areas) pays a fee to express gratitude for their assistance.

There used to be construction groups in every production team that helped neighbors to construct houses by offering labor. In site no. 2 during the Maoist era, all the members of the production team offered labor and prepared construction materials when any member built a new house. In the research area, these groups have changed into small-scale private agents that undertake construction in nearby villages. In site no. 2, some powerful agents grew larger and merged with smaller ones or delegated smaller jobs to them, while others have already folded due to severe market competition and currently QT Township in site no. 2 has several hundred construction teams. The construction team has already lost its function of mutual social aid and been totally changed into private enterprises.

Security maintenance

Night guard groups for the purpose of security maintenance were observed in almost all the researched administrative villages. The groups were voluntarily organized at the administrative village level in the 2000s, and the main reason for the establishment of these groups was the increased number of crimes caused by migrant laborers from outside; recently, the government has promoted these groups nationwide. In site no. 1, the members receive allowances, while in site no. 2, they are not paid; in most cases in the latter site, the chiefs of the village groups take over the post, because fewer and fewer villagers volunteer.

The differences between these and the night guards that existed in the pre-war period in the North China Plain (called *kanqing* and *dageng*) are: (1) the former night guard mainly watched farmland to protect the crops before harvest, while the present one watches only residents to avoid

property theft; (2) the former night guards were people from poorer families, or strong thugs or rogues in the village, who were hired by landlords to
protect their private property, while the present ones are voluntary groups
of villagers who protect the security of the residential area. There are no
night-watch activities for farmland any more, except for some orchards
containing high-value crops, as crop values are generally very low, and
most residents now depend on non-agricultural income. The most significant incentive to organize night-guard groups is to protect the private
property of the original residents from newcomers from outside. This is a
kind of negative collective action by local residents for self-defense.

Cultural activities
Observed cultural activities are divided into two categories. The first
category are traditional cultural activities, like music and dance, which
are performed at annual festivals or memorial events of the Chinese
Communist Party. The performing arts form in the North China Plain is
called *Yangge* and its origin is said to hark back to the Qing Dynasty. Such
groups are organized voluntarily at the administrative village in site no. 1
and at township level in site no. 2. They are funded by contributions from
local enterprises or group members. The second category is the day-to-day
activities for recreation or the promotion of good health. In site no. 1,
movie screenings, karaoke competitions, and sports competitions are often
led by the administrative village. In site no. 2, a recreational group at the
township level that is funded by contributions from local enterprises was
organized to teach singing, dance, and writing poetry.

According to the leader of a local administrative village, many cultural
activities used to be conducted at both the natural village and administrative village levels in this area decades ago, but they gradually disappeared as other recreational facilities like movie theaters and coffee shops
appeared in nearby cities. There are no fixed, daily cultural activities at the
administrative village or natural village levels, except playing cards, Mah-
jongg, or chess with friends in houses or on the street.

The changes to collective actions in the research area from the Maoist
era to the present are summarized in Table 8.4. As for agricultural production, what was collective farming under the people's commune system is
now run by individuals or by newly formed FPAs. Labor exchange has
almost disappeared because of the spread of machinery. Social mutual aid
used to be organized at the production team level in the Maoist era, but
most groups that provided such aid no longer operate, except for funeral
groups. Some such services are provided by market mechanisms, or by the
administrative village as formal public services. The activity of maintaining
security has been formalized into an institution, though security activities

Table 8.4   Changes to collective actions in the research area

	Maoist era	Post-Maoist era
Agricultural production	Collective farming	Run by individuals/FPAs
Social mutual aid	Production team	Disappeared/provided by market or government
Security maintenance	Production brigade	Institutionalized
Cultural activities	Voluntarily organized in production team	Voluntary groups organized at administrative village or township level, funded by government or enterprises

Source: Prepared by the author.

are still implemented at the administrative village level. Finally, cultural activities that used to be found at the production team level have now expanded to the administrative village or township levels. Organizations for cultural activities are basically initiated on a voluntary basis, and in some areas the administrative village and local enterprises provide facilities and funds to support them.

Resource Management in the Researched Areas

In this section, I will analyze the mechanism of common-pool resource management and the involvement of local residents and administrative organizations in the researched areas. The common-pool resources mentioned here include farmland and fishponds, the property rights of which belong to the collectives. Selected cases will be analyzed from the perspective of the roles of villagers, administrative villages, and village groups in resource management. Though the cases discussed in this section were formed recently and need organizational adaption, they provide some clues to understanding the local social system which residents participate in.

Case one: Land management by land shareholding co-operatives in the North China Plain
As shown in Table 8.3, there are two FPAs in site no. 1. Here, the one established in NF Village, ZZY Township, will be taken as a case study. ZZY Township has 42 administrative villages with a population of 26 300 under its jurisdiction. In 2003, an industrial park was established in the township, and administrative villages in ZZY aggressively promoted investment from

outside. As a result, about 40 enterprises (including from the furniture processing, musical instrument, and rubber processing industries) started operations in NF Village and provided major employment opportunities for local residents. More and more villagers began to abandon the cultivation of traditional grains because of sluggish grain prices and the increase in new job opportunities in the non-agricultural sector in the industrial park. In the whole of ZZY Township, the land area under wheat cultivation decreased dramatically, from 50000 to 18000 mu in the ten years 2000–2009.[15]

NF Village leaders established an FPA in 2006 to utilize abandoned farmland, which established large-scale wheat production on recollected lands from villagers who no longer had the will to use them for cultivation. In 2007, according to the newly published law governing FPAs, the administrative village formally registered as an FPA, which enabled it to apply for tax favors and subsidies. By 2009, there were 40 registered FPAs in ZZY Township, which means that each administrative village had an average of one FPA. Local leaders have a strong incentive to establish FPAs, because they can take political credit for the action. The breakdown of the 40 FPAs by business category is: cultivation (25), livestock farming (11), and agricultural machinery (4).

The base of this FPA is the administrative village, and the leadership and membership of the FPA almost duplicates that of NF Village, though the FPA is officially a newly founded organization that is independent from the administrative village. The leadership of the FPA discloses the body's financial situation during the semi-annual Villagers Representative Conference.

The FPA in NF Village is run by a land shareholding co-operative system. Villagers who invest their plots of land can join the FPA at the rate of one share of stock per 1.5 mu. Shareholders can receive dividends from FPA revenues according to the financial situation. More than 80 percent of all villagers in NF Village (1380 out of 1700) joined the FPA. According to administrative village leaders, this institutional reform passed the Villagers Representative Conference with more than two-thirds of votes in favor; the majority of villagers supported the introduction of this system, because it guarantees the land use rights of villagers, and the methods of profit distribution are transparent. Further, some villagers who work outside can also enjoy the benefits of the FPA. Some villagers do not participate in the FPA because they already run their own business on their land, or because their plots are remote from FPA farms. Recent migrants from outside NF Village, 1300 in all, cannot join the FPA because they do not appear on the local census register.

Another reason why villagers supported the introduction of this new system is the existence of strong trust in the leader's management ability, including administrative skills and connections with upper government. The cadre of NF Village, including the manager of FPA, has been rather fixed in recent years, except that the chairperson (who had been at the same post since the 1980s) was not re-elected in the last election in 2011. Connections with upper government are an important qualification for good leaders, because they may be advantageous to acquire subsidies and projects and attract enterprises.

The distribution of land use in NF is as follows (see Table 8.5). The land of NF Village consists of 3200 mu of farmland, 1100 mu of industrial land, and 500 mu of abandoned land. The farmland is divided into two categories: the first is distributed to individual households, and the second is pooled land with which to adjust for population change or help poor families. There has been no land duty or rent charged for the former category since the abolition of agricultural taxes in 2005, while the latter land category is often rented out for use for individual economic activity. As shown in the table, the FPA operates on an accumulated 1900 out of the 3200 mu of farmland; wheat cultivation accounts for 1100 mu, and the rest is dedicated to mushroom growing and tree sapling cultivation. Part of the wasteland is rented by villagers who dig for gravel and raise crabs.

Now, I examine the financial situation of NF Village in 2008 (Table 8.6). The largest income source of NF Village was land leases to factories, which accounted for more than 60 percent of total income (2.76 million RMB). The profit of the FPA itself was still rather small at that time, but the administrative village received a considerable subsidy of 0.61 million RMB for the FPA. The total expenditure is 0.8 million RMB, most of which is dedicated toward investment in the FPA. The agricultural line item of the NF Village budget was in the red at that time. Leaders plan to invest more in irrigation facilities and capital investment in grain storage facilities in the coming years to improve the quality of wheat produced with an eye toward the possibility of product branding.

The distribution of net profit ("A – B" in Table 8.6) for the investors in 2008 was as follows. About 73.9 percent of the total annual net profit (1.45 million RMB) was distributed to villagers; 0.34 million RMB and 0.17 million RMB were allocated to the administrative village and the FPA, respectively. The dividend per person in 2009 was about 1050 RMB, which is likely significant in light of the local per capita income. The manager of the PFA said that the body was exposed to strong pressure from the villagers' expectations of the dividends and mentioned their reluctance to accept decreased dividends, though he did not give a clear answer about compensation should the FPA go bankrupt. The current finances of the administrative village are highly dependent on revenue from industrial land use

Table 8.5   Land use in NF village, ZZY Township

Type of land	Type of management	Area (mu)	User	Land use
Farmland				
Farmland distributed for villagers	Managed by FPA	1 100	FPA	Wheat, corn
	Contract/FPA	800	Villagers/FPA	Trees, mushrooms
	Contract	900	Villagers	Crops, vegetables
Common farmland	Contract	400	Villagers	Vegetables, flowers and animal husbandry
Industrial land	Rental	1 100	Factories	Industrial use
Wasteland				
Land, fishpond	Contract	200	Villagers	Gravel digging, aquaculture
Land	Abandoned	300	–	–

Source: Prepared by the author.

Table 8.6   Financial situation of NF village in 2008

Income (A)	276
Land leasing	170
Income from FPA	30
Crop subsidies	61
Subsidy for FPA	15
Expenditures (B)	80
Cost of mushroom department	30
Cost of grain department	50
Fertilizer	20
Seeds	3
Machinery and labor	17
Pesticides	9
Water and energy	1
Balance (A − B)	196

Note: Unit: 10 000 RMB.

Source: Prepared by the author.

fees; these provide dividends to villagers instead of profiting the FPA. Land leasing is the easiest way to derive stable gain without any investment, but inherent in this development model is the risk of collapse due to the retreat of factories and other changes in economic circumstances.

Case two: Resource management by contract in the Yangtze River Delta
The common, collectively managed resources in site no. 2 comprised fishponds and farmland. Almost all collective resources in these areas are managed by individuals for fees. The owner and management method of each resource differs according to its historical background. Let us examine the details of the management of fishponds and land.

Many ponds in this area are used for aquaculture. Table 8.7 shows the size, background of construction, ownership, and profit distribution for eight plots of fishponds in the research area. The origins of these ponds are divided into four groups: (1) natural ponds; (2) those constructed in empty lots cleared by soil digging for residential construction in the 1970s–1980s; (3) empty lots formed by railway and highway construction in 1999–2001; (4) those converted from paddy fields in the early 1990s, when the price of rice was very low. A fishpond manager of SY Village (no. 5 in Table 8.7) said that he first asked the administrative village for approval to convert the paddy fields into ponds, and then he directly negotiated with each villager who owned the land use rights in the planned site. In the early 1990s, most farmers gave up hope of farming the land because paddy fields were damaged by severe flooding on a large scale, and abandoned, and it was easy for him to persuade the villagers to sell their land at very low prices or even without any fee.

The owner of a pond is either the administrative village or the village group; which of these two organizations has ownership is basically decided by the historical background of the construction and investment. All of the researched fishponds were managed by individual villagers on a contract basis at the time of investigation, and no pond is subject to joint investment or management by a village group. Four villagers without any blood relations in SY administrative village once invested in a 1300 mu fishpond, but all members of the group except one withdrew within a couple of years because of clashes of opinion among investors, and the remaining original investor undertook the entirety of its management. Joint investment in resource management does not seem to last very long here, and such arrangements ultimately tend to be changed into bilateral contracts.

The standard and method of distribution of rental fees differs from case to case. Most of the fees paid for the use of fishponds owned by village groups are paid to village groups in the form of cash or commodities, except in QT Village, where 85 percent of the fee is pooled into the

Table 8.7   Management of fishponds in each village

No. of plots	Location	Area (mu)	Background of construction	Owner	Manager	Rental fee per mu	Receiver of fee
1	QT	18	empty lots from railway construction in 1999 and highway in 2000	VG	individual	300	85% for AV, 15% for VG
2	QT	70	same as above	VG	individual	300	same as above
3	QT	30	same as above	VG	individual	300	same as above
4	SY	100	natural pond, reconstructed in 1970s	AV	individual	150 RMB	formerly AV, later the villagers (owner of land use rights)
5	SY	100	investment by villager in 1992	VG	individual	300 RMB or 15 kg of fish	VG
6	BZ	tens of mu	empty lots from railway construction in 2000	VG	individual	N.A.	VG
7	YS	156	N.A.	VG	individual	N.A.	N.A.
8	TL	60	investment by villager in 1993	AV	individual	200	villager (owner of land use rights)

Note: AV and VG are abbreviations for administrative village and village group, respectively.

Source: Prepared by the author.

administrative village's public fund. In QT administrative village, it was decided that ponds constructed in 1982–1998 would be owned by the administrative village, and those constructed later would be owned by the village groups or individuals. On the other hand, fees for the use of ponds owned by administrative villages are paid directly to the individual farmers who have the land use rights.

The land in this area is owned by the village group, and BZ is the only administrative village studied in which some village groups accumulate abandoned land and rent it to large-scale farmers both inside and outside the administrative village. As shown in Table 8.3, BZ Village has a nominal FPA. In 2012, six large-scale farmers who rent a total of 1000 mu of land in BZ Village applied for FPA registration with the local government. The group was headed by the largest farmer, who cultivates 800 mu of rice. Their objective was to apply for FPA registration mainly because they had difficulties securing funding from commercial banks; further, they can enjoy favorable policies as an FPA. Ultimately, the group was successfully registered as an FPA, but each member's business is separate: there is no integration in any farming process, like purchasing production materials or selling products.

Though TL Village also has an FPA, it has no function: it was established by the leader of the administrative village under strong pressure from the upper government. The leader of TL also mentioned that they created a shareholding co-operative only on paper due to strong encouragement by the government. In reality, the administrative village's leaders did not believe that they could accumulate land owned by village groups, nor persuade each village group to join shareholding co-operatives, as they would be too time-consuming, and administrative villages cannot assume the risk of managing the village group's resources. The resource distribution and structure of southern rural society are far more complicated than in northern villages, where the authority for ownership and management of resources is concentrated in the administrative village. The amount of land owned by the village group in site no. 2 is too small to establish organizations like FPAs, so bilateral contracts were chosen as a reasonable method of resource management.

CONCLUSION

In this chapter, I have studied communal resource management in Chinese villages to grasp the characteristic of Chinese rural society through analysis of the management system for fishponds and land in two research areas. One of the main findings of this study is that the local administrative unit, the administrative village, and the village group play the roles of host organization in resource management for historical reasons and because of the unique property system in China. As shown in Table 8.8, two patterns of resource management were observed. In site no. 1 the communal land was utilized by land shareholding co-operatives and the villagers participated in the management as shareholders. On the contrary, in site no. 2 the communal land and fishponds were utilized via bilateral contracts arranged by the village group.

These different methods of resource management originated from the

Table 8.8 The manager and method of rural resource management in researched villages

Site	Targeted Resource	Owner	Manager	Investor	Distribution of Profit	Role of administrative village in resource management	Role of village group in resource management	Type of popular participation
North China Plain	Land	Administrative village	Administrative village	Administrative village	Shareholders	Manager	–	Shareholding
Yangtze River Delta	Land	Village group	Individual	Individual	Contract	–	Broker/ coordinator	Contract
	Fishpond	Administrative village/ village group	Individual	Individual	Contract	Authorizer	–	Contract

Source: Prepared by the author.

210

different function of local society in each research area. The structure of village organization and resource distribution in the North China Plain (site no. 1) is much simpler than that in the Yangtze River Delta (site no. 2). Most of the resources and power are concentrated in administrative villages, which have formal ownership of and strong power to manage and mobilize local resources. In contrast, in the Yangtze River Delta village structure is more complicated: it is characterized by a two-tiered structure that consists of administrative villages and village groups. Resources are distributed in a more scattered way under such systems, mostly at the village group level, which has an inner self-governing mechanism. The administrative village, except as involves the portion of the resources owned by itself, only has the authority to monitor and authorize the village group's behavior.

As a result, the researched northern administrative villages re-collect the land at a certain scale and manage it via a land shareholding co-operative model, while in the south, administrative villages cannot become directly involved in resource management because the village group's ownership over resources is too strong. The key to encouraging villagers to participate in such groups is the existence of resources under a single authority and trusteeship to the authority by local people. The unique method of popular participation found in these case studies is that common-pool resources are entrusted to a qualified manager, usually an individual, and the majority of the business risk is borne by the manager, while the investors receive a portion of the revenue as a dividend or rental fee. Villagers are most interested in that ability, which does not entail merely management skills but also connections between organizers and authorities to facilitate resource management and transparency of profit distribution. If people regard the activity as worth their investment, they entrust their share of the resources to the manager.

NOTES

1. Farmers' Professional Associations were formalized by the Law of Farmers' Professional Associations, which detailed favorable policies for registered FPAs (including tax exemptions and subsidies), in 2007. For the policy background and current situation of the FPA, see Fock and Zachernuk (2006) and Hoken (2009). Li and You (2007) said that approximately 6000 water users' associations were formally registered in China in 2004, and more than 3 million households had joined them, but one-third of them do not actually perform any function.
2. Regarding the boundaries of Chinese villages, see Kobayashi (1986), Kojima (1996), Tahara (1997), and Skinner (1979).
3. For the characteristics and functions of local leaders in rural development, see Yu (2001) or the review by Tahara (2005c).
4. The land shareholding co-operatives system is one of the shareholding co-operative

systems which occurred in Guangdong and later spread to experimental sites in coastal areas in the 1990s (Zhou 2001; Po 2008; Zhang 2010). This system is broadly observed in suburban Beijing as one of the management methods of collective assets in these years (Li 2008).

5. According to Chen (2008, p. 183), the villages from Beijing to Shandong Province originated from compelled migration from Shanxi Province during the Ming Dynasty (early fifteenth century).
6. This perspective is inspired by a series of studies by Tahara (2005a, 2005b, 2009), Tianyuan (2012), Pei (1998), and Zheng et al. (2011).
7. For instance, the protest incident in Wukan (administrative) village, Guangdong Province attracted enormous international attention ("China's Wukan elects village committee months after protests," *Xinhua net*, March 3, 2012).
8. In 1996, the rates of administrative villages in which ownership of farmland was vested in administrative villages and village groups were 45 percent and 55 percent, respectively (Yan 2002, p. 53).
9. The law was partly revised in 2010 to reflect socio-economic change after its establishment. See Miyao (2011) for details.
10. RMB is the abbreviation of renminbi, the Chinese currency unit. It is also called the Chinese yuan.
11. All the information and data used in this study are sourced from face-to-face interviews by myself with local governmental officers, village leaders, and villagers or documents provided by them in April, November, and December 2009; January, April, and September 2010; July, November, and December 2011; and January 2012. I express my deep gratitude to the interviewees and fellow researchers, including Dr Dongqun Yang from the Chinese Academy of Agricultural Sciences, Dr Bin Cao from the Chinese Academy of Social Sciences in Beijing, and the members of the College of Environment, Nanjing University, who helped to arrange the field survey.
12. The influence of blood ties in village groups is not always conducive to the welfare of all members. Particularly, in a village group consisting of multiple families, less-influential families may be harmed by nepotism in favor of the majority (interview with former village group leader from TH Village Group, QT Administrative Village).
13. Agricultural machinery agencies travel all over China in the agricultural season every year. The central government aims to raise the degree of mechanization in farming, so it gives these agencies favorable treatment, including subsidies for trans-province highway fees.
14. In site no. 2, every production team used to have a funeral group. However, the group was changed to the administrative village level, and fewer than ten people remain members.
15. The mu is a Chinese unit of land area. One mu equals one-fifteenth of a hectare.

REFERENCES

Ako, Tomoko (2010), "Nouson shyakai no gyoushuuryoku: Kohokushyou S ken no koukyou seikatsu wo meguru jirei kenkyuu" ("The agglomerating power of Chinese rural society: Case study of public life in S prefecture, Hubei"), in Masaharu Hishida (ed.), *Chyuugoku: kisou kara no gabanansu (China: Governance from Grassroots)*, Tokyo: Hosei University Press, pp. 99–122.
Chen, Lixing (2008), "Cyuugoku no keiken" ("Chinese experience"), in Toshihiro Yogo and Takashi Sasaki (eds), *Chiiki syakai to kaihatsu: higashi ajia no keiken (Local Society and Development: from East Asian Experience)*, Nihon Fukushi University COE Program Local Social Development Series Vol. 1, Tokyo: Kokon Shoin, pp. 177–250.

Fock, Achim and Tim Zachernuk (2006), "China: Farmers Professional Associations: Review and policy recommendations," Departmental Working Paper Report No. 37430, Washington, DC: World Bank.

Fukutake, Tadashi (1946), *Chyuugoku nouson syakai no kouzou* (*The Structure of Chinese Rural Society*), Kyoto: Taigado Press.

Hatada, Takashi (1973), *Chyuugoku sonraku to kyoudoutai riron* (*Chinese Village and Theory of Community*), Tokyo: Iwanami Shoten.

He, Xuefeng (2002), *Zaoyu xuanju de xiangcun shehui: Jingmen shi di si jie cunwei-hui xuanju guancha* (*Chinese Rural Society Encountered Election: Observation from the Fourth Election in Jingmen City*), Xi'an: Northwest University Press.

Hoken, Hisatoshi (2009), "Noumin sengyou gassaku soshiki no hensen to sono keizai teki kinou" ("The transformation of the Farmers' Professional Association and its economic function"), in Akihide Ikegami and Hisatoshi Hoken (eds), *Chyuugoku nouson kaikaku to nougyou sangyouka* (*Rural Reform and Agricultural Industrialization in China*), Chiba: Institute of Developing Economies, pp. 203–232.

Kato, Hiroyuki (1995), "Nouson ni okeru shijyouka wo donoyouni toraeruka" ("How to understand the market economy in rural areas"), in Hiroyuki Kato (ed.), *Chyuugoku no nouson hatten to shijyouka* (*Development of Market Economy in Rural China*), Kyoto: Sekai Shisosha Press, pp. 2–26.

Kobayashi, Koji (1986), "Mura no tochi to kaihougo no nouson kaikaku" ("Land of the village and the rural reform after liberalization"), in Koji Kobayashi (ed.), *Kyuu chyuugoku nouson saikou: henkaku no kiten wo tou* (*Traditional Chinese Village Revisited: Inquiring the Start of Reform*), Tokyo: Institute of Developing Economies, pp. 195–224.

Kojima, Yasuo (1996), "Chyuugoku sonraku no kouchi bunpu no gendaiteki hensei" ("Distribution arrangement of farmland in modern Chinese Villages"), *Kenkyu nenpo* (*Annual Report on Foreign Studies*) No. 33, Kobe: Kobe City University of Foreign Studies, pp. 1–27.

Li, Junying (2008), *Beijing jiaoqu cunji jiti jingji zhidu chuangxin yanjiu* (*Study on Institutional Innovation of Village Collective Economy in Suburban Areas of Beijing*), Beijing: China Agriculture Technical Press.

Li, Qiong and Chun You (2007), "Minjian xiehui de jiti xingdong: yi guanshui xiehui weili de fenxi" ("Collective actions in private association: Case study of water user's association"), *Issues in Agricultural Economy*, 7, 41–45.

Liu, Fengqin (2005), *Nongdi zhidu yu nongye jingji zuzhi* (*Land System and Rural Economic Organization*), Beijing: Chinese Social Science Press.

Miyao, Emi (2011), "Chyuugoku sonmin iinkai soshiki hou no kaisei" ("Amendments to the Organic Law of the Villagers Committees of China"), *Foreign Legislation*, **247**, 111–123.

Oi, Jean C. (1992), "Fiscal reform and economic foundation of local state corporatism," *World Politics*, **45**(1), 99–126.

Okamoto, Nobuhiro (ed.) (2008), *Chyuugoku seinan chiiki no kaihatsu sen-ryaku* (*Regional Development Strategy of Southwest China*), Chiba: Institute of Developing Economies.

Pei, Xiaolin (1998), "Township-village enterprises, local governments, and rural communities: The Chinese village as a firm during economic transition," in Eduard B. Vermeer, Frank N. Pieke, and Woei Lien Chong (eds), *Cooperative and Collective in China's Rural Development: Between State and Private Interests*, Armonk, NY: M.E. Sharpe, pp. 110–135.

Plummer, Janelle and John G. Taylor (eds) (2004), *Community Participation in China: Issues and Processes for Capacity Building*, London: Routledge.

Po, Lanchih (2008), "Redefining rural collectives in China: Land conversion and the emergence of rural shareholding co-operatives," *Urban Studies*, **45**(8), 1603–1623.

Qian, Yingyi and Barry R. Weingast (1997), "Seido, seifu koudou shyugi to keizaihatten: chyuugoku kokuyuu kigyou to gouchin kigyou no hikaku" ("Institution, governmental activism and economic development: Comparative analysis of Chinese state enterprise and TVEs"), in Masahiko Aoki, Hyung-ki Kim and Masahiro Okuno-Fujiwara (eds), *Higashi ajia no keizaihatten to seifu no yakuwari: hikaku seido bunseki apurochi* (*The Role of Government in East Asian Economic Development: Comparative Institutional Analysis*), Tokyo: Nikkei Publishing, pp. 285–308.

Rozelle, Scott and Guo Li (1998), "Village leaders and land-rights formation in China," *American Economic Review*, **88**(2), 433–438.

Ruf, Gregory A. (1998), *Cadres and Kin: Making a Socialist Village in West China*, Stanford, CA: Stanford University Press.

Sasaki, Mamoru and Yukio Karasawa (eds) (2003), *Chyuugoku sonraku shyakai no kouzou to dainamizumu* (*The Structure and Dynamism of Chinese Rural Society*), Tokyo: Toho Shoten Press.

Skinner, G.W. (1979), *Chyuugoku nouson no shijyou to shyakai kouzou* (*Marketing and Social Structure in Rural China*), Kyoto: Houritsu Bunkasha.

Suga, Yutaka (2009), "Chyuugoku no dentouteki komonzu no gendaiteki gan" ("The modern implication of Chinese traditional commons"), in Takeshi Murota (ed.), *Kankyou gabanansu soushyo 3: gurobaru jidai no rokaru komonzu* (*Local Commons in Global Era*), Environmental Governance Studies Series Vol. 3, Kyoto: Minerva Press, pp. 215–236.

Sun, Yat-sen (1989), *The Three Principles of the People: San min chu I*, (with two supplementary chapters by Chiang Kai-shek), Taipei: China Pub. Co.

Tahara, Fumiki (1997), "Kaihougo no kousei nouson ni miru kouchi saibunpai patan" ("The farmland redistribution pattern in Jiangxi villages in the post-liberation era"), *Journal of History*, **42**, 52–70.

Tahara, Fumiki (2005a), "Chyuugoku sonraku seiji no akuta bunseki: douro kensetsu to sonyuu kigyou setsuritsu wo jirei toshite" ("Actor analysis in Chinese rural politics: Case study of road construction and establishment of village enterprise"), in Norihiro Sasaki (ed.), *Gendai chyuugoku no seiji henyou: kouzouteki henka to akuta no tayouka* (*Political Transformation in Modern China: Structural Change and Diversification of Actors*), Chiba: Institute of Developing Economies, pp. 59–95.

Tahara, Fumiki (2005b), "Chyuugoku nouson ni okeru kaihatsu to ridashippu: pekin shi enkou X mura no yasai oroshiuri shijyou wo megutte" ("Development and leadership in rural China: A case study of vegetable wholesale market of X Village, Beijing"), *Ajia keizai*, **46**(6), 16–39.

Tahara, Fumiki (2005c), "Chyuugoku sonraku seiji kenkyu no genjyou to kadai: sonraku seiji no akuta bunseki ni mukete" ("A survey of research on rural politics in China: A groundwork for the actor analysis of village governance"), *Ajia keizai*, **46**(1), 53–71.

Tahara, Fumiki (2006), "Chyuugoku nouson ni okeru kakumei to shyakaishyugi keiken: chiiki shyakai no genshika to soshikika" ("The revolution and socialism in rural China: The atomization and organization of local society"), *Historical Science*, **820**, 130–136.

Tahara, Fumiki (2009), "Nougyou sangyouka to nouson rida: nuomin sengyou gas-sakushya seiritsu no shyakaiteki bunmyaku" ("Agricultural industrialization and rural cadres: The social context of establishment of farmer's professional associations"), in Akihide Ikegami and Hisatoshi Hoken (eds), *Chyuugoku nouson kaikaku to nougyou sangyouka* (*Rural Reform and Agricultural Industrialization in China*), Chiba: Institute of Developing Economies, pp. 233–262.

Takida, Go (2005), "Chyuugoku nouson ni okeru koukyousei no kiki: kisou seiken no furyou saikenka to *kigyouka*" ("The crisis of the public in rural China: The bad-debtization and commercialization of the rural government"), *Japan–China Journal of Sociological Studies*, **13**, 53–72.

Takida, Go (2009), "Sonmin jichi no suitai to jyuumin soshiki no yukue" ("Decline of village autonomy and the future of the resident organization"), in Yoshihiko Kuroda and Yuko Minami (eds), *Chyuugoku ni okeru jyuumin soshiki no saihen to jichi heno mosaku: chiiki jichi no sonritsu kiban* (*The Reorganization of the Resident Organization and the Explorations for Autonomy*), Sino-Japan Sociology Series No. 6, Tokyo: Akashi Press, pp. 192–224.

Tianyuan, Shiqi (2012), *Riben shiyezhong de zhongguo nongcun jingying: guanxi, tuanjie, sannong zhengzhi* (*Rural Leaders in China: Connection, Cohesion and Agrarian Politics*), Jinan: Shandong Renmin Press.

Uchiyama, Masao (2003), *Gendai chyuugoku nouson to "kyoudoutai"* (*Modern Rural China and "Community"*), Tokyo: Ochyanomizu Shobo.

Yan, Shanping (1995), "Chiiki komyuniti no henyou: *shyaku* ha kaitaisuruka" ("The changing regional community: Will *Shequ* be dismissed?"), in Hiroyuki Kato (ed.), *Chyuugoku no nouson hatten to shijyouka* (*Development of Market Economy in Rural China*), Kyoto: Sekai Shisosha Press, pp. 199–228.

Yan, Shanping (2002), *Shirizu gendai chyuugoku keizai2: noumin kokka no kadai* (*Rural Issues of China, Modern Chinese Economy Series Vol. 2*), Nagoya: Nagoya University Press.

Yu, Jianrong (2001), *Yue cun zhengzhi: zhuanhuanqi zhongguo xiangcun zhengzhi jiegou de bianqian* (*Politics in Yue Village: Rural Politics in the Transformation Era in China*), Beijing: Shangwuyin Press.

Zhang, Xiaohan (2010), *Nongcun tudi gufen hezuo zhi de zhidu jiexi yu shizheng yanjiu* (*An Empirical Analysis of the Rural Joint Shareholding Co-operative System*), Shanghai: Shanghai Renmin Press.

Zhe, Xiaoye and Yingying Chen (2000), *Shequ de shijian: "chaoji cunzhuang" de fazhan licheng* (*Practice of Community Development of "Super-villages"*), Hangzhou: Zhejiang Renmin Press.

Zheng, Fentian, You Cheng and Rongping Ruan (2011), "Cong cunzhuang xing gongsi dao gongsi xing cunzhuang: hou xiangzhen qiye shidai de cunqi bianjie ji xiaolv fenxi" ("From village enterprise to enterprise village: An analysis on the boundary of village and enterprise and its economic efficiency in post-TVEs era"), *China Rural Survey*, **6**, 31–45.

Zhou, Xiaowei (2001), *Chuyuugoku ni okeru shyaku gata kofun gassaku sei no seiritsu to tenkai* (*A Study on the Development and Growth of Rural Community Type Shareholding Cooperative System in China*), Tokyo: Tsukuba Shobo Press.

PART III

Conclusion

9. Propositions for understanding local society for rural development

Shinichi Shigetomi

INTRODUCTION

The self-organizing activities of local people are prerequisites for community-based, participatory rural development. The research objective of this volume was to identify the mechanisms through which rural people organize themselves for their development needs. We assumed that such mechanisms exist in local society. We regard local society as a system in which locality groups mobilize local institutions and resources to form and manage organizational activities. To identify the local social system, we applied an organizational process approach. We investigated the process by which local people organize themselves for development in various cases from seven Asian countries and observed how the actors, institutions, and resources in these local societies determine how local people organize themselves.

In this concluding chapter, I synthesize the findings of the case studies to develop some propositions for understanding local society and the mechanisms that facilitate the self-organizing activities of rural people.

LOCAL SOCIETY MATTERS

Rural people choose the form of organization and the method of organizing based on local conditions. In this sense, the local society matters in the self-organizing process for rural development.

This proposition is affirmed in cases where the same development organization or project was implemented in different local contexts. The Indonesian case study shows this most eminently. Shimagami (Chapter 5) compares the performance of a microfinance organization that had nation-wide branches in the context of four regions. According to her findings, in cases of defaults, each region adopted different solutions. The Javanese village could mobilize the village's communal resources; the Banten village used the private resources of the village chief; the Torajanese village relied on the resources collected by kin groups; and the Central Sulawesi village left the matter to each voluntary organization.

Rural development projects that disregard the local mechanisms for developing organizations may fail. The community forestry program implemented nationwide in the Philippines is a good example. Hayama (Chapter 6) revealed that the fundamental cause of the failure of this program was not the policy, project design, support, or incentives, but the fact that the organization for this project did not match the organizational capabilities of rural local societies in the Philippines.

LOCAL SOCIETY MADE OF LOCALITY GROUPS

The local society consists of locality groups. It is not merely a venue or geographical unit but has some elements that have a function in the organizing process. Studies emphasizing the importance of "community" often pay little attention to how much the community actually matters. There must be actors who carry out the functions for organizing community members.

Our case studies identify various locality groups – local administrative organizations and social organizations – in each local society. As for local administrative organizations alone, Indonesia has the administrative village (*desa*), sub-village (*dusun*), *Rukun Warga* (RW), and *Rukun Tetangga* (RT), while Myanmar has the village tract, village, and ten-house group. Moreover, varieties of social organizations are added to the list of locality groups. In Thailand, the indigenous village and the temple supporter group exist along with the administrative village. In India, habitations and caste groups are important locality groups besides the *panchayat* village, which is the administrative village. In the case of the villages in Central Vietnam and the Torajanese area of Indonesia, kin groups are significant locality groups too. For the success of community-based development, it is important to identify locality groups as the elements of "community."

LOCALITY GROUP AS THE HOST ORGANIZATION

Among the locality groups, one group plays the role of host for organizational activities. It is very important for development assistance agencies to identify this group to avoid overlooking the relevant target group for their project.

In the Indian case studies of Venkateswarlu and Shigetomi (Chapter 7), for the mobilization of resources for collective actions, a habitation is a more relevant locality group than a *panchayat* village. In Myanmar, according to Okamoto (Chapter 4), the village, not the village tract, is the host of the community forestry program. The host locality group may be different within the same country, depending on the local context. In Northern China, the administrative village is the possible candidate for local resource management, while the village group would take over this role in Southern China. Social organizations can play the host group as well. We saw that the kin groups and temple supporter group became the basis of development organizations in the case of the lower central Thai village.

The same case study on Thailand reports that a savings group formed at the sub-district level failed to attract participants. Here, the government was wrong to believe that the sub-district could be a host organization. The relevance of the locality group depends on the type of development organization. The network-type social organization of the rural Philippines may match the management of Grameen Bank groups, but not community forestry.

INSTITUTIONS, RESOURCES, AND LOCALITY GROUPS

Each locality group has its own institutions and resources that function in the organizing process. The local society plays a significant role in the organizing process through these institutions and resources.

In his case studies in rural Thailand, Shigetomi (Chapter 2) identified three locality groups – the administrative village, the indigenous village, and the temple supporter group – and found that each has different functions in the process of organizational development. The administrative village has an institution for proposals and for building consensus for organizational activities; the indigenous village has an institution for mobilizing collective identity; and the temple supporter group has an institution for accumulating organizational experiences. Each group has resources that can be mobilized for collective action. For example, the administrative village might own a swamp that can be used for fund-raising through fish farming, while the temple can provide assets for a co-operative shop building.

In Indonesia, local administrative organizations have different functions at each level. In Java, the *desa* (administrative village) works to receive outside resources and manage them for its communal needs. The *dusun* (sub-village) is the unit that hosts organizational activities. The RT has an institution for mobilizing residents for collective actions.

In the case of China (Chapter 8), Yamada identified that the administrative village and the village group had different roles in communal land management. In Northern China, the administrative village is both the resource owner and the manager of resource utilization in the village. The institution of local administration is utilized for land management. In the Southern Chinese village, the village group owns the communal land and commissions it to someone in the village. In the Indian case, in which the habitation lacked an institution for collective decision-making, the local leaders formed a village development council to compensate for the missing institution.

In some cases, the resource is the factor that triggers the organizing process. Chinese villagers might not have initiated collective actions if their villages had not had communal land. Indeed, Yamada found very few instances of collective actions in her surveyed villages other than the management of communal land.

COMPOSITION OF LOCALITY GROUPS

It is already understood that a local society consists of locality groups, while each locality group may differ in function. The composition of locality groups accordingly affects the organizational capabilities of local societies.

The local administrative organizations alone make a difference in such capabilities. For example, a Myanmar village has a local administrative organization called the ten-house group. The ten-house group works to mobilize residents for collective works, while the village is the unit that local residents consider the host organization for collective actions. A similar relationship exists between the RT and *dusun* (sub-village) in Java, Indonesia. With this combination of local administrative organizations, the local societies of Indonesia and Myanmar seem to be better facilitated to organize collective works at the village level than other local societies that do not have such local administrative organizations possessing mobilization mechanisms. In the habitation of India, there is no such subdivision, and the village administration hires local residents for public services rather than mobilizing them for communal work.

The combination of local administrative organizations and social organizations is also important to determine the organizational capabilities of local societies. The Thai case is a clear example of this. The lower central village could not mobilize the sense of unity or experience of collective actions, since the social organizations that may provide the latter elements did not coincide with the sphere of the administrative village. The Torajanese village in Indonesia could mobilize the resources owned by the ritual community of the kin group for the development project of the administrative village because both units overlapped geographically. In this situation, the ritual community works for the benefit of the village and vice versa. In the case of villages in Central Vietnam studied by Iwai (Chapter 3), each village has formal social organizations such as the Women's Union that were uniformly introduced by the national government. This means that exogenously formed social organizations overlap with endogenous social organizations. When the formal social organizations were assigned to be the host of development projects, such as microfinance programs for the rural poor, they relied on the sense of unity and the institutions of consensus-building shared among the people in the same village. As a result, the government agency could enjoy a high repayment ratio without intervening in the administration of the project at the grassroots level.

TYPES OF LOCAL SOCIAL SYSTEM

The local social system takes various forms. Focusing on the characteristics of the host organization for collective actions, we found the following three types from our case studies.

First, the natural or administrative village has an institution for building consensus, and another for mobilizing villager participation in collective actions. As mentioned earlier, some villages – such as those in upper Myanmar and the Javanese regions of Indonesia – facilitate labor mobilization through sub-village organizations. Social organizations also enhance the sense of participation. The sense of unity among the residents of the administrative village in northeast Thailand came from the sense of belonging to the same indigenous village – a locality-based social organization. The area of the ritual community in the Torajanese village in Indonesia happened to coincide with the area of the administrative village, and as a result, communal resources were provided for the administrative village's projects. In Central Vietnam, the combination of exogenously formed social organizations and indigenous villages functions to ensure participation and mobilization.

The so-called community-based or participatory development programs may be a relevant choice in this type of local social system. The development assistance agencies may be recommended to leave the task of organizing people to the local administrative organization. Indeed, the organizing activities in the northeast Thai village were initiated by local leaders, although outside agencies provided some ideas, advice, and resources. The Myanmar government gives some room for local residents to form their organizations for the administration of community forestry.

Second, the natural or administrative village has an institution for consensus-building, but lacks an institution for mobilizing the participation of villagers. The cases of India and China represent this type. In the case of villages in China, collective actions were observed in communal resource management, which does not require the participation of each villager. This nature of activity needs only the leaders to have the ability to administer resources for communal benefits. The villagers may participate in checking the performance of the leaders. In India, the natural village or habitation showed its capability clearly in resource procurement from individuals rather than persuading each villager to participate. The village leadership monopolized some economic opportunities in the village and tapped rent for communal funds. This is similar to a government collecting taxes from the population and using the revenue for public purposes.

In this type of local social system, the hierarchical social structure, or the power of control, may help rather than hinder resource procurement. In other words, it is questionable whether promoting popular participation in such local societies would produce satisfactory results. Rather, a policy that stimulates communal resource procurement and utilization may be effective for local development. In this sense, the matching grant policy in India should be appreciated. At the same time, the capability of leadership in resource procurement and management becomes crucial for successful local development. Conversely, illicit management of resources might occur if there is no adequate system for monitoring and controlling the leaders' behaviors.

Third, the administrative village works only as a receiving tool. At the onset of a development project, this type passes the task of organizing to relevant social organizations. The headman of the lower central Thai village was capable enough to pass the government policy for organizing local residents to the leader of a kin group. In the rural Philippines, the village chief let outside agencies organize the people. Since local people usually cooperate with each other through dyadic ties, forming an organization with a few members, such as a Grameen Bank group, is a reasonable approach. In this type of local society, the front-line development workers ought to be more closely committed to the process of organizing local people than in the village of the first type of local social systems.

CONCLUSION

Our case studies in seven Asian countries show that the mechanisms in local societies yield differences in organizational activities among local people. We found that local society is a composition of locality groups such as local administrative and social organizations. Each locality group has its own institutions and resources to regulate and facilitate human interactions. A local society as a whole, therefore, is regarded as a set of interrelated locality groups, institutions, and resources. People rely on the social system of their locality to form and manage their organizations. Exploring various case studies in Asian rural societies, we found certain types of local social systems that shape development organizations and the means of organizing collective actions among local people. Some local societies have the system facilitating both consensus building and the mobilization of residents at the village level. Organizational activities calling for the participation of entire villages are widely seen in this type of local social system. Another type of local society shows significant capabilities in procuring and utilizing resources as opposed to mobilizing popular participation in collective actions. In certain other types, the local administrative organizations work only as tools for receiving projects, and the social organizations in the locality work as the main actors for creating development organizations. When only network-type social organizations are available in the local society, short-term or small-group projects may be the popular forms of development organizations. Thus, in assisting participatory rural development, approaches should be adopted according to the types of local social systems in each project site.

This volume has shown that rural people shape their self-organizing activities by relying on existing local social systems. However, we have yet to develop a model or ideal type of local social system that could be applied to a wide range of local societies in developing countries. Such a model would help rural development practitioners find an appropriate mechanism for organizing local people in their project sites. This study is a preliminary step toward future attempts to mediate scholarly investigations and development practices for a better understanding of communities and the scaling up of community-driven development.

Index